Language, Space and Power

BILINGUAL EDUCATION AND BILINGUALISM
Series Editors: Professor Nancy H. Hornberger, *University of Pennsylvania, Philadelphia, USA* and Professor Colin Baker, *University of Wales, Bangor, Wales, Great Britain*

Recent Books in the Series
Language and Literacy Teaching for Indigenous Education: A Bilingual Approach
Norbert Francis and Jon Reyhner
The Native Speaker: Myth and Reality
Alan Davies
Language Socialization in Bilingual and Multilingual Societies
Robert Bayley and Sandra R. Schecter (eds)
Language Rights and the Law in the United States: Finding our Voices
Sandra Del Valle
Continua of Biliteracy: An Ecological Framework for Educational Policy, Research, and Practice in Multilingual Settings
Nancy H. Hornberger (ed.)
Languages in America: A Pluralist View (2nd edn)
Susan J. Dicker
Trilingualism in Family, School and Community
Charlotte Hoffmann and Jehannes Ytsma (eds)
Multilingual Classroom Ecologies
Angela Creese and Peter Martin (eds)
Negotiation of Identities in Multilingual Contexts
Aneta Pavlenko and Adrian Blackledge (eds)
Beyond the Beginnings: Literacy Interventions for Upper Elementary English Language Learners
Angela Carrasquillo, Stephen B. Kucer and Ruth Abrams
Bilingualism and Language Pedagogy
Janina Brutt-Griffler and Manka Varghese (eds)
Language Learning and Teacher Education: A Sociocultural Approach
Margaret R. Hawkins (ed.)
The English Vernacular Divide: Postcolonial Language Politics and Practice
Vaidehi Ramanathan
Bilingual Education in South America
Anne-Marie de Mejía (ed.)
Teacher Collaboration and Talk in Multilingual Classrooms
Angela Creese
Words and Worlds: World Languages Review
Martí, P. Ortega, I. Idiazabal, A. Barreña, P. Juaristi, C. Junyent, B. Uranga, and E. Amorrortu
Language and Aging in Multilingual Contexts
Kees de Bot and Sinfree Makoni
Foundations of Bilingual Education and Bilingualism (4th edn)
Colin Baker
Bilingual Minds: Emotional Experience, Expression, and Representation
Aneta Pavlenko (ed.)
Raising Bilingual-Biliterate Children in Monolingual Cultures
Stephen J. Caldas

For more details of these or any other of our publications, please contact:
Multilingual Matters, Frankfurt Lodge, Clevedon Hall,
Victoria Road, Clevedon, BS21 7HH, England
http://www.multilingual-matters.com

BILINGUAL EDUCATION AND BILINGUALISM 55
Series Editors: Nancy H. Hornberger and Colin Baker

Language, Space and Power
A Critical Look at Bilingual Education

Samina Hadi-Tabassum

MULTILINGUAL MATTERS LTD
Clevedon • Buffalo • Toronto

Library of Congress Cataloging in Publication Data
Hadi-Tabassum, Samina
Language, Space and Power: A Critical Look at Bilingual Education
Samina Hadi-Tabassum.
Bilingual Education and Bilingualism: 55
Includes bibliographical references and index.
1. Education, Bilingual. 2. Language acquisition–Social aspects. I. Title. II. Series.
LC3715.H32 2005
370.117–dc22   2005027484

British Library Cataloguing in Publication Data
A catalogue entry for this book is available from the British Library.

ISBN 1-85359-879-8/ EAN 978-1-85359-879-1 (hbk)
ISBN 1-85359-878-X/ EAN 978-1-85359-878-4 (pbk)

Multilingual Matters Ltd
UK: Frankfurt Lodge, Clevedon Hall, Victoria Road, Clevedon BS21 7HH.
USA: UTP, 2250 Military Road, Tonawanda, NY 14150, USA.
Canada: UTP, 5201 Dufferin Street, North York, Ontario M3H 5T8, Canada.

Typeset by Florence Production Ltd.
Printed and bound in Great Britain by the Cromwell Press Ltd.

December 5, 2006

Contents

v

Introduction

The goal of *Language, Space and Power* is to richly describe the sociolinguistic and sociocultural life of a dual language classroom in which attention is given to not only the language learning processes at hand but also to how race, ethnicity and gender dynamics interact within the language acquisition process. Much attention has been given to the quantitative research supporting the academic success of dual language programs (Collier, 1989; Gandera & Merino, 1993; Lindholm & Gavlek, 1994; Lindholm-Leary, 2001). However, critics of dual immersion programs state that there has been relatively little in-depth examination of the contextual factors in dual immersion development: (1) the quality of education in the minority language; (2) the effects of dual immersion instruction on intergroup relations between students; (3) how dual immersion programs define the relationship between language and power; and (4) how that relationship may affect both language majority and language minority students in the dual immersion classroom (Valdes, 1997). In this book I hope to fill a gap in qualitative research focusing on bilingual education by presenting a close examination of a fifth-grade, Spanish/English, 50/50 dual immersion classroom located in a large urban public elementary school that will be known as PS 2000 in this book. Theoretical issues pertaining to language, space and power frame the book as I examine the power-based tensions and conflicts over the established border between the Spanish and English language in this fifth-grade dual immersion classroom and the kinds of discursive spaces that allow students to talk openly about these border-boundary tensions and conflicts.

The overall focus of the book is to first come to an understanding of the day-to-day discourse in a fifth-grade dual immersion classroom in order to determine where the borders and boundaries lie between Spanish and English; then locate particular classroom spaces, places and times

1

when the dual immersion students collectively voiced their resistance and counter discourse toward the established structural boundary between the Spanish and English language and the unequal division and distribution of the two languages in their classroom; and ultimately, observing whether the dual immersion students' metalinguistic discussions ever went through a process of negotiation, mediation, resolution and empowerment that lead to a transgressive, empowering *third space* in which they could overcome the inequitable borders and boundaries between the two languages and in which language use and production in the classroom was no longer structured according to a strict binary but was instead fluid and hybrid (Bhabha, 1994). By focusing on how bilingual students conceptualize and understand linguistic divisions and differentiations and whether or not they ever resolve their metalinguistic conflicts over linguistic borders and boundaries, this book explores the ideas and beliefs held by the dual immersion students on language itself and how their heightened self-awareness of language raised them toward a critical consciousness – toward an awareness of linguistic inequities and toward a transcendental understanding of language.

To accomplish these goals, I used a critical ethnography methodology, which allows the researcher to locate points and times of discourse and counter discourse. I sought those metalinguistic discussions and disruptions that openly addressed issues of power struggles over language use and resistance toward linguistic borders and boundaries. I then mapped the spatial trajectory for these metalinguistic discussions and disruptions by locating sites where and when there existed a potential third space of radical openness, a liminal space where differences can be articulated and where critical thinking is encouraged – a third space where micro-revolts can occur beyond the centered binary of the dual immersion model (Bhabha, 1994). Thus, as a cartographer of metalinguistic third spaces, my terrain was the contested terrain of resistance, opposition, tension and negotiation – where the instability of the Spanish/English linguistic borders and boundaries heightened to a great concern in which perhaps the transgression or maintenance of borders and boundaries was magnified (Soja, 1996). Instead of measuring and counting the students' language proficiency rates, this book directs attention to the ideological aspects of linguistic differentiation and inequities and further posits that the dual immersion classroom can be a decentered, fragmentary place of conflicting voices that coexist and collide together and sometimes deconstruct the false binary between the two languages. The following research questions on metalanguage, power/resistance and the discursive third space help frame the ethnographic endeavor of this book:

(1) When and where do the fifth-grade dual immersion students use metalanguage to voice their resistance towards the structural borders and boundaries between the Spanish and English language and thereby overtly express a conflict with the established borders and boundaries?

(2) How do the dual immersion students interpret the border and boundaries between the Spanish and English language and its dichotomizing and partitioning process? How do they recognize and account for the differentiation between the two languages through their metalinguistic discussions (e.g., "Why isn't Spanish used during informal social spaces such as the lunchroom or gym class? Why is English used more often during group work?").

(3) What are the students actually *saying-writing-doing-being-valuing-believing* about the borders and boundaries between Spanish and English during their metalinguistic discussions (Gee, 1992)? What kind of discourse and counter discourse is produced during these metalinguistic discussions?

(4) What types of power relations and power differentials are established during these metalinguistic discussions? Do the power relations between students and teachers ever shift during the metalinguistic discussions? How do the power relations and power differentials relate to the spaces in which the metalinguistic discussions occur most often?

(5) Do the students ever reach a threshold point in their metalinguistic discussions, through a process of mediation and negotiation, which can be labeled as a transgressive third space where the structural border between the two languages has opened, shifted, and transformed itself so that the dual immersion students arrive at a transcendental understanding of the two languages that then subsequently allows for hybridization and fluidity between the two languages?

The following sections constitute the theoretical foundation for this book and unfold in layers to reveal how imperative it is to see a dual language classroom as a polysemic text to be analyzed in its many conflicting domains. The metaphysical distance between theory and practice will dissipate soon as we examine a real dual language classroom over an extended period of time, reflecting and describing its topoi, in which even ordinary classroom phenomena have revelatory force. A description of the matrix of linguistic border and boundaries in the dual language immersion model will be the point of origin in our journey to then explain the structure and spatialization of power in this dual language classroom – all the while revealing something concrete about human nature, the human subject, race and culture.

Borders and Boundaries: Dividing Languages Structurally According to Time and Space

Two-way immersion (TWI) bilingual education is an integrated language immersion program in which students who speak a majority language, such as English, study and learn together in the same classroom with students who speak a minority language, which is often Spanish but can include other minority languages such as Mandarin, Korean and Arabic – depending on the geographic location. Both the language majority and language minority students learn the two languages simultaneously and acquire academic content knowledge through both L1 (English) and L2 (Spanish, Korean, etc.). Dual immersion education is another term used more often to describe TWI bilingual programs but both terms signify the same type of bilingual education program in which two distinct sociolinguistic student groups are fully immersed in learning both the majority and minority language across all content areas and within the same classroom setting. The fundamental aim of a dual immersion program is to teach English-dominant students a minority language such as Spanish in all subject areas, starting early in elementary school, in the same classroom setting, and at the same time that language minority students are learning the English language along with their own native language – thereby building upon both academic proficiency and linguistic proficiency in the majority and minority language for both student populations. There is also reputedly a greater likelihood of cross-cultural dialogue between the two distinct sociolinguistic student groups, both native and nonnative speakers of English, in a dual immersion elementary classroom. Thus, there is potential for a cross-pollination and gestation of both languages and cultures in a dual immersion model that is not inherently found in other types of bilingual programs.

According to researchers at the Center for Applied Linguistics (Christian, 1994), the traditional methods for dividing classroom instruction equally between the majority and minority languages in a dual immersion classroom include the following: (1) division by time in which instruction of each language can occur during half-day, alternate days, or alternate week intervals; (2) division by content in which the language chosen for instruction depends on the subject matter, for example, when Spanish is used solely to teach mathematics and science and English is used solely to teach language arts and reading; and (3) division by staff in which either there are two teachers who teach the dual immersion class with at least one teacher fluent in the minority language and one teacher fluent in the majority language or where one teacher who is fluent in both languages teaches all the students. The instructional use of bilingual materials also promotes the development of a balanced bilingualism in both student groups.

The two languages in a dual immersion classroom are in turn organized in a structurally parallel way, despite the cultural and historical differences between Spanish and English. Even though English is often endowed with greater power and prestige than Spanish, the two languages are not hierarchically ordered; rather, the dual immersion model configures the Spanish and English language in separate and contrasting but equal and symmetrical relations. Perhaps most important in marking this distinction is the division and distribution of the two languages according to equal numbers of alternate days, half-days and weeks; content area; and teaching staff. A dual immersion classroom can divide the two languages into structured equal halves during the school day by having Spanish instruction in the mornings and English instruction in the afternoons, as well as divide the content areas and teaching staff according to equal linguistic divisions. The dichotomy between Spanish and English subsequently produces a linguistic differentiation through its border-making design in which each language is separated and segregated into its own discrete space and time and is not allowed to mix with the other.

In order to create equal power relations between the majority and minority language, the dual immersion model essentially uses underlying structuralist methods and principles to create a structured linguistic equilibrium in the teaching of the two languages. That is, in order to form a dual immersion program, there is an elementary structure of binary signification, Spanish:English:: – Spanish: – English, on which a dual immersion program rests so that each language is equally recognized and valued (Levi-Strauss, 1976). Like all cultural binary oppositions, the Spanish: English::–Spanish:–English binary constitutes a structure of mutual entailment, one language deriving meaning and existence from the opposite language. A binary axiology is built based on two categories – Spanish and English – and this bifurcation is supported by a structure of classification that has two units made up of both antagonism and similarities, binaries manifested by history and constituted by different sorts of cultural and literary discourse. Structuralism is known as the first wave of *sphere scholarship* that used the separate sphere model to map out real social spaces such as classrooms and schools by separating them into specific bounded spaces associated with ideological and opposing binary forces, both antagonism and similarities, such as maleness and female-ness, whiteness and blackness and Spanishness and Englishness (Kerber, 1988).

Furthermore, the theoretical approach offered by structuralism empha-sizes that elements of language, for example, must be understood in terms of their relationship to the entire system of language, thus there is a part-to-whole relationship formed between the Spanish and English parts and the whole dual immersion model in itself (Saussure, 1965). Moreover, an essential premise in structuralism is that social and linguistic phenomena, like the Spanish and English language in a dual immersion classroom, do not have inherent meaning in themselves but rather can only be sensibly defined as parts of larger governing systems and that the meaning of these languages can be revealed only when larger systems are recognized and understood structurally – the notion that the whole (a dual immer-sion model) is greater than its parts (Spanish and English). The parts then can only have meaning if they are a fragment of the whole system and are meaningless if they stand on their own explanatory power as parts. In dual immersion classrooms, as well as in other bilingual classrooms where there are two functioning languages, a structuralist model would suggest that the Spanish and English language can only be meaningful in relation to each other and cannot be understood in and of themselves since they cannot stand alone. In order to have meaning in a dual immersion classroom, the majority and minority must form a signifying structural whole; the model is dependent on each of the parts for its iden-tity and does not want a Spanish-only or English-only type of language instruction program. Thus, signification relies on the totality of a dual immersion structure as opposed to solely its internal parts.

Given the situated patterns of equivalence and equality in a dual immersion classroom, the theoretical approach offered by structuralism also emphasizes that meaning in a dual immersion classroom is contin-gent upon the established strict borders between the Spanish and English language – hence the obsession with classifying and counting instructional time equally according to each language (Calderon, 1996). In turn, the structure of a dual immersion model has to emphasize linguistic "order, accountability, systematization, rationalism, expertise, specialization, lin-ear development, and control" in order to implement a truly democratic program in which each language has equal time and space and follows a binary path of parallel construction (Cherryholmes, 1988: 9).

Furthermore, two key structural notions help establish the democratic character of dual immersion programs: the notion of polarities and the notion of equivalence (Jakobson, 1990). Polarities constitute the metaphysical force of binary opposition between the Spanish and English language in a dual immersion classroom. Yet, the polarities between Spanish and English share equal ground because of the stated equivalent status between the two languages, especially in a 50/50 dual immersion model. Thus, in order to have equivalency between the two languages, there needs to be a polar opposition between them as well. In other words, structuralism focuses more so on the intermingling relationship of polarity and equivalence between the two languages rather than on the languages themselves as the subject of study. Spanish and English have value or meaning not in themselves necessarily but in virtue of the polar relationship between them; they can only be seen as equals when they are kept at polar opposites within the classroom discourse, separated by days, times, people and content areas. However, what happens when it is necessary to duplicate a structural object such as a dual immersion classroom that is inherently bound by notions of polarity and equivalence?

Even though the objective of dual immersion programs is to create structured equality between the Spanish and English language, the structure of the classroom itself can only be an imitation of equality because that equality between majority and minority languages has never been actually present historically within our national discourse, which still structures society and social institutions according to a monolingual framework in which English is the language of hegemony and dominance and thus has a higher position in the sociocultural hierarchy:

> The goal of all structuralist activity, whether reflexive or poetic, is to reconstruct an "object" [the dual immersion classroom] in such a way as to manifest thereby the rules of its functioning of this object. Structure is therefore actually a simulacrum of the object, but a directed interested simulacrum, since the imitated object makes something appear which remained invisible or ... unintelligible in the natural object. (Barthes, 1992: 65)

It is this recognition that language itself has a history that leads us away from the claim that structures of meaning can be essentially reconstructed in their simulacrums. The structuralist paradigm does not address the historical aspects of inequality between the Spanish and English language, not to mention present inequalities, because structuralism mainly seeks to construct a contingent relationship between the various parts of a structure without recourse to any historical basis for explanation. The equality of languages is achieved in a dual immersion classroom through the polarity and equivalence of languages; however, it is still an imitation or simulacrum of democracy because Spanish and English did not start off from a historically equivalent space.

Furthermore, there are many other concerns that a structuralist paradigm overlooks such as a lack of concern for the play of difference between languages and how that difference affects the binary structure. The totalizing nature of language as found in structuralism ignores the possibility of referring to the majority and minority language in a dual immersion classroom in terms of their dispersion and differentiation. Instead of emphasizing the principle of difference and disparity between the Spanish and English language, structuralism views a dual immersion classroom design as a normative structure that follows an organizing principle of holism where Spanish and English come together in a complementary form and congruent manner.

In addition, by treating language as a symbolic structure that follows established codes, structuralism also turns away from the speaking subjects of language and their contradictory or conflicting voices as they may be found in the lived experience of everyday speech within a dual immersion classroom. Instead, structuralism constitutes itself as a self-referential system so that "language speaks of itself, its forms, and its objects" and is in turn able to generate connotations that are remote from real human experience in the everyday classroom (Williams, 1999: 58). This, of course, shows how structuralism strips away the speaking subject and the role of discourse and instead turns the study of language into a discipline separated from an actual observation of language use. In treating it as such, structuralism seeks to divorce language from all that lies outside of its system, from all external causes and determinations that may act upon language, from external classroom reality itself.

Structuralism's emphasis on systemic thought further constrains social structures by classifying, ordering and programming them in order to determine and control every aspect of their lives so that there is no room for innovation, creativity and non-conformity (Lefebvre, 1999). Its technocrats or architects presuppose that society should be a rational system and they plan thereafter to make it one as well. Structuralist systems, such as the dual immersion model, with their proposed rational coherence and transparent cohesion, are a technocratic ideal because in practice they attempt to predetermine borders and boundaries and stipulate norms and rules to formulate efficient bilingual education models.

However, the research in this book suggests that the binary between Spanish and English is a false binary; just like all binaries, it can only produce a false consciousness. This book describes instead a fundamentally unstable and shifting classroom that knows no permanent or solid place for linguistic equality and where the utopian impulse to purge, homogenize and to relocate problematic inequalities is dispelled. By examining the unequal production of language in the classroom as well as the unstable social ties between majority and minority language students, this book takes on a post-structuralist framework by analyzing the non-utopian tensions and struggles along the shifting borderland between Spanish and English. A post-structuralist study then would call into question the binary coherence and stability of a dual immersion classroom by drawing awareness that the bilingual classroom can be a fragmentary place where shifting borders between two putatively equal languages can destabilize and decenter the binary structure proposed in the original model.

The work of post-structural thinkers such as Jean-Francois Lyotard and Michel Foucault has cast great doubt upon the classic, structural notions of what constitutes objective truth, reality, meaning and knowledge in the study of language. Post-structural theorists find it necessary to subvert structuralism by focusing instead on the heterogeneous, the diverse, the subjective, the spontaneous, the relative and the fragmentary since they believe that there is no one objective truth, reality, meaning and form of knowledge within the study of language. Rather, language for post-structuralists is in a constant state of flux where the creation of new and multiple meanings is possible through a series of oppositions and transformations of language itself. They argue that there are no definitive, closed structural boundaries that can build logical categories of language by means of binary contrast; rather, language has a history that becomes a part of the process by which new ideas and meanings come into existence and change its original structure (Bannet, 1989). Moreover, post-structuralists have characterized language and thought processes according to gaps, discontinuities and suspensions of dictated meanings in which difference, plurality and multiplicity and the coexistence of opposites are allowed free play and are not confined by strict borders and boundaries.

The following section is intended to provide a post-structuralist framework for dual immersion programs that abandons the quest for a structural theory of language learning and its discrete analysis of language proficiency and acquisition. Instead, the post-structuralist framework for this book concentrates on situated disunity and metalinguistic conflicts over language use and linguistic borders and boundaries, and how certain speaking subjects within the dual immersion classroom challenged these linguistic borders and boundaries and sometimes shifted them in a different direction. However, the book should not be seen as an attack or a criticism of dual immersion programs and bilingual education in general. Instead, this book aims to open up the dual immersion discourse in bilingual education research to a post-structuralist sensibility that works at the local classroom level and grounds post-structuralism in the social dynamics of a specific dual immersion classroom extended over time and across multiple spaces.

A Post-structuralist Framework for Dual Immersion Programs

Structuralism is continually criticized by post-structuralist thinkers because its theoretical construct does not account for individual human action or agency, which may conflict with a deterministic structure, such as a dual immersion classroom (Lyotard, 1984). Instead of seeing structures such as dual immersion classrooms as an organized reality that behaves mechanistically in that its structure is rigid with tightly defined relationships, post-structuralists see the structure as a product of individualized human creation or *habitus* that is not necessarily universal in thought processes. Instead, the locally situated dual immersion classroom can be open to dynamics, change, fluidity and even self-contradiction in its meaning-making: "I wanted to react against structuralism and its strange philosophy of action which . . . made the agent disappear by reducing it to the role of supporter or bearer of the structure" (Bourdieu, 1977: 179). Post-structuralism advocates a dissolution of totalizing structures that they feel are falsified and non-subjective; instead, they place emphasis on the subject or agent and its sense of agency and power (Williams, 1999).

Furthermore, in the post-structuralist framework, there is no definitive one-to-one correspondence between Spanish and English in which both languages can be divided equally so that they have equal representation in the dual immersion classroom. In fact, a post-structuralist would claim that there is no determinable relation at all between the two languages because post-structuralism would be highly critical of the proposed unity of dual immersion programs as being always stable. Post-structuralists also refuse the stability of meaning often assumed with structures such as the dual immersion program; instead, they stress its fragmentation – of language, of time, of human subjects, of the dual immersion classroom structure itself. For post-structuralists, all total systemic thought is suspect to a sense of falseness and untruth. Rather, the post-structuralist paradigm consciously acknowledges that classroom reality is fragmented, multidimensional, uncertain, decontextualized and differentially valued in a manner that promotes conflicts and agonistics (Sarup, 1993). Thus, a post-structuralist paradigm depends on individual meanings and the contexts in which dual immersion programs are applied. This realization, in turn, results in an attempt to reassert the fragmentary nature of classroom reality. Instead of depending on universally structured dual immersion truths, these individual fragmentary meanings are constantly shifting and destabilizing the consistency of its own binary structure. There are no concrete egalitarian dual immersion structures that can create definitive borders and boundaries between one language and another. There are only shifting borders and boundaries, and moving, destabilizing, decentering structures with no false unity. A post-structuralist study then would call into question the coherence and autonomy of dual immersion programs, drawing awareness that the dual immersion classroom can be a fragmentary place.

Within this definition of post-structuralism, Middleton (1995) further states that within one structure there are multiple truths that do not necessarily coalesce with each other and may differ in terms of how much power they each command. Theoretically, a post-structuralist framework states that terms such as *equality* and *egalitarianism* cannot be placed in a structural position. Instead, these concepts are merely tokens in the interplay of power relations between majority and minority languages and majority and minority students since there no longer exists a grand narrative of egalitarianism stating that all dual immersion classrooms are necessarily democratic in nature. The result is a plurality of shifting categories of equality in a dual immersion classroom in which the degree of equilibrium between Spanish and English is always moving and changing within the lived everyday classroom life.

However, an important category in Middleton's definition is *power*, which is a central focus point in post-structuralist thought. Power will be defined in this book according to the argument that power is not a possession or capacity; power is an institution, a structure, or a force that is endowed in certain people and not in others (Popkewitz & Brennan, 1998). There are many focal points of power within a system that are not contained indefinitely within one structure and one person. Instead, power is a shifting and moving category that constantly changes within a structure: "Power is exercised from innumerable points, in the interplay of non-egalitarian and mobile relations" (Foucault, 1972: 94). For example, in a dual immersion classroom, there is no duality between those who possess power and those who do not; rather, power passes through and is exercised by individuals and structures alike at all levels of the social system and at various places and times within the classroom life. In turn, Foucauldian power has the characteristic of a network relationship in which threads or ties of power extend everywhere like a web or mesh and are not confined to a specific centralized location (Sarup, 1993). In relation to this spatial definition of power, Foucault also suggests that the analysis of power should concentrate on the point of application of power rather than on the possession of power.

The purpose of this post-structuralist study was also to problematize power differentials and networks, and attempt to locate shifting places and times when power is actualized in a dual immersion classroom. Power no longer operates from solely the top-down authority of the teacher to the student or from solely the English language to the Spanish language. Instead, complex differential power relationships extend to all aspects of the classroom life because power is everywhere; it filters up from below and is produced at every moment in the classroom life:

> Power must be understood in the first instance as the multiplicity of force relations immanent in the sphere in which they operate and which constitute their own organization; as the process which, thorough ceaseless struggles and confrontations, transforms, strengthens or reverses them; the support these force relations find in one another, thus forming a chain or a system, or on the contrary, the disjunctions and contradictions which isolate them from one another; and lastly, as the strategies in which they take effect, whose general design or institutional crystallization is embodied in the state apparatus, in the formulation of the law, in the various social hegemonies. Power's condition of possibility, or in any case the viewpoint which permits one to understand its exercise . . . and which also makes it possible to use its mechanism as a grid of intelligibility of the social order . . . is the moving substrate of force relations, which, by virtue of their inequality, constantly engender states of power, but the latter are always local and unstable . . . One needs to be nominalistic, no doubt: power is not an institution, and not a structure [like language or signification]; neither is it a certain strength we are endowed with; it is a name that one attributes to a complex strategical situation in a particular society. (Foucault, 1978: 93)

According to Foucault, power is always coexistent with strategic resistance, not as an outside force, but internalized within power itself so that power and resistance work alongside each other. Foucault wrote extensively from a historical standpoint that power and resistance are ever present in our society, both within the organizations we are a part of and outside these formal organizations. His view is that power and resistance exist in multiple forms and are acted out by individuals daily in local settings such as bilingual classrooms. He asserts that "power reaches into the very grain of individuals, touches their bodies and inserts itself into their actions, their discourses, their learning processes, and everyday lives" (Foucault, 1978: 39). Foucault views power and resistance as coexisting within the same social relationship, and thus strongly refutes the idea that power can be easily labeled as good or bad because power is multidimensional:

> Are there no great radical ruptures, massive binary divisions, then? Occasionally, yes. But more often one is dealing with mobile and transitory points of resistance, producing cleavages in society that shift about, fracturing unities and effecting regroupings, furrowing across individuals themselves, cutting them up and remolding them, marking off irreducible regions in them, in their bodies and their minds. Just as the network of power relations ends by forming a dense web that passes through apparatuses and institutions, without being exactly localized in them, so too the swarm of points of resistance traverses social stratifications and individual unities. (Foucault, 1978: 96)

In turn, wherever there is power, there is also resistance that spreads itself about like a network. The points of resistance within power, however, are not stable, structured entities. They too are fluid, moving and ambiguous, and can never be self-contained within social structures, just like power itself cannot be self-contained. Foucault himself believed in and supported the microlevel politics of localized struggles and specific power relations within history that traversed larger social structures. Acts of resistance at the local level are *micro-revolts* in which there is a multiplicity of dispersed micro-power relations. Furthermore, the existence of power relations presupposes forms of resistance that create a locus of opposition and conflict through such a counter discourse. Just as power is fluid and present everywhere in the social network, so is resistance; there is a multiplicity of resistance that is constantly shifting and regrouping. However, Foucault also stated that power is a positive and productive force that has the capability to transform and transgress structures. This post-structuralist study also attempts to locate places and times of both opposition and negotiation within shifting power relations to find individualized meanings in a dual immersion classroom. Instead of asking which subjects within the classroom structure possess absolute power, this book shifts attention to the discourse processes by which speaking subjects are seen as effects of power relations within the dual immersion class.

Furthermore, post-structural theory claims that these acts of resistance and differential power relations are constructed through discourse, which is directly linked to power because discourse constitutes power. Since human beings use speech acts for social reasons and not only to convey linguistic meaning but also to convey who they are as individuals, discourse is indeed tied directly to subjective concepts of power, knowledge and resistance. The post-structural framework combines concepts of power and resistance with discourse to explain "the workings of power on behalf of specific interests and to analyze the opportunities for resistance to it" (Weedon, 1987: 34). Classroom discourse then becomes the medium for expressing and negotiating power/resistance relationships that develop in the everyday classroom life. Sites where the dual immersion students constructed their own form of power/resistance to the dominant dual immersion discourse were examined in this study for the kind of metalanguage students used to develop and voice a counter discourse that would be able to bypass or resist the dominant, binary, structural opposition between Spanish and English. Thus, in this post-structuralist study, the students' use of metalanguage provided the form of analysis that best expressed and articulated local concepts of power, resistance and conflict over language use and linguistic borders and boundaries within the dual immersion classroom.

Discourse and Counter Discourse: Getting Meta About Language

This book, which is grounded in a sociolinguistic and ethnographic research approach, focuses on the study of discourse instead of language acquisition because it looks at fifth-grade students' values, beliefs and intentions toward language use in the classroom and linguistic borders and boundaries between Spanish and English. The focus of this book is also on when and where conflicts occurred over language use and linguistic borders and boundaries, and how students mediated these linguistic conflicts. By recording how students talk and interact in conflict-ridden metalinguistic discussions in which topics related to language use and linguistic borders and boundaries are the disputed objects of conversation, the analysis of the study is on the students' discourse about language and not language itself. James Paul Gee (1992: 164) describes this phenomenon as the study of "language-within-discourse" because the object of the discourse is how the dual immersion students theorize language practices. Rather than recording how students explore the grammatical systems of the English and Spanish language or the students' acquisition of language and literacy in Spanish and English, the focus on discourse as a means of inquiry in this book attempts to understand the complexity of how students use language in a social context to talk about the ideology of language itself. Gee (1989) also reminds us that discourses are always embedded in ideologies and that inquiries into discourse and schooling entail difficult questions about the social values in instructional practices and theories. In this study, the established border between the Spanish and English language within the classroom discourse and the boundaries produced from such borders were ideological concerns addressed in the students' metalinguistic discussions throughout the school year.

Whenever the two languages came together into relevant contact, whether it was during a formal class lecture or in the production of a class play, the students' use of metalanguage sometimes had the effect of ultimately undermining attempts to draw exclusive or impenetrable boundaries around any single language and its use in the classroom discourse. For example, the dual immersion students often posed critical questions aloud as to which language should be used for a specific context, and those types of questions or comments lead to the conflict-ridden metalinguistic discussions investigated in this book. Significantly, their questioning of the social context of language use or of the variable relationship between the Spanish and English language – between linguistic practices and their social formations – led to metalinguistic discussions regarding how borders and boundaries are socially constructed and reconstructed between the two languages (Gal & Irvine, 1995).

Metalanguage can be defined as *reflexive language* that is used when speakers overtly remark on language, report utterances on language and describe aspects of language such as linguistic borders and boundaries (Lucy, 1993). These uses of language are metalinguistic in that they treat language as an object of reference and description, and also carry a judgment about the purpose and use of language. Furthermore, the use of metalinguistic discourse provides a way to document or to report the ways speakers understand and evaluate language as an object, especially in the presence of another contrasting language (Hanks, 1996). By observing how dual immersion students use one language to foreground and describe another or the same language, the researcher is able to document places and times in the everyday classroom life when the subject and object of the classroom discourse is language itself. However, metalinguistic activity takes place all the time in a bilingual classroom to help structure ongoing linguistic activity in daily speech (e.g. Why are there accent marks in Spanish and not in English?). In this study, the focus was on the students' use of metalanguage to express power/resistance relationships toward the Spanish and English linguistic borders and boundaries and even voice recognition of the different kinds of conflicts and contradictions between the Spanish and English languages (e.g. Why is Spanish used less in the class play?).

The following chapters in this book clearly show how the students in this fifth-grade classroom did take a position toward linguistic borders and boundaries in their classroom discourse; however, they predominantly voiced their position-takings solely in the English language. Yet, the position toward the English and Spanish borderlands was nonetheless voiced directly through metalanguage as students talked about mediation between the two languages within the dual immersion classroom and between their binary oppositions. Such metadiscourse is a reflexive mode of communication that can raise the students' critical consciousness about language, ideology and power. The dialogical interaction and interplay during metadiscourse provided revealing insights into how the dual immersion students actualized and interpreted the language relationships in their classroom. Their insights into language relations, ideology and power differentials are noteworthy for implications in bilingual education because they suggest that metalinguistic elicitation of the two languages from the students themselves can produce highly revealing results and provide direct evidence of their interpretations of everyday language use and the linguistic borderlands found between minority and majority languages.

Furthermore, reflexivity occurs when individuals voice a critique that becomes a *critical turning*, which can then lead to eventual ruptures within structures, such as a dual immersion classroom, and open up the *space of possible questions and answers* (Bourdieu, 1990). For example, if a dual immersion student exerts overt resistance toward a certain boundary, her/his use of metalanguage to express this resistance has the reflexive potential to force a rupture or breach in the structured binary between the two languages. Subsequently, this rupture can be seen as a positive phenomenon because it has the potential of leading students to that threshold point where unequal and uneven borders and boundaries no longer exist between the two languages and where it is possible to pose critical questions and subsequently shift linguistic borders and boundaries in different directions. By examining the position of the two languages through the analysis of students' metadiscourse and the field of power where these positions are often voiced, we can determine whether a critical turning in the students' metadiscourse led to eventual ruptures and opened up the space of possible questions and answers regarding the structure of the dual immersion classroom itself.

James Paul Gee (1989: 6) also proposes that metalanguage (e.g. meta-words, meta-values, meta-beliefs, metadiscourse) can be a *liberating and powerful force* that has the potential to analyze, resist and transgress over conflicts and tensions that are inherent when two or more languages, such as Spanish and English, are present. Gee's overarching definition of metalinguistic discourse includes a broader combination of *saying-writing-doing-being-valuing-believing* about language. According to Gee, when two languages are present together, they are bound to interfere with one another in terms of what the subjects are saying-writing-doing-being-valuing-believing about each language (e.g. the students' values toward Spanish use versus English use). This interference might possibly be resolved when metalinguistic discourse is used to analyze and critique language use through a type of dialectical discussion that allows participants to be consciously aware of how languages function in their classroom.

Within such metalinguistic discourse, overt talk regarding language as an object of contemplation can be powerful in terms of getting students empowered enough to truly transgress over structured binaries, borders and boundaries. In fact, such a *transgression* of binary oppositions can result from a rupture or overturning during the metalinguistic discussion so that the discussion now attempts to overcome any resistance and conflict between the majority and minority languages. The explanatory and interpretive principles of metalanguage in turn create an empowering classroom discourse accompanied by a greater reflexivity that has the potential to lead to a *critical turning* of linguistic binaries, borders and boundaries. Bourdieu (1990: 197) defines this empowering discourse as a *field of strategic possibilities* where the dual immersion students can possibly resolve the regulated system of differences inherit in a dual immersion structure by placing dynamic ruptures in effect, overcoming contradictions, and then moving toward a direction of restructuring change – a direction toward the search for non-binary solutions for language use and toward a transcendental understanding of language. Even though it is optimistic to believe that such a radical transformation can occur, this book captured when and where metalinguistic micro-revolts reached a threshold point that led to some structural changes in the unequal and uneven linguistic borders and boundaries between Spanish and English.

The Third Space: A Discursive and Empowering Space

According to cultural theorist Homi Bhabha (1994), once post-structuralist thought has deconstructed the false binary between the Spanish and English languages through student-led, conflict-ridden metadiscourse, the now infinite points of intersection between the Spanish and English language in a dual immersion classroom can then be recon-ceptualized in the *third space*. This liminal third space connects the two languages but also separates them through a tense and contradictory opposition to create a new, in-between, hybrid, fluid metaphysical space that is more open and inclusive of critical reflection regarding the linguistic borders and boundaries between the two languages. Within the third space, which is grounded mostly in a transcendental under-standing of language, it is possible for the speaking subject to not only differentiate between the two languages, but also to discuss how the two languages can condense together at once to create a new fugal space of language learning in which one language or culture does not gain a privileged status over the other. Rather, the languages can mix together freely and randomly in hybrid forms within the third space where constant back and forth *liminality* between borders and borderlands leads to fluctuating languages, cultures, discourses and spaces (Bhabha, 1994).

The theoretical framework of liminality originally comes from the work of anthropologist Victor Turner (1967) whose research on the perform-ances of rites of passage ceremonies in the traditional rural culture of the Ndembu tribe in Africa led him to define the protagonists in his research study as the *liminal persona*:

Their condition is one of ambiguity and paradox, a confusion of all the customary categories [. . .] We are not dealing with structural contradictions when we discuss liminality, but with the essentially unstructured (which is at once destructured and prestructured) and often the people themselves see this in terms of bringing neophytes into close connection with deity or with superhuman power, with what is, in fact, often regarded as the unbounded, the infinite, the limitless. (Turner, 1967: 96)

The liminal persona enters a liminal state through these performances of rites and rituals; this is a temporal state that is described by Turner as a period initiated through ritual in which the initiated is in a state of stasis between two borders:

During the liminal period, neophytes are alternately encouraged to think about their society, their cosmos, and the powers that generate and sustain them. Liminality may be partly described as a stage of reflection ... Liminal entities are neither here nor there; they are betwixt and between the positions assigned and arrayed by law, custom, convention, and ceremonial. (1967: 95–105)

Thus, liminality is an important category strongly related to the concept of cultural hybridity. For Bhabha, liminal as an interstitial passage between fixed identifications represents a possibility for a cultural hybridity that entertains difference without an assumed or imposed hierarchy. The concept of liminality as a quality of *in-between* space and/or state is important in describing some of the most interesting and highly specific social and cultural phenomena: the transcultural space, the transgeographical space, the transgender space, the translinguistic space, etc.

Furthermore, by describing space in terms of an in-between space, a philosophical mode and metaphor for thinking about space and spatiality and how it constitutes structures, power, knowledge, subjects and languages is created. The third space also shifts away from a one-dimensional and two-dimensional view of bounded spaces of thesis and antithesis and instead moves beyond this binary into a polysemic, synthesis space that is open to differences, otherness, anomalies and nonsynchronous entities. Viewed from this Hegelian perspective of dialectics, the hybrid third space allows for linguistic multidimensionality, non-linearity and scaled spaces to be more fully expressed through metalinguistic discourse that attempts to deconstruct the false binary between Spanish and English. Furthermore, the third space valorizes the existence of multiple subjectivities and perspectives, provides forms of analysis that express and articulate difference, that encourage critical thinking, even if it is disputatious and leads to potential sites of resistance. Unlike the modernist paradigm where dominated space is closed, sterilized and bifurcated, the postmodern third space is an appropriating space that serves the meta-needs of bilingual students so that they are able to voice their concerns about language use and linguistic borders and boundaries.

This book applies the abstract notion of the metaphorical third space to the everyday life of a fifth-grade dual immersion classroom. Empowering change in the classroom is possible through the third space because it blurs the linguistic borders and boundaries between the Spanish/English binary and exposes the non-hybrid, structuralist nature of the dominant dual immersion discourse. Yet, the empowering change leading up to the third space is possible only through *negotiation* – a process in accordance with mediation and communication. Bhabha (1994) claims that negotiation can bridge the differences among heterogeneous entities for progressive ends but without negating their differences either. Negotiation must not simply take place within the discursive space of enunciation, but between the ever-shifting lived space of the classroom so that the third space is being appropriated continually, as differences in ideology and power are being mediated. In turn, Homi Bhabha's third space can be read as a metaphorical space that complicates the established linguistic borders and boundaries in order to instigate critical consciousness of those borders and boundaries. It is as though opening up a discursive third space is necessary for critical consciousness to occur in the democratic classroom and will eventually lead to student empowerment that can potentially bring about the changing of structural borders and boundaries between Spanish and English. When students are given the opportunity to explore their own classroom structure, the third space becomes a powerful and evocative metaphor for the transformative engagement that happens in empowering dialogue when students argue, discuss and negotiate in a democratic classroom that allows for such possibilities to happen. Thus, in order to develop a third space that has potential consequences in the dual immersion classroom, it is also important to acknowledge the forces that keep the third space open and the classroom conditions that allow the third space to be found.

In an attempt to further ground the abstract notion of the third space, the postmodern geographer Edward Soja (1996) states that the epistemology of the third space is indeed a transgressive space that is open to new possibilities and insights that have moved beyond the first space–second space duality through a deconstructive, meaning-gathering, appropriating process such as a metadiscourse. Soja's third space is also a dominant post-structural, metalinguistic space that is looking for differences and Otherness since it has transgressed beyond the structural binary forces of a first and second discursive space. The third space is further defined by Soja as an all-inclusive geography that has extraordinary openness and a wide range of critical metalinguistic exchange that allows it to accept multiple perspectives. Once it overcomes the binary opposition, it is capable of becoming limitless:

> Everything comes together in the Thirdspace: subjectivity and objectivity, the abstract and the concrete, the real and the imagined, the knowable and the unimaginable, the repetitive and the differential, structure and agency, mind and body, consciousness and

unconsciousness, the disciplined and the transdisciplinary, everyday life and unending history. (Soja, 1996: 56)

Critical theorist bell hooks (1994) also defines the concept of the third space as a transgressive space where the rupturing of borders is needed in order to empower students to *voice* their resistance through dialectical discussions that are indeed metalinguistic in nature. In order for such dialectical discussions to occur in the classroom, bell hooks states that it is necessary to have a democratic exchange of ideas from the students that is fundamental to the transgressive third space. However, bell hooks also states that during such critical dialogue and dialectical discussions, it is important that the students' positions toward language use and linguistic borders and boundaries are neither silenced nor given preference over other positions or it would not be an empowering third space.

Gutierrez (1995) has also investigated the possibility of the theoretical third space within the bilingual and bicultural classroom. Gutierrez and Reyes first published an article in the *Harvard Educational Review* that located the third space in the conflicting dialogue and social interactions between the classroom teacher and the students. By recording classroom dialogue scripts and using discourse analysis to review the scripts, Gutierrez and Reyes were able to locate moments when the teacher discourse and student discourse stumbled upon the third space, which they define as "the only space where a true interaction or communication between teacher and student can occur in the classroom . . . a middle ground or third space" (1995: 447). Here the term *middle ground* connotes a process of mediation and negotiation between the teacher and the student that then led them to the third space. By locating when and where the teacher and student discourse truly intersected, overlapped, and coexisted throughout conflict and contestation, the researchers were able to examine patterns of classroom discourse over an extended period of time within this bicultural classroom. Through *thick descriptions* of classroom interactions, Gutierrez and Reyes presented evidence of the third space by examining student and teacher conflicts about domination and resistance and how those conflicts were negotiated and resolved within the transgressive, empowering third space. Thus, it is critical to first locate transgressive, third spaces in the open and reflexive classroom where students can take part in a metadiscourse on language – a new space that renders, makes visible, vocalizes and questions that which is otherwise transparent, silent and unquestioned about language use and linguistic borders and boundaries in a dual immersion classroom.

Social Cartography: Constructing a Trajectory of the Third Space

In this book, I located the classroom contexts that best illuminated the full power and utility of metalinguistic reflexivity by focusing on when and where students in the fifth-grade dual immersion classroom organized their conversations and social activity around metalinguistic discussions related to language use and linguistic borders (Gee & Green, 1998). In particular, I located classroom spaces where students attempted to situate themselves in a lived third space through such metalinguistic discussions. However, it cannot be assumed that all metalinguistic discussions will necessarily lead to a transcendental understanding of language via negotiation of linguistic borders and boundaries within the third space. Rather, it is imperative to examine the dialectical development of the metalinguistic discussions to determine whether or not they eventually led to the restructuring of extant linguistic borders. Only by the means of a critical ethnography will the researcher be able to construct a *social trajectory* of the third space by observing how the dual immersion students position themselves in successive metalinguistic discussions throughout the school year in order to locate if and when the third space is ever appropriated (Paulston, 1996). When each point in the social trajectory is combined with others, it will provide a holistic, context-dependent and integrative analysis of conflicts related to linguistic borders and boundaries and the appropriation of the third space within this dual immersion classroom.

Chapter 1 provides background information on the research setting, the classroom teacher and the dual language students. Chapter 2 focuses on the events related to the Spanish spelling bee episode and the Reading Buddies episode, which both highlight the tension between the use of Spanish versus English in the language arts curriculum. However, in these two episodes, I also examine the kinds of spaces and places in which such metalinguistic discussions surrounding language use and linguistic borders and boundaries had occurred most often throughout the school year. In particular, the rug area was one of those central places in the classroom that allowed for the flow of intersubjective discussions surrounding language use amongst the students and teachers, especially during class meetings that were held on the rug every Monday and Friday mornings. Chapter 3 focuses on the cheers episode in which the dual immersion students had to create a pep rally cheer to best represent their identity as a dual immersion classroom in front of their fifth-grade, monolingual peers. Chapter 4 focuses on the drama episode in which the students produced and presented a colonial Cuban play examining race, class and gender, as well as the performativity of primitivism and the folklorization of blackness in Spanish children's literature. Chapter 5 focuses on a school music program in which a Puerto Rican teacher came into the dual immersion classrooms to teach the students how to sing traditional Spanish folk songs. Within all these chapters, the tensions and contradictions inherent within language use and linguistic borders and boundaries resurfaced in the metadiscourse and grounded the book's theoretical foundation.

In Chapter 6, the book's conclusion, I analyze how all the chapters related to each other intertextually; for example, the development of the metadiscourse in the drama episode differed ontologically in many ways from the other three episodes. Here the use of a dialectical framework allowed me to analyze the movement and direction that the metalinguistic discourse took throughout the duration of each specific episode. The dialectical discussions surrounding language use and linguistic borders and boundaries sometimes led to the maintenance of existent borders and boundaries between the Spanish and English language, even until the very end. Sometimes these dialectical discussions led to the restructuring of the existent linguistic borders and boundaries to produce a hybrid third space where both languages could coexist simultaneously. While at other times, the dialectical discussions were held in suspension at the end of the episode and subsequently repressed in the class memory, such as in the cheers episode, so that no restructuring of linguistic borders and boundaries was possible thereafter in the larger context of the classroom discourse. In turn, I attempted to describe what type of transformations the metadiscourse underwent in each chapter, if any, as the discourse surrounding particular events and episodes changed over time, moved through different spaces and places, and dealt with the different levels of power and resistance. By examining each chapter according to whether structural changes were actualized, we can better understand how the dialectics within the metadiscourse at times led to transformational changes while at other times they remained stagnant or repressed.

Lastly, even though the language-space-power dynamic remains the main theoretical lens of this book, at the heart of these articulations of language-space-power, there were larger looming questions of community, identity, agency and epistemology. Classroom culture, cultural change and continuity, the emergence and functioning of power relationships, and the shaping of cultural identities are phenomena investigated and analyzed in this book through an interdisciplinary cultural studies framework in order to better understand not only the possibility of how, when and where language use patterns and linguistic borders and boundaries could change but also for a better understanding of how differences in class, gender, race, ethnicity and language shape how we analyze a classroom and how classrooms are seen through these *differences*.

Chapter 1
The Research Setting

Why Critical Ethnography?

Influenced by neo-Marxist theory, critical ethnography places human participants at the center of analysis and examines their interpretive and negotiating abilities in social settings (Holston, 1989). Critical ethnography has borrowed its focus on thick descriptions of human participants interpreting and negotiating amongst themselves from interpretivist ethnography. In this yearlong research study, I also studied the social reality of a local dual immersion classroom and wrote thick descriptions on how the dual immersion students, teachers, parents and administrators interacted socially to construct and negotiate the meaning of language use and linguistic borders and boundaries in their local classrooms and school. Critical ethnography also interrogates specific and local meanings in a social setting and presents multiple and perhaps incompatible perspectives of that lived social reality through a heterogeneous recording of differences between and amongst the negotiated meanings. It also seeks to identify contradictions, gaps, inconsistencies, slippages and other paradoxes between actual and perceived social realities in order to initiate empowering change in existing asymmetrical power networks (Le Compte & Priessle, 1984).

Furthermore, the human participants in a critical ethnography are seen as empowered agents who can change the structure of their social realities through acts of resistance (Gore, 1992). In this study, the complexities of the dual immersion students' resistance to the linguistic borderlands was documented through metadiscourse in order to provide an understanding of the contradictions they perceived between the two languages within the classroom discourse and how they went about negotiating and mediating these conflicts, even though these sites of resistance toward, and negotiation of, linguistic borders are assumptions that the critical ethnographer often makes as an outsider. Nonetheless, critical ethnography calls for giving voice to the viewpoints of informants who are often marginalized or silenced in research. It also stresses the need for asking questions that have never been formulated before and tries to address them through unconventional methods. Next, it asks the researcher to interpret the research results through new theoretical lenses and present them in novel ways that portray the multiple viewpoints and perspectives that can constitute the social reality of a dual immersion classroom. In order to increase the validity of these theoretical assumptions, the critical researcher must consult and collaborate with the researched subjects and co-define the data together by seeking the informant's perception of these sites of resistance and the theoretical construct of the third space, which may seem quite abstract to the informants.

By conducting informal interviews throughout the data collection phase with key student participant-informants and then formal post-interviews at the end of the study, this study replayed "the multiple voices that created the original scene . . . and presents the informants' comments in such temporally situated, multiple-coexistent ethnography, in a sense, to parallel the presentation of disparate perspectives as found in cubist paintings and polyphonic music" (Quantz & O'Conner, 1988: 20). My role as the researcher was to "understand the meaning of their experiences, to walk into their shoes, to feel things as they feel them, to explain things as they explain them" (Spradley, 1980: 9). Instead of making preconceived evaluations and judgments before the observation process, I came to discover the students' ways of speaking about the linguistic borders and boundaries between the Spanish and English language through classroom observations as an outsider, non-participant observer who strictly observes and describes the classroom without using a structured format for recording data through predetermined codes (Erickson, 1980). In the end, the researcher's theoretical constructs, the student participant-informant's commonsense notions of these constructs and the research data containing the metadiscourse came together to make sense of the linguistic borderlands and the possibility of a third space within this fifth-grade dual immersion classroom.

In the Foothills of Dual Immersion Country

I first found out about PS 2000 through a bilingual education course assignment in which I had to analyze a dual immersion school in the city. I was given a list of schools by the instructor and told to contact the schools myself. PS 2000 was the first school that I had telephoned and I immediately received a warm reception from the school secretary who recommended that I come observe Roberta's fifth-grade classroom because she was an exemplary teacher who was used to having visitors observe her teaching. After setting up an appointment with Roberta and meeting her in person, I realized that both she and the school would be open to me coming in regularly throughout my graduate coursework at the local university to observe her classroom teaching on an ongoing basis. For the first two years of our relationship, I would visit Roberta's classroom every so often in order to validate a number of thesis papers I wrote in my beginning graduate courses. As I started approaching the stage in which I had to develop a qualifying paper and state my initial dissertation research interests, I visited Roberta's classroom more often and one day accidentally stumbled across a classroom event that then led me to pursue the theoretical framework for this book. The students were situated on the rug during a classroom meeting in which the student council president, Anna, a Puerto Rican female, brought up a heated topic for group discussion – the regulation of Spanish in formal and informal spaces. Anna became quite emotional and began crying over the fact that she found her peers, even her Spanish-dominant peers, continually resorting to the use of English rather than Spanish in informal spaces such as the hallway, cafeteria, playground and activity classes. The discussion continued with a volley of shots from students both in favor of and against the patrolling of linguistic borders by the students themselves in these informal spaces. When I walked away from the class meeting in which the issue was never really resolved but had dramatically affected the classroom ethos, I knew then and there that this was what I wanted to research for my dissertation – locating when and where dual immersion students talked reflectively about the uneven and unequal borders and boundaries between the Spanish and English languages.

When I first entered the field setting in September 1999 for my dissertation research, I was there on average two to three full days throughout the school week and for a full academic year ending in June 2000. By observing both English and Spanish days equally, I stayed grounded in the competing classroom discourses from the very beginning. During this yearlong study, I observed and described everyday classroom life starting from the very beginning of the school year by using both informal data recording strategies such as field notes, and formal observation instruments such as videotapes and audiotapes. In addition to identifying patterns and summarizing weekly field reports, I used the field notes to develop hypotheses in regards to how the students used metalanguage to negotiate the linguistic borderlands. After I had observed that a certain classroom space, such as the weekly class meetings that were held in the rug area at the beginning and end of each school week, had the potential to lead toward the targeted metalinguistic discussions, I then made a concerted effort to formally record these metalinguistic places on audio-tape and videotape. As the researcher, I was constantly aware of changing classroom contexts and subsequently located those points in the social trajectory of the classroom life that contained potential for metalin-guistic discussions. Thus, I came to an understanding of the classroom discourse by first entering into the full social context of the classroom and then documenting how the student participants debate and interact within specific metalinguistic discussions during and in specific times and places.

Furthermore, according to Patton (1990), a qualitative research design needs to remain sufficiently open and flexible to permit exploration of whatever phenomenon under study offers for inquiry. By observing class-room conversations when the dual immersion students acknowledged each other and engaged each other in metadiscourse, I observed features and patterns of language use that were situational and spatially defined in the classroom (Heras, 1993). Since classroom talk can be both ordinary everyday talk and specific talk, I focused on specific words, phrases and uses of language that reflected ways of speaking about the linguistic borders and boundaries between Spanish and English. In other words, as the teacher and students constructed the classroom discourse, my posi-tion was to observe and record *interactional spaces* where they interacted in a particular place, at particular moments in time, and with particular configurations of participants (e.g. whole class, table groups, pairs and individuals) in relation to metalinguistic discussions concerning linguis-tic borders and boundaries (Heras, 1993). In order to draw on extensive ethnographic data over a yearlong period, the study first examined a range of interactional spaces and relationships within and amongst multiple classroom spaces (desk area, rug area, drama class, hallways); then focused on differences in patterns of classroom discourse (teacher talk vs. student talk); and finally found where opportunities for border-land metalinguistic discussions occurred most often. The recording of everyday classroom life and the social and discursive processes and prac-tices that make up its existence allowed me to understand how language, space and power intersected on a diurnal basis.

After charting the classroom spaces and their discourses, I targeted and located focal places and times when and where metalinguistic discus-sions occurred often in the classroom discourse. Then I devised a plan of investigation that entailed selectively recording and collecting written, audiotaped, and videotaped observations of these metalinguistic-filled spaces. As I analyzed this initial set of data, I came up with questions that guided the next cycle of data collection and interpretation – whether or not the classroom participants ever reached a transgressive third space in which they overcame the inequities of false linguistic binaries. Some of these questions were also used during informal interviews with some of the students and teachers to help guide me further during the formal interviews I conducted at the very end of the study.

While I was carrying out regular observations, audiotaping and video-taping the metalinguistic discussions, I also tried to identify participant-informants who played a key role in the different metalinguistic discussions and who also had a strong influence in the establishment of power relations during these discussions. After choosing six key participant-informants, I conducted in-depth, open-ended interviews at the end of the yearlong period in order to record how these key informants defined the tensions and contradictions between the Spanish and English language and how they perceived their role within these metalinguistic episodes. After conducting broad initial observations, I searched for participant-informants who could provide me with insider information from the perspective of a classroom native. Instead of becoming the sole authority in the research process, I wanted to negotiate with the participant-informants regarding the representation and signification of these meta-linguistic episodes and the possibility of a third space. Participants accepted as insiders are likely to have access to languages and social inter-actions different from those observable to the researcher (Milroy, 1987).

The factor that was most theoretically important for this study was finding participant-informants who were negotiating between the linguis-tic borders and boundaries and were generally struggling with issues of language and power, thus the sampling frame for this study was based mostly on theoretical grounds (Johnson, 1990). For example, the selected six participant-informants were struggling to keep the Spanish lan-guage from slipping from their grasp by negotiating and reformulating language constructs of domination and difference. The participant-informants were also attempting to situate themselves in that fluctuating, fluid third space where they could transgress over linguistic borders and boundaries. However, instead of being characterized as marginal figures in the classroom, all six participant-informants were central figures who were involved in leading and initiating the border skirmishes throughout the academic school year. Oftentimes, their voicing of these skirmishes opened up the carefully patrolled linguistic borders and boundaries in this dual immersion classroom. These classroom natives in many ways were attempting to redefine the local dual immersion classroom structure through their "self-making acts of exclusion and inclusion within and across the third space" (Tsing, 1993c: 9). In this process, the divide between the Spanish and English language had dissolved in some metalinguistic episodes, as the participant-informants moved beyond the linguistic binary pulling at them. Their authentic, partial voices were speaking from the in-between, fluid third space, where there was a "critical exchange that could become the location of resistance struggle, a meeting place where new and radical happenings can occur" (hooks, 1994: 30).

Thus, it was important to find student participant-informants who were able to help reduce the ethnographic data so that the data were representative of this study's theoretical framework of the third space. By having them review and analyze either videotaped or audiotaped episodes in which they could locate themselves in specific metalinguistic discussions, calling attention to the complexity and specificity of sociolinguistic intersections in the dual immersion classroom, this study first recorded their interpretations of the metalinguistic discussions and then transcribed them. Furthermore, the reciprocal affirmation and endorsement of the data from equally significant student participants disavows any one regime of truth as devised solely by the researcher; instead, multiple truths are documented from various participant-informants. By checking their understanding of what transpired in the metalinguistic discussions, the discourses of resistance, and the third space, as exhibited in the data, I was able to strengthen the study's validity due to the fact that my observations were triangulated with six student responses and understandings of the same data. All the interviews were conducted in English but students could have responded in either English or Spanish, depending on their preference. However, the interview instrument remained the same for all students, regardless if they were language majority or minority students. The formal interviews marked the end of the research study.

The School Setting: An Exemplary Site

The site for this research study was an exemplary, public elementary school (Pre-K-5) located in a large urban city on the East Coast, and it will be referred to as PS 2000 throughout the book. Located in a neighborhood with mostly historic three-story brick apartment buildings dating from the late 1800s, brownstone apartments, and active upscale businesses catering to a predominantly white, upper middle-class residential area, this 1959 neighborhood school is a four-story brick structure located within walking distance of major cultural centers, corporations, museums, restaurants and public parks. Inside the school, there is a wide array of student work displayed in the hallways and on classroom doors, and several awards won by individual students and teachers are displayed in glass showcases. The student population at this school is diverse in terms of both socioeconomic status and racial and ethnic backgrounds. The school enrolls 1000 students in grades pre-kindergarten through fifth. Of those students, 47% are White, 22% are Hispanic, 23% are African-American and the remaining 8% are Asian, Pacific Islander, or Native American (Hemphill, 1997). The majority is upper middle class based on the school's reported socioeconomic status; however, 25% of the students are in the free and reduced lunch program. Even though most of the students are from the local neighborhood, there is still a one-third student population living outside of the neighborhood that commutes to the school from more impoverished parts of the city. This one-third of the student population that resides outside of the school zone must apply for student enrollment through a lottery system in which there are usually 300 applicants for 150 positions in the kindergarten class.

In its school board listing, PS 2000 has been described as the following:

> Within this heterogeneous setting, students learn and flourish from a cadre of unusually creative, dedicated and talented teachers. Working with interdisciplinary units centered on core themes, this school's teachers develop curriculum based on established guidelines. Several of our staff work as mentor teachers to their younger colleagues, and have been actively involved in professional development programs. A number of teachers have been videotaped in their classrooms and used as models at teaching institutions throughout the country. In addition to an unusually diligent teaching staff, the school boasts a uniquely actively, committed parent body.

In a parents' guidebook to the city's public schools, Clara Hemphill (1997) wrote a lengthy description of this school in relation to its school environment and culture, student demographics and school curriculum. She describes the school as a big, noisy school with creative and enthusiastic teachers and a hyperactive parent association that raised funds over $180,000 in the past year. The school curriculum is defined as progressive and mirrors the liberal and eclectic philosophy of this particular city neighborhood. In terms of the school's philosophical outlook, Hemphill describes the school as aggressively egalitarian because it earnestly tries to implement a multicultural and multiethnic curriculum. Even though it is one of the most popular public schools in the city, the students attending the school range from those whose parents own the local hardware store, to professionals in the corporate world, and to artists, actors and musical composers who cannot afford to send their children to expensive private schools. In terms of what is happening in the classroom, Hemphill states that the students are having lots of fun and seem happy and relaxed because of the kind of curriculum being taught in their classrooms. She raises the following points: (1) the children work on a project-based curriculum; (2) they paint, sing, work on the computers and write their own stories and books; (3) the curriculum is interdisciplinary and uses thematic units; (4) the children move at their own pace; (5) mathematics is taught using hands-on manipulatives; (6) there are no textbooks, only authentic literature; (7) the curriculum units begin with extensive discussions; (8) the students utilize basic research techniques and skills often; and (9) the students are totally immersed in the subject matter and the subjects come alive for them.

The following text is a speech written by a parent at PS 2000 who was involved with the school's afterschool programs. The speech provides an insider's view of the school as seen through the eyes of the many visitors who come to observe the school from all over the world:

As a parent, too, I owe this wonderful PS 2000 community so very much. Think of it. My children went to a school that was named one of the top ten in the country by *Child* magazine and twice named the best school in this city by *Redbook* magazine. Their classmates included a girl who became a national finalist in the Intel Talent Search, and a boy who in middle school went to the White House and interviewed the President on education issues.

I was your PA president during my younger daughter's last two years at PS 2000, and part of the job I most enjoyed was welcoming visiting journalists and educators from all over the world. Their presence in our school gave me a great gift: the chance to see PS 2000 through fresh eyes, and to marvel again at what happens in our classes and halls.

From the education minister at the University of Ghana, to educators from the Republic of China, Russia, Japan, Sweden, and France, they came to see at this school what we often take for granted: a place where children are treated with respect and caring, where they are encouraged to feel a sense of pride and ownership in their school, where there is creative and exciting learning literally jumping off the walls.

In a school newsletter that the parent association publishes weekly, members of the school community can send in a written entry that they want to publish. At the end of the school year, one of the school newsletters printed the following caption that highlights the multicultural mission of the school: "Welcome Banner. Please help our school say 'welcome' in different languages. If you know how to say 'welcome' in another language, please send it in to your teacher or leave it in the marked box in the office." The school calendar was also listed in the newsletter and included the notation of multicultural events as the *Dual Immersion Pot Luck Picnic* and the *Multicultural Learning Group Pot Luck*, along with other inclusive school-wide events such as the performance of plays, afterschool activities, weekend retreats, dance festivals, cultural events, tutoring services, babysitting services, money-raising events and semi-annual auctions. The reactions to these events were also posted in the newsletters for those parents who were unable to attend any of the events:

> On Wednesday, April 12, over 25 people filled the library for the **Multicultural Learning Group** breakfast. The real nourishment was the discussion of goals and projects aimed at helping us learn more about just who we all are here at PS 2000. Among the items discussed were a reading group, diversity and sensitivity training, potluck dinners in the park and at one another's homes. And of course, planning for the *Cinco de Mayo* International Family Dinner and Dance is well underway!

The school administration also sent out flyers to students announcing upcoming multicultural events held during the evenings for students and their families:

> This Friday ... *Cinco de Mayo* International Family Dinner and Dance. D.J., Dancing, and Dance Instruction in the PS 2000 Gym. Food, Drinks, and Air Conditioning in the Cafeteria. Children: $5.00. Adults: Free. Sign-up to bring a covered-dish to feed 6–8 people and your whole family gets in for free! Friday, May 5th from 6:30–10:00 p.m.

The flyers sent home were translated into Spanish for the dual immersion classrooms; however, it is evident to a proficient Spanish reader that there are spelling errors, word usage problems and a lack of accent marks in the original Spanish translations:

> Pan American Week Celebration
> April 10–14, 2000
> The Pan American week celebration is upon us and it is the Dual Immersion Program's responsibility to organize the bake sale, among

other activities. The class representatives will be in charge of recruiting volunteers from each class to bake/bring goods typical of the Americas to sell during that week. Things like muffins, breads, fruits, nut mixes, pastelillos, or any baked goods that are easy to eat and carry around would be wonderful. We will also need people to help with the set up, sale, and clean up that day. It is still not known when will the bake sale take place but it will probably be on the same day as the show/entertainment. We will keep you posted on any developments. We TRULY appreciate your help. The money made will go toward the Dual Immersion Program.

Celebracion De La Semana Pan Americana
Abril 10–14, 2000
Se esta acercando rapidamente la semana Pan Americana y le corresponde al Programa en Dos Idiomas organizar la venta de biscochos y postres, entre otras actividades. Los padres representates de cada clase se encargaran de organizar un grupos de voluntarios que puedan traer los biscochos y ayudar con la venta ese dia. Los biscochos deben ser tipicos de las Americas, pero principalmente deben ser faciles de comer y transportar. Algunas sugerencias son muffins, pastelillos, galletas, obleas, frutas o nueces mixtas. Todavia no sabemos que dia especificamente se hara la venta de bizcochos pero muy posiblemente sera el mismo dia de la presentacion artistica que se contrate. Se las agradece enormemente su ayuda. El dinero que se recoja sera utilizado por el Porgrama de Dos Idiomas. Ojala todos participen.

The District's Dual Immersion Program

PS 2000 decided to pioneer a dual immersion program when the US Department of Education gave federal funding to expand dual immersion programs because of their reported academic effectiveness. Now the school district's dual immersion program attracts many diverse students throughout the city since its inception in the early 1990s. In the following local newspaper article, the district's dual immersion program was highlighted for its ability to enhance language learning, especially for young children:

When Hattie Evans hailed a taxi in Midtown recently and the Spanish-speaking driver struggled to understand English, her 9-year-old son, Maurice Julius Evans, suddenly perked up and gave the driver directions to their uptown apartment house in Spanish.

The moment was pivotal for both mother and son, because it was one of the first times that Maurice was confident enough to speak Spanish outside of his fourth-grade classroom. And Hattie had the opportunity to witness firsthand the benefits of her son's school's relatively uncommon language-instruction program known as dual language.

"All of a sudden I was telling the driver in Spanish how to get from Stern's department store to our apartment in Sugar Hill," Maurice, who is African-American, recalled recently during an interview at the school. "Now, I help my mom and neighbors at the *bodega* when they need a translator." (Holloway, 2001)

The dual immersion program at this particular school grew nearly by one grade per year until it reached its current configuration of a PreK-5 dual immersion model. At each grade level, there is only one Spanish/English dual immersion classroom and five other English monolingual classrooms. Each graduating class of dual immersion students stays together as a self-contained group from kindergarten to fifth grade throughout each school year. Each class in the dual immersion program ideally tries to enroll half Spanish-dominant language minority students and half English-dominant language majority students. The vision at this particular school is that Spanish-dominant and English-dominant students could become bilingual and biliterate in an environment that honors and celebrates the languages and cultures of both its student groups. The school also believes that the best time to learn a second language is early in life, and with appropriate instruction and the necessary home/school support, all students can become bilingual and biliterate by the end of the fifth grade. The dual immersion vision grew, developed and has been passed down for nearly ten years. However, faculty, parents and the principal have refined the dual immersion program over time, based upon immediate language development concerns and needs. In the following school newsletter, there is a bilingual advertisement for the dual immersion program in which accepted families with Spanish-dominated children are asked to apply especially to the school's dual immersion program:

PS 2000 Programa de Dos Idiomas
Atención: Familias con Niños Que Hablan Español
PS 2000 tiene un programa de immersion de dos idiomas. Los alumnos aprenden los cursos en inglés y español cada día. Es un programa ideal para niños que son fluentes en el español y vienen de familias que

quieren que sus hijo(s) continuen el desarollo del español mientras esten aprendiendo el inglés. PS 2000 esta cometido a la diversidad de culturas, y tienen un grupo de padres muy activo en el programa. Si esta interesado que su hijo (a) forme parte de un programa enrequecido come este, porfavor llamar a nosotros si tienen preguntas o necesita información.

PS 2000 Dual Immersion Program
Attention: Families with Children Who Speak Spanish
PS 2000 has a Dual Immersion Program where children are taught certain subjects in Spanish each day, as well as other subjects in English. This is an ideal program for children who are fluent in Spanish and who come from families who support Spanish speaking at home. The school is currently accepting applications for the 4th and 5th grade classes. Overall, the school is excellent and committed to diversity. It has an active parent group. If you are interested in having your child in an enriching program, please call us if you have questions or need information.

Furthermore, PS 2000 was seen as having an exemplary dual immersion model during the time of this study. The term exemplary is defined hereafter in accordance with the factors and variables identified by Carrasquillo and Rodriguez (1996) in their research of three bilingual schools. After visiting the schools, observing bilingual classrooms, interviewing bilingual students and their teachers, administrators and their parents, analyzing test data and academic records, evaluating student work and conducting teacher questionnaires, the team of researchers indicated ten characteristics that contribute to the academic success of exemplary bilingual education programs: (1) a positive school climate; (2) an administration with leadership and commitment to bilingual education; (3) teachers' high expectations of students; (4) teacher effectiveness and empowerment; (5) clearly defined curriculum; (6) extracurricular and co-curricular activities; (7) high student self-esteem and expectations of themselves; (8) academic growth; (9) satisfactory attendance; and (10) parental involvement. PS 2000 qualifies as an exemplary dual immersion school because it has been the recipient of many awards and honors in recent years based on the criteria listed above that has given the school district-wide recognition for its language education.

The district is committed to the dual immersion program at PS 2000 and works closely with a local school of education to provide teachers and parents professional development workshops on the dual immersion model. At least four times during the school year, the local school district held all-day Saturday conferences for all dual immersion parents and teachers from the four dual immersion elementary schools to attend. However, most of the conference participants were parents and a few district officials; it was rare for the dual immersion teachers in the district to attend these Saturday conferences. The conferences often began with the district officials and professors of education giving an overview of where dual immersion bilingual programs stand in relation to language policy at the national, state and local levels. After their introduction, the conference participants often listened to a nationally recognized keynote speaker and expert on the topic of dual immersion education; then they attended morning workshops related to classroom practices and district policies; ate a catered lunch; attended afternoon workshops; and then came together as a whole group at the end of the day to listen to closing remarks and provide feedback and evaluation on the conference proceedings.

According to the local school district, the goals of the Saturday dual immersion conferences were to (1) support the professional growth of dual immersion teachers; (2) to foster the exchange of ideas across schools; and (3) to create partnerships among teachers and administrators across dual immersion schools. The following transcript narrates the opening introduction of one of the Saturday dual immersion conferences held at the local school of education in which one district official states that the children in the dual immersion program do as well as and even outperform students in the monolingual English programs on the district's English reading tests. The district officials and professors were fluent in English and Spanish and translated what they said first in English into Spanish for the Spanish-dominant parents:

District Bilingual Coordinator: Children who read and write in two languages have a major advantage. Now we see that here in our own district . . . in the scores . . . in the reading . . . in the English reading tests results that we get from the various schools throughout the district . . . that children from the dual immersion program do as well . . . and in many cases . . . even better than children who are learning only English . . . so we have firsthand experience with that . . . *Primero quiería decir que la última vez ustedes aprendieron muchos de las características de las programas de dos idiomas y es el método que tener éxito y competencia en dos idiomas . . . tanto en el segundo idioma para los estudiantes. Aprendieron también del proceso de aprendizar el otro lenguaje . . . y sobre todo de los estudios nos demuenstran que niños que lean y escriben dos idiomas tienen una gran* *ventaja y nos vemos aquí en nuestro distrito . . . con los resultados de los exámenes de lectura en inglés y los niños en el programa de dos idiomas hacen bien y en muchos casos superior a los . . . demas estudiantes que son . . . que estan en programas de solo inglés.*

Since I attended all four of the all-day Saturday conferences in the district, I was able to interview parents as to why they wanted their children enrolled in a dual immersion program as well as take note of what kind of discourse was produced during these weekend conferences. Oftentimes, research on dual immersion education neglects to focus on the black and Asian parents who send their children to dual immersion programs. The following transcript shows how a few black parents sent their children to dual immersion schools due to their own personal histories and ancestry in postcolonial nations such as Jamaica and Panama where multiple languages coexist in the African diaspora:

Author: Why did you decide to put your children in the dual immersion program?

Yolanda [black female parent]:   Well . . . I have family . . . that . . . from Panama . . . I had grandparents . . . Panamanian . . . and no one ever . . . like once I left their home . . . no one ever . . . continued . . . and here we are . . . we have Spanish-speaking people . . . within the city . . . and . . . here I don't know anything . . . and I feel very lost . . . 'cause I feel I should know something . . . and since I don't feel that I have . . . the mentality to learn this because I always felt . . . umm . . . ashamed . . . because I didn't know something . . . uh . . . like I said . . . I don't know how to roll my tongue . . . to pronounce certain words . . . so . . . I want my children to have that . . . and I want them to have that extra step . . . if they can receive extra money in the field . . . by knowing a second language. I want that for them. So . . . that's how I feel . . .

Author: Similar reasons for you two . . . ?

Jerome [black male parent]:   Yes similar reasons. I grew up in a home where my grandfather lived in Cuba for a long period of time until his early adult stage. And . . . my son . . . I think . . . in a way . . . it would be good . . . for him to be able to speak two different languages. His kindergarten teacher . . . advised us at some point . . . that he had a knack for Spanish. He learned a couple of songs in school. Then he came home . . . he was singing those songs.

Nadine [black female parent]:   He had the tongue for it also. I mean . . . pronouncing . . . like . . . so. Unfortunately, the kindergarten teacher

had a terminal illness and she died. So . . . you know what I mean . . .
things were topsy-turvy. And . . . in the end . . . we decided let's go for
it. I mean . . . if it doesn't work you have the option of pulling away.
Let's see how . . . I mean . . . for me . . . I learned Spanish in high school.
I can sit and listen to someone talk. I know what they talking . . . I'm
not fluent speaking . . . but . . . can understand the whole conversation.
So I mean . . . if he could at least do that . . . as a teenager or as an adult
. . . it's good.

Author: Where are you from originally?

Jerome and Nadine [husband and wife]:   Jamaica . . .

Author: You grew up with . . . ?

Nadine: Spanish. You had to do Spanish. It was compulsory. It is the
second language in Jamaica.

Jerome: It is mandatory now in the schools. At the kindergarten stage
you start.

Nadine: It is not so far away from Cuba. But everyone is introduced
and it's done as a subject. Not like . . . you know a program where you
learn both languages. It's a subject area that you have to do. So . . . at
least you have a knowledge of what Spanish is.

Jerome: And Latin is mixed.

Nadine: 'Cause I have an older son now who is in the eleventh grade
and he's doing Spanish. And he's doing better in Spanish than English.
'Cause he was introduced in Jamaica at an early stage. It's done in
elementary. Now when I was in school . . . it was high school. But now
they're introducing it early.

It was evident from attending the district-organized conferences that
the district officials, professors of bilingual education and parents all
wholeheartedly supported the district's dual immersion program and
often reported on its merits. However, throughout this study, tensions
developed within the school district between groups of participants who
supported the dual immersion program in its extant form and groups of
participants who wanted to change the dual immersion program due to
a variety of reasons.

The teachers at PS 2000 made up one group of participants who
did not wholeheartedly support the dual immersion program at their
school because of the added pressure and responsibility of preparing a
curriculum in two languages, as well as the inconsistency between the
degree of Spanish taught at the different grade levels. The principal at PS
2000 did not wholeheartedly support the dual immersion program for
various reasons such as the fact that the school was held accountable only

for the English proficiency levels and there was no testing required in the Spanish language as of yet; teacher turnover and the difficulty of finding teachers fluent in both English and Spanish; and the responsibility of finding external resources and finances to supplement the school's dual immersion program. Even though the teachers and school administrators supported bilingualism and multiculturalism, they nonetheless wanted to make changes to a program that the district touted as one of its best and thus did not want changed.

Throughout the school year, the dual immersion parent association, led by two upper-middle-class, English-dominant, white female parents, met often with the principal, district officials, other parents and teachers in advocacy of greater Spanish representation within the dual immersion curriculum. However, it was primarily the upper-middle-class, English-dominant, white parents who took on an active role in the change process and became leaders in the petition for Spanish language equity. Many of these parents stated that they wanted their upper-middle-class, English-dominant, white children to become fully fluent in Spanish because of the linguistic capital it afforded them (Bourdieu, 1982). Meanwhile, the lower-middle-class, Spanish-dominant, Hispanic parents wanted their children to mostly maintain Spanish fluency while learning the English language and thus enrolled their lower-middle-class, Spanish-dominant, Hispanic children in the dual immersion program for the human capital it afforded them. Nevertheless, both groups of parents came together to form the dual immersion parent association and often discussed the economic capital behind the dual immersion program. The dual immersion parent association helped raise money throughout the year for much needed resources and materials, as well as for a few weekend retreats for the dual immersion teachers. Even though two white parents administered and ran the dual immersion parent association, there were several Spanish-dominant parents also represented in the organizational meetings. In the beginning of the school year, I was able to attend the first dual immersion parent meeting of the year and recorded field notes capturing who the parents were, as well as the mounting tensions surrounding the school's dual immersion program:

Earlier in the afternoon, I called the parent who was organizing this meeting and gained her approval for coming to the meeting. When I arrived at the meeting, there were only a few parents there. I asked the parent coordinator, Sandy, a white English-dominant mother from the local neighborhood, if it would be okay to take field notes. She said that I could take notes. So, I took a seat off to the side because I was directed to do so by Sandy who stated that the parents are sitting at the main table in the center. More and more parents started coming into the room and introducing themselves to each other. They seem to already know each other. Some of them brought their children also. Julia's mother, who is Dominican, is speaking in Spanish with another Spanish-dominant parent. The meeting is being held in the 2nd grade dual immersion classroom. The teacher has Spanish text all over the walls. There is a Spanish poem about PS 2000 on the wall and a Spanish poem about *insectos* [insects]. Sandy puts up a newspaper article on the chalkboard that talks about how parents in the city are enrolling their children in Spanish language programs because Spanish is becoming so important to the city. Subsequently, Sandy hopes that some money and attention will trickle down to the dual immersion program from the school's larger budget.

At this moment, there are 17 parents in the room. There seems to be more kindergarten parents than any other grade level. I took note of some informal conversations occurring throughout the room. One of the parents is talking about the lack of activity teachers who speak Spanish at PS 2000 and how this limits the amount of time spent on Spanish. She also says that the big issue is that Spanish is not on the same level as English because there is not enough content emphasis on Spanish. At 6:45 p.m., more parents are coming into the room. The parents seem to know each other and are very friendly. However, the Spanish-dominant parents are sitting at the same table and are speaking only in Spanish with each other. Now the meeting is about to begin. Maude, who is the head of the dual immersion parent association, a white English-dominant mother from the local neighborhood, begins by saying that they have to keep in mind what they have in common throughout the meeting. She commends the dual immersion classrooms because they have the most "vitality and diversity." The parents then go around in a circle and introduce themselves and state why they chose the dual immersion program at PS 2000.

The first white female parent talks about how she speaks 5 different languages herself and her husband is from Puerto Rico. Now more parents are filtering into the room. Maria goes next and says that they speak quite a lot of different languages at home with Spanish being one of them. She likes the diversity as well in the dual language programs. Meredith, another parent, says that her child came from Peru at three years old. Rita, the next parent, says that she believes in dual immersion and bilingualism. Marie remembers her earlier years as an exchange student in high school and her wonderful exposure to languages and cultures. Alex's son is Chicano and he also believes in a "dualistic mind frame." Another Mexican-American parent wants her child to learn Spanish. Another couple, father is German and mother is Mexican, says that they want their children to learn Spanish. Another white male parent was influenced by his business connections in Indonesia, where they speak 5 languages. Another white male parent has a Colombian wife who wants her children to speak Spanish. A black mother who teaches Spanish at the high school level and has an Ethiopian husband wants her children to also speak Spanish. Another black female parent states that she wants bilingualism in this country and supports dual immersion programs. The next mother is an English woman who enjoyed the linguistic diversity in Europe and wants to the same open mindedness toward languages here. Bob, a white male parent, says he knows someone who did her dissertation on dual immersion programs and was fascinated by them. Julia's mother says she wants her children to learn more languages. Another parent states that she knows this bilingual program is good from hearing other parents talk about it. She also states that she wants to become fluent in French herself for professional reasons but knows that it is harder when you are older. Another parent states that she travels extensively as an opera singer and meets people from different cultural backgrounds. She says that languages open people to different kinds of people. At this point, there are twenty-eight parents in the room and more are still coming in the room. Peter goes next and states that his kids pick up English so quickly that he wants them to learn more Spanish. Another parent, Kevin, has a sister who is a linguist and who sent him articles on how learning languages helps build the brain. John's father says that he never expected John to learn a second language "honestly" but that it does broaden John's way of thinking. Another white parent talks about how her son is able to read in Spanish and hopes that he will soon be comfortable enough to speak Spanish with his Spanish-dominant peers in the dual immersion classroom. Another parent, who was the former dual immersion coordinator for the school, says that she wants her children to maintain their Latino history. Yet, she does not expect fluency in Spanish either for her child. She states that she has no high expectations but hopes that when they go to Central America this summer that her children will be able to functionally communicate well in Spanish.

After the parents introduce themselves and their reasons for sending their children to the dual immersion program at PS 2000, Maude introduces the parent association's chairperson, Maria, a Hispanic

Spanish-dominant mother, who speaks about the great turnout of parents at this meeting and the great dual immersion teachers at the school. Maria offers more support on the part of the parent association. Then she continues talking about the "spectacular and wonderful teachers" at PS 2000. After Maria finishes, Maude introduces the first item on the agenda that is the "enrichment position idea." This is in reference to the hiring of an activity teacher who is Spanish-speaking. She states that finding Spanish speakers on the school staff during the teachers' prep periods is hard. She says that activity teachers in drama, art, gym, and computers are not Spanish speakers. Now the parent association will even give them money from their own budget to hire an activity teacher who speaks Spanish. The parents have the right and initiative to find a Spanish-speaking activity person. They are interviewing people such as people who can teach music in Spanish. But they will be paid $75–$100 a day. The parent coordinators state that they need advocacy on a daily effort in order to pursue the issue about getting Spanish speakers. They talk about how parents need to be active and talk to the administration. They also state that they are hoping to improve the quality of their children's education and improve the quality of the world.

Sandy, who is the second parent coordinator in addition to Maude, states that the school staff needs an activity person but that they have to somehow come up with the rest of the money. She states rhetorically how they are going to pay for what they want. Sandy says that there are not enough books in Spanish either for the kids in the library. They need to raise money for these books so that they can "really create a great feeling in this school ... there is a perception that they are isolated." The German parent speaks up at this time and asks Sandy a question about how the prep periods and activity periods are structured. Sandy explains that the teachers get 50 minutes a day for their prep periods and then grade-level prep periods once a week for grade-wide teacher meetings. Other parents soon raise their voices and state that they are not happy that the majority of the prep periods [art, drama, computers, conflict resolution] land on Friday, which should be a Spanish day. They met with the principal about this situation, and he reassured them that they will get a Spanish-speaking prep person but he hasn't followed through with this promise. The principal also stated that he wants Spanish on Fridays as well. Then Sandy talked about how this dual immersion program at PS 2000 is not a really a 50/50 model and that Spanish is being marginalized. So now they have an opportunity to hire a Spanish-speaking activity person with a $4500 budget in order to overcompensate for the marginalization of the Spanish language.

Since the parent association really didn't have that much money, one parent suggests that they get corporate sponsorship from a Spanish-speaking corporation. Then Sandy talks about the dual immersion bulletin board in the lobby and how the parents should keep looking there for more information. Sandy also mentions that the new school board committee favors the dual immersion program and wants to help. They are now looking for more money and better standards for dual immersion. Sandy states that the test scores at PS 2000 will help them to get more resources. She also wants the parents to attend the November 18 school board meeting so that they know what is going on at their school. In terms of fund raising, Sandy presents a book of grant listings that they can apply for through the district. She wants people to look at it and help write grants for the district. Sandy then mentions the forthcoming Pan-American week when the dual immersion program raises money for itself. They put on performances and have a bake sale. They were talking about connecting this week with the Mardi Gras parent coordinator since timing is important. They can make tons of money but it is a lot of work. She says that since PS 2000 is a public school and nothing happens until they [the parents] do it.

Then Sandy mentions how most people at the school don't even know that the dual language parent association even exists and that they have regular meetings. As they get more cohesive, they will then get the school administration and district's ear. But she says that money is still a big issue. At this point, another parent mentions that they need to meet on a regular basis so that they can speak with the school administration and how they need to share each other's concerns. Then Sandy mentions how the parent association also wants a Spanish translator for the school newspaper because there are over a 100 Spanish-dominant households at PS 2000. Also, the school needs to make signs that are bilingual and that they need a bilingual banner at the front of the school. Since time is running out, Maude mentions that it would be better if they broke up into smaller committees and meet more often with each other in these smaller groups. So now all the parents in the room break into groups, brainstorm ideas, and decide when to meet again in small groups.

Then all of a sudden, the mood in the classroom changes from its initial optimism when a parent asks whether they can meet with the dual immersion teachers as well because he feels as if his child is not being challenged in the classroom. Maude says that the teacher support committee should also invite the teachers to their next meeting. Julio, the Filipino parent, states that before anything else the parents need to know what is essentially a dual immersion program. Since he asked around, Julio says that he has heard many questions about dual immersion programs. Rita, the Spanish-dominant parent representative, says that the district is working on implementing a standardized curriculum in Spanish and a standardized Spanish proficiency test. Then the parents suggest that they should go directly to the district level and go straight to the teachers themselves. Rita then interjects and states that they can't just say this is what we want. John's father then raises his voice and says, "Why not?" At this point, there is a heightened sense of tension in the room and the parents and parent coordinators bring forth important issues and questions regarding the objectives of the dual immersion program. Then John's father suggests that they also have a curriculum committee. Parents keep saying that they want to talk to the teachers. Sandy warns against this because they will be going against the teachers in this way. Instead, she suggests that a teacher support group do this job. Then a parent shouts out and asks how long this dual immersion program has been in place at PS 2000. Rita answers at least 10 years. Rita then agrees also that they need to talk to the teachers.

However, the discourse becomes even more contentious when the parents disagree over how much expectation should be placed on this school's dual immersion program regarding the amount of Spanish that the students should know. The German parent suggests the "snake method" found at the other dual immersion school in the district is an ideal model because the day is split into consecutive languages. If it is Spanish in the afternoon, then it's English the next morning. The parents agree in unison that the teachers should follow a 50/50 model as closely as possible. Other parents say that the teachers don't have time to do this. Another parent then makes a suggestion that they should monitor and assess the program as opposed to using standardized tests. John's father then screams out that the school has a "Don't ask. Don't tell" policy toward the dual immersion program, toward Spanish proficiency, and how much Spanish the students should really know.

At this point, Maude realizes that the English-dominant parents have been dominating the conversation and turns to the Spanish-dominant parents, who are seated together, and asks them how they feel. Rita helps translate what the Spanish-dominant parents are saying. Mercedes says that she is happy with the program because her child is acquiring some form of Spanish. Julia's mother then states that it's unrealistic for English-dominant students to speak fluent Spanish.

She says that there can't be 100% fluency in Spanish. She says if Julia, her Spanish-dominant daughter in Roberta's classroom, would learn French then she would face the same situation. Since time is running out, and in order to end the contentious nature of the discussion and move toward a positive turn and bring back a productive feel to the room, Maude suggests that they break into groups now. She states that she wants as many people talking as much as possible in order to "stay active, connected, and vocal." Afterwards, I walked around and talked to the curriculum and grant committees and offered them ideas and suggestions, as well as answering questions they had about dual immersion programs.

The field notes from the first dual immersion parents' association meeting highlight key issues that kept resurfacing throughout the school year. Overall, most of the dual immersion parents at PS 2000 wanted to expand the Spanish component of the dual immersion curriculum, whether if it was through hiring a Spanish-speaking activity teacher, approaching the district officials and teachers about the need for more challenging Spanish curriculum, implementing a standardized Spanish curriculum and Spanish proficiency test, changing the present model to a snake model with consecutive languages every day, or buying more Spanish books for the school library. However, at the same time, it is interesting to note that many of the Spanish-dominant parents disagreed with the English-dominant parents, who were the most vocal about increasing the Spanish component, and stated that it is impossible to achieve total fluency in Spanish for their English-dominant kids. Yet, the Spanish-dominant parents appreciated the additive component for their own children. Furthermore, throughout the meeting, the English-dominant parents had the greatest voice and say and realized only at the very end that the Spanish-dominant parents were being marginalized in the discussions. This inequity highlights the very paradox that the parents were alluding to earlier within their own children's education and the marginalization of the Spanish language in their classrooms. The issues and concerns brought up in this first dual immersion parents' association meeting resurfaced periodically throughout the school year and are described at length in the following chapters in this book.

The Classroom Setting

The fifth-grade classroom selected for this study claims to implement a dual immersion model of bilingual instruction in which class instruction is taught in Spanish all day Tuesday and Thursday every week and in English all day Monday, Wednesday and Friday. By having Spanish instruction only two days a week, once again we see how this particular model of dual immersion education did not originally begin with a truly 50/50 model because of the marginalization of Spanish, which was brought up in the parents' meeting highlighted in the earlier section. However, during this particular school year, Fridays was designated as an activity day because students spent most of the school day outside of the classroom in activity classes such as computers, peace education and conflict resolution where they spoke in English with English-dominant activity teachers.

Furthermore, there was usually a sign posted outside the class door stating whether that day was a Spanish day or an English day. Thus, the students transitioned from one language to another on a day-by-day basis throughout the week and in all core subject areas. The Spanish language was integrated across the weekly curriculum and in all content areas such as science, mathematics, social studies and language arts so that students were learning the same content in two languages. The following box clearly outlines a week of instruction and shows how the languages changed daily.

	Monday	*Tuesday*	*Wednesday*	*Thursday*	*Friday*
8:30 to 9:30	Class meeting	*Vocabulario*	Math	*Escritura Creativa y Circulo Creativo*	Class meeting
9:30 to 10:00	New vocabulary	*Escritura Creativa*	Ethics	*Companeros de Lectura*	Peace education
10:00 to 11:00	Drama	*Matematicas*	Music	*Español con Ciencias*	Computers
11:00 to 12:00	Spelling	*Sociales*	Reading	*Computadora y Projectos*	Conflict resolution
12:30 to 1:00	Reading	*Lectura*	Vocabulary	*Lectura*	Social studies
2:00 to 3:00	Math	*Arte en Accion*	Recreation	*Matematicas*	Creative time

In terms of classroom culture, the teacher in this study, Roberta, created a progressive learning environment distinct from traditional classrooms.

Students assumed responsibility for their learning, served as resources for one another, got feedback on their work from a peer audience and engaged in teaching experiences with students in the second-grade dual immersion classroom. Since PS 2000 works closely with a local graduate school of education where the pedagogical approaches have been designed to support student-centered learning, the curriculum and teaching practices used by Roberta also created a progressive learning environment: thematic instruction, whole language instruction, writer's workshop, cooperative learning, problem-based learning and integrated content area instruction in mathematics, science and social studies. Roberta often took her students to the world-renowned museums in the city and emphasized an experiential learning approach. On Friday afternoons, the students were often presented a slide show of famous artwork and photographs and conversed with intellectually about the meaning of art. Twice during the week, students were given independent student work time in which they solved math, science and social studies inquiry questions in their journals. In addition, Roberta, a former anthropology student, emphasized the study of diverse cultures, and she extensively included the study of Hispanic cultures, especially how Hispanic history and culture have influenced the Americas. The Aztec and Maya civilizations were studied through thematic units that emphasized the Hispanic influence in many areas of study such as architecture and agriculture. In science, students investigated topics such as simple machines, the human body, geology, and then gave an oral report in both English and Spanish, as well as a written report in both languages.

Roberta also used student project work to incorporate several progressive pedagogical approaches in which the students worked in heterogeneous cooperative groups to research and report on a topic in many different subjects throughout the school year. There was constant emphasis on social and affective learning and less emphasis on individual centered class work. Spanish-dominant and English-dominant students often spent a majority of the school day talking, listening, writing, reading and thinking together in cooperative groups. Roberta did not create a hierarchical system in her classroom either in which there was an internal tracking system that ranked students according to their abilities. Rather, Roberta set high expectations for all her students. Her role as a teacher sometimes fluctuated as well so that she appeared as a mother and friend to her students, especially during troubling times such as family divorce or death.

Whole language practices were also evident in this fifth-grade dual immersion classroom. Students used language to create meaning in journals and reports as opposed to solely studying language structures such as grammar. Whole language practices advocate students using language to reflect real-world purposes and functions that are authentically related to their life experiences. Creative writing journals were a regular feature in the language arts instruction, and students usually wrote and shared their creative writing stories on a voluntary basis every week on the rug area. Students wrote and read their stories in either Spanish or English. They chose whatever topic they liked to write about. After sharing and editing their stories, they published their entries on either of the two computers available in the classroom and shared their final publications with everyone in class. In this way, writing was thought of as a process in which students write, edit and publish their stories based on feedback from peers. However, Roberta also emphasized vocabulary, and the students learned and practiced at least ten vocabulary words a week. If it was a Spanish week, they studied Spanish words; for example, one week the list included words like *sistemas, organos, ciclos, circumferencia, respiracion, circulacion, digestion, reproduccion, musculos* and *adaptacion*. During the next week, the vocabulary words included organs, muscles, cycles, system, respiration, circulation, adaptation, reproduction, circumference and circulation. Almost all the vocabulary words were tied into the different content areas such as science, social studies and mathematics. Also, every day Roberta read a popular children's book aloud to the students during the last fifteen minutes of the day. In terms of formal assessment, students took standardized tests administrated by the district at the end of the school year; however, most classroom assessment was teacher-designed and portfolio-based.

Moreover, it is also imperative to note what kind of ethos and culture Roberta produced in the classroom. She truly believed that students should seize control of their learning and this philosophical approach of emancipation often lead the students to become conscious of their own agency and engage in genuine discourse with one another, as well as take part in student-centered learning following an inquiry-based, discovery-based, constructivist methodology. There were times during the school day and different places in the classroom where and when students were given the freedom to take on the full ownership of their own knowledge acquisition. Roberta was not a teacher fond of developing complex systems of administration and instruction for the sole purpose of surveillance and disciplining students. Rather, the students were given many opportunities to discuss with each other; for example, the rug area during biweekly classroom meetings and during the creative writing circle opened up a democratic space in which different student voices were heard. The students were given the freedom and opportunity to confront each other, to engage with their differences, and become altered by that dialogue throughout the school day and in many classroom spaces (Muldoon, 2001). Roberta also stated that all student voices have an equal right to be heard and need to be recognized by the teacher for their equal worth. Within this dynamic of intersubjective dialogue and a dialectic of mutual recognition amongst students, a democratic personality formed to characterize Roberta's classroom ethos. The students participated in a social environment that ideally attempted to build solidarity amongst them through such intersubjective relations. But they also had the freedom of walking across the classroom to grab a drink of water during a lecture, raising their hands to ask any question they wanted, and an openness to question even the teacher. By the end of the school year, the students had developed the capacity and agency for reflexivity and learned how to mediate conflicts and tensions that arose naturally within these intersubjective spaces of dialogue.

The Classroom Teacher

The teacher in this study, Roberta, is a native Spanish speaker of Puerto Rican and Portuguese heritage and has excellent Spanish and English language proficiency skills – a true balanced bilingual. Roberta's father was a descendent of the Portuguese royal family but was sent by his mother to Brazil, one of the Portuguese colonies, during the fearful times of World War II. He worked on a rubber plantation in Brazil before becoming a prized pugilist and subsequently winning a free boat ride to the United States, where he decided to stay forever and not return to Brazil. Roberta remembers her father telling her stories about becoming a middleweight champion in Brazil with his renowned knuckles, fighting giant ants and trying to survive in the Amazon jungle, as well as the physical abuse of life on the rubber plantation. In the United States, her father became an illegal immigrant but worked at a relative's mechanic shop where Roberta's maternal aunt first spotted him. The aunt then called her sister in Puerto Rico, Roberta's mother, who was about to marry a lieutenant the very next day, and told her to call off the wedding because she found a hardworking, handsome foreigner for her. Roberta's mother took the next plane to the United States and married her father after a few months, even though she had difficulty becoming accepted into the Portuguese community at first. After growing up in an urban enclave with her brother and sister, Roberta's family moved out to the suburbs where they were one of only a few minority families. In the suburban schools, the students made fun of Roberta because she was a Latina and thus Roberta didn't tell people thereafter that she spoke Spanish and was of Puerto Rican and Portuguese descent, since she was light-skinned enough to pass for being white.

In high school, where she had a strong academic standing, Roberta also became heavily involved with several extra-curricular activities such as gymnastics, cheerleading, the girl's basketball team, field hockey, baton twirling and the school newspaper. She made note of the fact that she joined cheerleading because all the pretty girls at the school were cheer-leaders. After high school, Roberta went through a phase of extreme nostalgia for Puerto Rico and decided that she would attend college in Puerto Rico and took on a leadership role at the university where she began teaching English classes and declared anthropology as her major. However, Roberta noted that the freedoms she enjoyed as a teenager in the United States during the 1960s were now gone because she had to be chaperoned everywhere in Puerto Rico by her relatives and was also restricted as to what she could wear such as the length of her skirts. Then the political and social movements of the 1960s pushed her to return back to the United States where she eventually began teaching in an urban, inner-city Puerto Rican community as one of the city's first bilin-gual teachers. After ten years of classroom teaching, Roberta acquired a Masters degree from a local progressive school of education, became a staff developer, taught as an adjunct in various schools of education, and wrote several local and federal grants to implement science programs in inner-city schools. After becoming frustrated with the bureaucracy and politics at the district level, Roberta decided to return to the classroom and found that she enjoyed working with children better than with adults, even though her cynicism toward adults in education was still there underneath the surface.

In turn, eight years ago, Roberta joined PS 2000 and has been teaching the fifth-grade dual immersion class ever since. Roberta also plays a key leadership role in the school because the school's philosophy advocates a decision-making framework in which teachers work together in collab-orative structures to implement change through shared leadership. Roberta can be attributed with certain characteristics associated with teacher leaders: community building, modeling good practices, mentor-ing new teachers, practicing reflection, caring for others and conducting critical inquiry. Furthermore, as a teacher leader in the school, Roberta has the freedom to make her own decisions as to what type of curriculum to use instead of following a strict regimented curriculum. In addi-tion, preservice teachers are placed at this school, and in this particular classroom, there is at least one student teacher placed each semester. The student teachers work and collaborate with the classroom teacher on most activities and projects; however, Roberta always pleaded to have a Spanish-speaking student teacher in her classroom. In addition to being a cooperating teacher in the preservice program, Roberta is also a National Board Certified teacher who conducts mentor workshops on weekends for those who are in the process of receiving their national certifications. Recently, she spoke at a national conference on behalf of national certification and is involved in promoting this policy.

However, Roberta also had a creative side to her outside the classroom. During her free time, Roberta worked on her visual art and often visited and befriended other local visual artists in the city. Another art form she embraced was dramatic performance. Toward the end of my research, I went to see Roberta perform on stage as Hamlet's mother in an off-off-off Broadway production of this Shakespearean classic that was reconfigured into a modern-day context with a barrio setting, Puerto Rican characters and a plot set around gang violence. The following excerpt from Roberta's formal interview conducted toward the end of the year highlights Roberta's educational philosophy as well as her philosophy toward life:

Author: What do you want your students to be able to do at the end of the year?
Roberta: I want my children to be life long learners . . . I want them to be curious . . . creative . . . resourceful people. I try to create an atmosphere that encourages individualism . . . independent thinking . . . and my philosophy is to help these people become the best learners that they can be . . . to ask questions . . . to dare to be different . . . no matter how silly it might seem. I was a lousy student sometimes because I did not conform. I want to make sure that they are the best people that they can be.

The Student Population

In this fifth-grade dual immersion classroom, nearly half the student population is white with English as the only language spoken at home. The other half of the class is Hispanic and speaks mostly Spanish at home; moreover, in this particular academic year there was only one black female student in the class and no Asian students. The Hispanic students come from various countries in the diaspora: Ecuador, Cuba, Mexico, the Dominican Republic and Puerto Rico. Some of the Hispanic students are recent immigrants but most have lived in this country for several years, with a few who were born in the United States. The majority of the white students are from a middle-class/upper-middle-class background while the Hispanic and sole black student are from a middle-class/lower-middle-class socioeconomic background. There are nearly an equal number of boys and girls. Also, most of the children in the program come from either divorced households in which they are shuffled from one parent's home to the other parent's home and are dependent on a baby-sitter/nanny to move them from one to the other, or they are from single-parent, female-run households with occasional support from extended family members such as grandparents, aunts, stepfathers and boyfriends.

Throughout the following chapters, several students from this fifth-grade dual immersion classroom will be highlighted as both social actors and social agents within the classroom. The reader will be exposed to many different kinds of actions and speech events in which the students had a central role. Since this study utilizes a critical ethnography methodology, the focus is mainly on how the students themselves, who are often marginalized in ethnographic studies, challenge the discourse in their classroom. Yet, the study focuses on mainly a mix of six Spanish-dominant and English-dominant students who challenged the linguistic borders and boundaries between the Spanish and English language more so than the other students, otherwise known as the border crossers due to their ability to move between the two languages much more fluently. Border crossers can be defined specifically as people who move in and out of borders constructed around coordinates of difference and power (Giroux, 1993). Throughout the school year, Yolanda, Jose, Shakima, Alice, Claudio and Scott were seen as border crossers who were able to take a critical view of teacher authority and challenge existing borders of knowledge to create a third space by constituting themselves and others in different cultural codes, experiences and languages. Nonetheless, each student in the classroom became a part of the collective identity of this larger classroom and had a presence in the classroom episodes, events and metalinguistic discussions that took place throughout the school year. The two tables that follow classify the students in this classroom according to their language dominance, socioeconomic status and residential status; however, the purpose of the tables is to better inform the reader about each student's sociocultural and socioeconomic background as opposed to replicating a modernist taxonomy of human subjects.

English-dominant students	
Alice	A white upper-middle-class female student who is a single child from a divorced family. She lives in the immediate neighborhood.
Scott	A white upper-middle-class male student who is from a divorced family. He lives in the immediate neighborhood.
Joshua	An ethnic white upper-middle-class male student who is from a divorced family. He lives in the immediate neighborhood.
Pierre	A white upper-middle-class male student who is from a divorced, French-speaking family. He lives next door to the school.
Brian	A white upper-middle-class male student who is from a divorced family. He lives in the immediate neighborhood.
Sunny	A white upper-middle-class female student who is from a divorced family and lives in the immediate neighborhood.
Lisa	A white upper-middle-class female student who is from a two-parent family and lives in the immediate neighborhood.
Mary	A white upper-middle-class female student who is from a single-mother household because she lost her father to cancer that year. She is an only child and also lives in the immediate neighborhood.
John	A white upper-middle-class male student who is from a two-parent family and also lives in the immediate neighborhood.
Shakima	A black, lower-middle-class student who is from a single-mother household and commutes to the school from a nearby low-income black community.
Susana	An upper-middle-class Hispanic female whose separated parents are from South America but she sees herself as English-dominant. She is an only child and lives in the immediate neighborhood.
Claudio	An upper-middle-class Hispanic male student who was adopted by white parents and lives in the immediate neighborhood.

Spanish-dominant students	
Yolanda	A lower-middle-class Hispanic female student whose large two-parent family is Puerto Rican and lives in the nearby Puerto Rican community.
Javier	A lower-middle-class black Puerto Rican male student who comes from a single-mother household and lives in a nearby black community.
Jose	A lower-middle-class Hispanic male student whose mother is Dominican and whose father is Puerto Rican. He lives with his divorced mother and two sisters in a faraway Dominican community.
Anjelica	A middle-class Hispanic female student whose two-parent family is from the Dominican Republic. She lives in a faraway Dominican community.
Belinda	A lower-middle-class Hispanic female student from a large, single-mother Puerto Rican family who lives in the nearby Puerto Rican community.
Juana	A middle-class Hispanic female student from a single-mother Dominican family and only child. She lives in a faraway Dominican community.
Julio	An upper-middle-class Hispanic male student from a two-parent family from Guatemala. He is an only child and lives in the immediate neighborhood.
Alicia	A lower-middle-class Hispanic female student who recently arrived from the Dominican Republic. She comes from a two-parent family and lives in a faraway Dominican community.
Julia	An upper-middle-class Hispanic female student from a two-parent Dominican family who lives in the immediate neighborhood.
Maria	An upper-middle-class Hispanic female student who was adopted by a two-parent white family and now lives in the immediate community.

Chapter 2

Language, Space and Power: Examining Metalinguistic Conflicts Along the Borderlands

To Mix or Not to Mix: Examining the Language Interference Debate

While growing up as a young girl in Hyderabad, India, I had mastered the ability to listen, speak, read and write in five different languages: (1) Hindi, the national language of India and the language of movies and songs; (2) Urdu, the language of my Persian ancestors who had conquered India in the past thousand years and the language of home; (3) Telegu, the regional language spoken by the local indigenous group and the language of markets and shopkeepers; (4) Arabic, the language of my religion and the language of the mosque; and (5) English, the colonial language of the British Empire and therefore the language of my schooling. It was only after my family had immigrated to Chicago, Illinois when I was seven years old that I gained the mastery of Spanish, the language of my newfound immigrant friends and neighbors. Unfortunately, along the way, I lost language proficiency in Telegu since I was no longer surrounded by the local Hyderabadi streets and shops where I bought food and clothes with my family and friends. The maintenance of Hindi, Urdu and Arabic has nonetheless been difficult for me since my immigration to the United States, especially as I become more and more immersed in the English language, the language of my academic surroundings.

Yet, when my graduate students ask me how I am able to still maintain the usage of languages from my forgotten homeland and the languages of my new host country, the answer comes very easily – the ability to switch smoothly from one language to another is based upon a change in context, person and time. Throughout our global world, children as young as five years old are able to master multiple, different languages because they can switch languages based upon contextual factors such as where they are currently situated physically, what time of the day it is and with whom they are speaking. Subsequently, when one examines successful forms of language education here in the United States, the programs that immerse the students in one language at a time and then switch languages based upon a change in context, person and time have been shown to be the most successful in terms of long-term language proficiency gains.

The dual immersion program is one example of a successful bilingual education program that brings together language majority students who are English-dominant and language minority students who are often Spanish-dominant and immerses them equally well in both languages and in all curriculum areas but in separate contexts. According to national policy centers such as the Center for Applied Linguistics (Christian, 1996), there are three traditional ways of dividing instruction equally between the two languages in a dual immersion program: (1) division by time in which instruction of each language can occur during half-day, alternate days, or alternate week intervals: so if Monday is a Spanish-speaking day then Tuesday is an English-speaking day and if the afternoon instruction ends with Spanish then the morning instruction the following day is in English with the afternoon returning to Spanish; (2) division by content in which the language chosen for instruction depends on the subject matter, for example, when Spanish is used solely to teach math, social studies and science and English is used solely to teach literacy; and (3) division by staff in which either there are two teachers who team teach the dual immersion classroom with at least one teacher fluent in the minority language and one teacher fluent in the majority language or where one teacher who is fluent in both languages and teaches all the students. The dual immersion program in turn separates the two languages into strict separate systems as opposed to integrating the two languages in an intermittent fashion (Lindholm-Leary, 2001).

Research in language education states that English has a unified set of speech sounds and Spanish has a unified set of speech sounds, and thus these two separate speech sounds should never mix with each other in order to develop a purified acquisition of each language. There is a great effort to separate the two language systems as much as possible in the dual immersion classroom so that the words from one language are not allowed to mix with the words from another language through the use of either code-switching, in which the two languages are mixed intermittently, or constant consecutive translation, in which text is translated in tandem from one language to another (Baker, 1993). Interference from code-switching is defined as the transference of elements of one language to another at various levels including phonological, grammatical, lexical and orthographical (Berthold *et al.*, 1997). Phonological interference occurs when the stress, rhyme, intonation and speech sounds from the first language such as Spanish influence the second language such as English through differences in accents as well as when English language learners often pronounce English words as if the vowel shift never occurred. Grammatical interference is defined as when the first language influences the second in terms of word order, use of pronouns and determinants, tense and mood, for example, placing the adjective before or after the noun. Interference at a lexical level occurs when an individual borrows words from one language and converts them to sound more natural in another language, and orthographic interference includes the spelling of one language altering another such as the use of Spanglish words and phrases, e.g. "You've got a nasty *mancha* on your *camiseta*. [You have a nasty stain on your shirt.]." Therefore, the use of English during a Spanish lesson and the use of Spanish during an English lesson are not sanctioned by a dual immersion program because of its beliefs that students will lack competency in either language through hybrid language practices such as code-switching and consecutive translation. Instead, dual immersion students are encouraged and expected to speak only in Spanish during a Spanish lesson and only in English during an English lesson, thus they are constantly separating the two languages in both theory and practice. Yet, the separation of languages is applied more strictly to the dual immersion teacher's utterances rather than the students' early language learning attempts. Moreover, the dual immersion teacher is instructed to accept whatever language the student chooses to use in her/his response, as long as the dual immersion teacher repeats what the student has said in the language that is currently being utilized in that particular context (Torres-Guzman *et al.*, 2005). If the dual immersion student responds to the teacher's question in English during a Spanish lesson, then the teacher is expected to paraphrase what the student just stated in Spanish for the rest of the class with the hope of avoiding needless repetition.

Nonetheless, language interference from one language to another is believed by some bilingual educators to lead to the inadequate development of both languages because linguistic interference may affect the order of acquisition of specific aspects of language, such as the learning of phonological processes, grammatical rules and vocabulary (Kessler, 1971). Furthermore, researchers fear that the bilingual student may rely more heavily on the stronger language, which often is English, during classroom instruction and choose not to use the weaker language as often as needed in order to gain a balanced proficiency level in both languages.

By giving each language its own separate context within the classroom curriculum and instruction, the dual immersion model hopes to ensure linguistic equity by equalizing the ontological and linguistic footings of the two languages and making them adjacent to each other spatially and temporally. In turn, it creates two sundered territories of equal worth that attempt to reverse the hierarchical model of inherent *difference* between Spanish and English that is often grounded in a power-based system in which one language occupies the center while the other lies in the margins. The paradox lies in the fact that a dual immersion model tries to equalize the two languages but can only do so by fragmenting them and dividing them into equal yet separate symmetrical halves that are integrated into a whole. A multiplicatory approach, on the other hand, would advocate the intermittent dispersion of the two languages across space and time, which in turn negates the structural divisions between the two languages and the binary spatial schema as found in a dual immersion model (Kirby, 1996).

Even though it seems quite natural for one language to interfere within another language from time to time, some purists state that any form of linguistic interference will lead the bilingual speaker to conclude that s/he does not know either language equally well. Other researchers state that the interference is less significant when the essential meaning is translated and conveyed perfectly from one language to another. Genesee (1989) presents evidence supporting the mixing of languages by bilingual children as normal behaviors and states that the mixing stems from the supposition that there can never be a truly balanced bilingual speaker because one language will always be either hierarchically stronger or weaker than the other and thus the languages should be allowed to mix together in order to stabilize speech patterns.

However, purists fear that the stronger language, such as English, will intrude into the weaker language, such as Spanish, and fill in the missing gaps even though the bilingual child might have been exposed to both languages equally well. Asymmetrical interlanguage connections are in turn produced when the first language always mediates access to conceptual meaning for the second language and dominates access to that conceptual meaning. If an English-dominant student sees the Spanish word *arbol* (tree), for example, then s/he is likely to access the word "tree" in the first language instead of in Spanish and thus strengthen the parallel conceptual processing of tree/*arbol* as a sign of unified signification. As the level of proficiency increases in Spanish, however, the English-dominant student becomes less dependent on the lexical mediation between the first and second language as the concept of tree/*arbol* grounds itself in both languages. In turn, according to purists, the two languages cannot be represented as a single system since the linguistic production for the weaker language is not equal to the linguistic production of the stronger language, due to the inherent power differential between the two languages (Kroll, 1993). When the dominant language and the weaker language are mixed together through differentiated degrees of code-switching, the bilingual speaker is essentially differentiating between the two languages as separate entities with the stronger language determining the syntactic frame for the weaker language; yet bilingual speakers are also exhibiting pragmatic competence by code-switching and mixing languages, which is a normal feature of bilingualism (Bialystok, 2001). Nonetheless, even if bilingual children are mixing the languages and recognizing the differences between the stronger and weaker languages, it does not necessarily resolve the fundamental question of how those languages are represented conceptually in the human mind. Should we think of the cognitive processing that occurs in bilingual minds in terms of separate linguistic storage areas in which there is no interference and connection between the two languages due to stringent borders? Or should we unify both languages under one conceptual system of meanings in which there is direct linguistic mediation between the two languages in terms of phonetics, syntax and semantics? Is the mental representation of the two languages organized then as either a discreet and separate representation of language or as a combined representation of language?

Mapping Languages in the Bilingual Brain

The reasoning behind the fixed separation of the two languages in a dual immersion model lies in psycholinguistic research conducted within the last few decades that states the need for students to clearly distinguish between the two languages cognitively in order to balance the two languages on equal footing in linguistic practice. The psycholinguistic model conceives of the two languages operating separately without transfer from one to the other and with a respective, restricted space and temporal distanciation from one language to the other language. Cummins (1981) refers to this as the *separate underlying proficiency model of bilingualism*, which proposes that in order to develop bilingual academic proficiency, clear, separate and meaning-enriched contexts for each language must be created during instructional time. The separate proficiency model of bilingualism states that bilingual children begin to learn the two languages with distinct, autonomous representational systems for each language that do not interfere with one another. The two languages may or may not interact with each other systematically, thus there is no qualitative difference between a bilingual child's acquisition of language and a monolingual child's acquisition of language. Moreover, research focusing on young children who simultaneously learn two languages states that they acquire both languages by distinguishing two distinct contexts for the two languages such as knowing when to speak in which language with which parent, i.e. the one parent one language rule (Romaine, 1989). Eventually, children become aware of language choice and are able to separate the two systems if they want to convey speech that is purified and homogeneous, in which one language does not qualitatively interfere with and influence the other.

Even though at first the two languages mix and merge in the initial stage of language acquisition, between the ages of three and five, linguists believe that young children can clearly separate the two language systems (Hakuta, 1986). The functional autonomy of the two language systems emerges at this definitive stage in the child's speech development and the evolution of two distinctive sets of language patterns is alternatively actualized. Furthermore, children who learn languages at different rates, for example, children who learn one language at birth and one language later in life also separate the two languages because they too gain knowledge of the two languages in different contexts and at different times. The two languages are thus represented differently as a function of being learned first or second and as the function of where and how the languages were being taught and used. Thus, young bilingual children generally go through different stages in the language acquisition process and eventually learn to separate the two languages due to contextual and temporal differences: (1) the first stage occurs when the child has only one lexical system comprising of words from both languages; (2) the second stage is when two distinct systems for lexicon begin to develop for pragmatic reasons, even though the syntactical structure remains the same for both languages; and (3) the last stage is when the child uses linguistic strategies in speech to separate the syntax and lexicon for the two different languages (Grosjean, 1982). According to some researchers, bilingual children pass between these stages and shift from a dependent to an independent language representation.

However, Cummins (1981) states that there is considerably more interdependence between the two languages, and it is a fallacy that the two languages should be kept apart in two separate containers situated inside the mind. Cummins states that bilingual research shows evidence contrary to the separate underlying proficiency model because language attributes in one language are not kept strictly apart from language attributes in another language within the cognitive system. Rather, transfer occurs readily from one language to the other and the two languages are highly interactive with one another inside the bilingual mind. The various attributes of language, such as phonology, syntax and semantics, are not isolated in relation to an individual immersion. Instead, some cognitive theorists in bilingual education state that the various attributes of language are all stored in one area of the brain and are shared by multiple languages that have alternative labeling systems for the same linguistic concepts; thus, there is a shared system of semantic meanings for more than one language. Lambert and Tucker (1972) also contend that a higher level of abstract cognitive processing exists alongside the transmission of information between languages because the two languages are contingent and thus there is always mediation and transfer between the two languages. The cognitive skills used for the development of one language do not necessarily depend upon the development of the second language because they both depend upon the same kinds of cognitive skills and processes needed to understand all linguistic codes. For example, when a teacher presents a lesson in Spanish, the student is not solely using the Spanish part of the brain; in fact, there is no designated place inside the brain where one language resides by itself. Rather, a Spanish lesson can readily allow a student to transfer that content knowledge into the English language and vice versa within the bilingual brain because the rules for phonology, syntax and semantics are the same regardless of which language is in use.

Research studies have also found that as bilingual learners gain a greater acquisition of lexicon in the second language the degree of concept mediation between the languages also increases while the level of lexical mediation decreases between the two languages (Kroll & Tokowicz, 2001). Thus, according to Cummins (1981) and other bilingual researchers who share his views, both languages exist within the same underlying cognitive space and utilize the same set of cognitive skills. However, instead of validating an initial mixed language stage where students are allowed to use one language during the presentation of another language before they can transition into the slow separation of the two languages, dual immersion students are expected instead to shift immediately from one language system to another both temporally and spatially but without allowing for either the mixed language stage or the inclusion of a transition period from one language to the other. In turn, the dual immersion model does not acknowledge the need for conceptual mediation and transfer between the two languages, nor does it allow for a pattern of linguistic interchange such as code-switching and consecutive translation that can offer alternative possibilities for language education.

Yet, the debate concerning how knowledge of the two languages is stored and represented within the brain is still a mystery for many researchers in linguistics, psycholinguistics and neurolinguistics, where there are competing theories of language and cognition and where theoretical arguments are still waged. However, there are several variables that need to be taken into account before we can designate a specific spatial representation for a particular language within the terrain of the human brain. How the languages are learned, how the languages are used, the age and manner of acquisition of the second language and how we are made conscious of our bilingual language use are all factors that can determine how children build up spatial representations and mental organizations for both languages. Yet, current technology has allowed researchers to use functional neuroimaging to inquire directly into how languages are represented in relation to each other within the brain's left and right hemispheres and observe the cognitive processes of language use through the imaging of cortical involvement, thus challenging the earlier oversimplification of languages and their production functions in discrete binary hemispheres (Pinker, 1994). The research produced from this new technology has produced two outcomes: some studies show that subjects responded differently in terms of cerebral dominance patterns to the two languages, with the second language producing a delayed stimulus response, and some studies showed that the subjects responded with the same pattern for the two languages (Bialystok, 2001). Thus, one must be cautious of methodological impurity even within research studies using precise neuroimaging to visualize linguistic activity in the bilingual brain.

Whether or not the two languages are stored independently or integrated into one spatial area, many researchers do agree that both language sources are active even when only one language is in use. Even if the bilingual brain maintains separation among the languages being used within the mind, the cognitive system is believed, at the same time, to allow for a free and fluid interchange between the two languages: separation while allowing for the intermixing of the two languages (Palij & Homel, 1987). Thus, whether the two languages are represented in a single system or in an interdependent system, it is believed that both languages are always active and open to surface-level cues from the environment that determine language choice. Both languages influence linguistic performance, even if the bilingual speaker is only using one language at that moment. Along with the acquisition of the two languages, researchers state that the bilingual speaker also gains access to control mechanisms and processes that allow the bilingual speaker to activate and modulate the two languages when and where s/he desires to do so in accordance to a change in context, person and time.

Mapping Languages in the Dual Immersion Classroom

The nature of language representation in the mental space of the bilingual brain is fundamental to virtually every theoretical framework in bilingual education, and each theoretical framework posits a representation with its own discernible structure. In the dual immersion model, the representation of the two languages as separate entities structured as a strict dichotomy in the mental space of the bilingual brain has transferred over to all other aspects of the dual immersion model: curricular space, physical space, material space, and metaphorical and symbolic space – they all mimic the binary representation of languages in the mental space of the bilingual brain. For the dual immersion model, it seems as if there is no difference between the structural details of linguistic representation in the brain and the functional use of those linguistic representations in student processing within the everyday life of a dual immersion classroom. Linguistic representation in the brain and linguistic representation in the classroom are related to each other in a parallel fashion, and thus, dual immersion teachers represent the two languages as spatially distinct in the physical space of the classroom; if the two languages are distinct within the bilingual brain, then the representation of them must also be distinct in the classroom. Even if Spanish and English are forced to use the same physical space, it is the separation of the two languages that determines the knowledge structure and acquisition of languages within the dual immersion classroom.

Thus, the dual immersion model has determined its own proper architectural configuration for the two languages: a binary architecture that is purported to be the same as the separate underlying proficiency model of bilingualism in which the two languages are spatially kept apart within the mental space of the bilingual brain. The dual immersion model in turn endows the mental space of the bilingual brain with specific properties, orientations and symmetries, just as Noam Chomsky (1988) materialized an a priori universal mechanism for language production within the mental space of the human brain. Furthermore, the architectural framework for the dual immersion model is definitely not multidimensional and dynamic because it does not believe that multiple arrangements of language representation should coexist in the mental space of the bilingual brain and subsequently within the ideological space of the dual immersion classroom. Instead, the dual immersion model reinforces a strict dichotomy between the two languages in which there is no sanctioned mutual interactivity and overlap between the two languages in the classroom. Consequently, the binary representational format for the two languages in a dual immersion model has serious implications for the pattern of language activation found in the dual immersion classroom and for the behavioral experiences of students using the two languages in the classroom.

By supporting the differentiated language systems hypothesis, the dual immersion model concludes that the bilingual student's earliest and most basic notions of language should be demarcated into separate Spanish and English territories. The dual immersion model does not comply with the unitary language system hypothesis, which states that the bilingual student's early linguistic representations are not separated and not specified according to a particular language. Starting in the kindergarten classroom, the dual immersion model advocates a formal separation of the two languages by demarcating where they begin and end. It also creates an absolute division of languages leading to perhaps a sense of a false divide between the two languages. In doing so, it does not allow for a more functional theory of language learning that supports a dynamic, multidimensional representation of linguistic knowledge within the bilingual brain. The dual immersion model does not believe that several variations of organizational schemas for language representation can coexist together and that language representation within mental space can change developmentally over the several years of formal schooling in the bilingual classroom, thus keeping the binary framework intact throughout all the K-5 years of schooling in a dual immersion model.

Furthermore, the binary division of languages within the conceptual space of a dual immersion classroom claims to represent natural divisions of language acquisition in which the two languages are separated into halves so students acquire higher proficiency levels in both languages by processing the two languages separately. Yet, these structural divisions of language acquisition eventually can construct material as well as metaphysical divisions and rifts within the everyday life of the classroom. Standardized ways of measuring and mapping language use onto the daily and weekly class schedules is one common practice found in the dual immersion model that excludes any kind of deviation from the dual immersion norm and thus language use is homogenized according to time and space. Furthermore, the varying degrees of need of different language use are rarely accepted in the dual immersion philosophy, even though it does happen naturally so that the teacher can overcompensate the Spanish language if s/he feels as if there is a greater need for Spanish that particular afternoon, day, or week. In this particular research setting, the two languages were kept apart by the days of the week because once again the dual immersion model states that languages are spatially kept apart within the mental space of the bilingual brain and thus should be kept apart spatially and temporally in the classroom space. Mondays and Wednesdays were designated as English days and Tuesdays and Thursdays were designated as Spanish days. The language of choice on Fridays, however, was English, but Roberta, the classroom teacher, did not feel as if she was losing instructional time in Spanish because, during this particular academic year, Fridays were designated as an "activity day" in which students mainly attended classes outside of their regular classroom and with other activity teachers in art, drama, music, peace education and computers.

Yet, in her classroom, the temporal patterning of classroom life and the constant rotation of formal lessons from one language to another, from one day to another, were done for the stated purpose of separating English and Spanish spatially and temporally. For example, a lesson on fractions may be conducted initially in English on Wednesday and then continued in Spanish on Thursday. However, the area of focus might change from one day to another so that the students might learn equivalent fractions in English one day and then improper fractions in Spanish the next day. Furthermore, the rate, speed, sequence and timing of lessons and activities were often determined by the classroom teacher, but the school also set parameters according to each grade level so individual dual immersion classrooms did not follow arbitrary conventions of bracketing the lessons and activities by language. Thus, the temporal structure of Roberta's classroom was defined by modernist, linguistic borders and boundaries that marked the beginning and end of each language and thus standardized the segmentation of classroom time according to languages (Zerubavel, 1979). The periodic mobility from one day to another followed a cyclical rotation and soon the students became familiar with the shifting process from language to another. Oftentimes, these temporal borders were rigid so that the class progressed from one phase of the learning cycle to the next one without any transgressions. Moreover, dual immersion teachers are often pressured to not resist the absolute authority of the school bells, clocks and timetables that mathematically measure the space and time allotted for each language. The generalized timetable of daily classroom routines was designed initially after the factory model, which imposed strict rhythmic time upon the workers through the use of archaic temporal and spatial regulations that restrained any deviation from external governing orders (Kliebard, 1986). The timetable or agenda is one mechanism that is still used today to not only to structure the events and activities that are to take place that day in chronological order but also to essentially organize and control time and space within the classroom. The school then becomes a metaphorical machine for learning in which each pupil, each grade and each moment in the school day are regulated in syncopation so that the school runs like clockwork.

By separating the two languages according to the days of the week and creating timetables designating the amount of instructional time for each language, linguistic borders and boundaries were produced within this dual immersion classroom. The border is where the teacher draws a line and says this is where one language ends and another begins. Boundaries are the bounded spatial confines produced by borders and give shape to the world of the classroom by designating Spanish spaces and English spaces. Linguistic markers in the classroom were used to construct the Spanish and English borderlands, and by breaking the dual immersion classroom into Spanish parts and English parts, these markers produced a Cartesian space consisting of a grid-like demarcation of languages according to time span and subject matter. The dual immersion students were expected to move through this grid-like Cartesian space when they transitioned from language to another, from one day to another, from one subject to another, from one coordinate to another (Foucault, 1970). The logic of the Cartesian space psychologically dominates students and teachers through its regulated mechanisms of time and concise tabulations of the spatial and physical realm. The regular daily and weekly routines in a dual immersion classroom are subsequently also tied spatially to different locations inside and outside the classroom, such as the student seating area and music class, where the two languages move back and forth across the Cartesian grid.

In the next section, we will examine the dual immersion classroom through the space-time continuum in order to further examine how languages are mapped in the classroom. Space-time relations are connected together due to the simultaneous intuition of both of them, space and time, situated together within a particular setting, thus, the coordination of languages across space cannot be achieved without their coordination in time and vice versa (Giddens, 1986). The dynamism between space and time in turn determines how space will be stretched out over a specified period of time; time and space are not separated from each other and are instead constructed through their interrelationship.

There is no antagonistic dichotomy produced between time and space because they are mutually dependent upon each other; they collapse onto each other to co-construct a working dualism throughout the external world, including the external world of the dual immersion classroom (Massey, 1994).

Moreover, the foundational understanding of human geography can further be conceptualized as a triumvirate of space-time-place in order to say that time and space are social constructs embedded in the materiality of the world through particular places (Harvey, 1996). Within the dual immersion classroom, human geography is also dictated by a space-time-place continuum that is closely connected to how the two languages are divided and distributed across space and time and within particular places. By examining the space-time-place triumvirate in the dual immersion classroom, one can better understand where and when the linguistic dualism found in Cartesian borders and boundaries materializes itself – both real and physical borders and boundaries as well as imaginary, metaphysical and psychological. In the following sections of this chapter, we will examine the manifestation of the Spanish/English borders and boundaries in relation to the space-time-place triumvirate in this fifth-grade dual immersion classroom and eventually how student-initiated counter discourse lead to the possibility of transgressing beyond these Cartesian borders and boundaries.

The Space-Time-Place Triumvirate

In *The Production of Space* (1991), Henri Lefebvre defines three main categories for understanding the concept of space: (1) space as conceived; (2) space as practiced; and (3) space as lived. In the first category, the conceptualization of space involves the intellectual theorizing of space through coded language, planning schemes and design discourse; the order of construction, the order of materials, the order of time and the order of space all come into play in the conceptualization phase. The value of a given space, such as a dual immersion classroom, is created and signified through this process of conceptualization. For example, as the teacher decides where and how the student desks are to be arranged, where her/his desk will sit in relation to the students' desks, where s/he will post the daily agenda, etc., s/he is generating a template or a generative schema for the conceptualization of the classroom space but is also symbolically defining its social and political identity and values via this process of conceptualization. Deciding which language will be taught in the morning versus the afternoon is another example of spatial

conceptualization. In the second category, on the other hand, spatial practice refers to the material and functional reproduction of everyday spatial
routines in a classroom such as the practice of getting in line for lunch or
moving from one center area to another center area. Lastly, in the last
category, lived space refers to the space that the human imagination seeks
to change and appropriate through the social construction or production
of new kinds of space.

   In forthcoming sections of this chapter, the triad constructed by
Lefebvre will be used to analyze the conceptualization of the geometric,
architectural space in this particular dual immersion classroom; the
symbolic meaning, signification and function of particular places in the
classroom; the practice of everyday spatial actions, behaviors and routines
in the classroom; the connections between physical, material, social,
linguistic and metaphorical spaces; and the actions of resistance used to
change and redefine the spatial borders in the classroom and thus allow
for the political redefinition and mutation of the lived classroom space.

   Before we begin examining Roberta's fifth-grade dual immersion classroom, it is important to distinguish between *space* and *place* and differentiate how one defines these two distinct spatio-temporal dimensions
(de Certeau, 1984). Places can be identified in the classroom as specific and
particular locales or dwellings that have material and territorial qualities.
The Heideggerian (1971) concept of *dwelling* can be used to expand the
definition of place as an active mode of dwelling with other humans and
things or dwelling with action with one's environment in a certain locale:
to dwell is to exist in the basic character of Being. Once we have rooted
ourselves, our Being, in a place, we begin to dwell in it authentically and
cultivate a sense of place within it such as a classroom library. On the other
hand, spatial relations are defined by the many kinds of spatial practices
evident in multiple places, meaning that the multiple practices enacted
within various places come to define that collective space: walking in and
out of that space, moving around in that space, defining its parameters,
etc. Thus, place connotes a specific location while space is relational and
multidimensional. David Harvey (1996: 316) further argues that there is a
dialectical relationship between space and place and states that "what goes
on in a place cannot be understood outside of the space relations which
support that place any more than the space relations can be understood
independently of what goes on in particular places." Harvey believes that
there is a dialectical tension between space and place because when spatial
barriers are removed, for example, they have an effect upon particular
places within that space. The removal of spatial barriers can create differences in the quality of the places contained within that space, in turn,

shifting spaces result in shifting places and vice versa. Even though place connotes a specific locale and space connotes a global production, they are mutually dependent upon one another and exist within each other as part-to-whole relations. Multiple, heterogeneous places in the classroom can be construed as abstractions from the totality of the unified classroom space; classroom space then is defined by all the dynamic places in the classroom taken together simultaneously as a whole: the seating area, the centers, the blackboard area, etc. In addition, the plurality of classroom spaces challenges the universality of a single space and these multiple, malleable spaces in turn are relative to human experiences so that they cannot be codified as absolute truth. In turn, spaces and places are more likely to change over time to create a palimpsest of human geography (Kern, 1983). Subsequently, the heterogeneity of space permits spatial production to vary from one social group to another, and even within that social group, there are multiple variations of space due to the multiple subjectivities determining that collective space. Classrooms then need to be seen not from a series of fixed settings in a homogeneous space but from a multitude of qualitatively different spaces that vary with the shifting ethos and with the shifting perspectives of its lived everyday human experiences and its multiple human subjects.

Yet, before we begin examining the subjectivity of a classroom space, let's examine its physicality. The physical space of the classroom is essentially a space in which movement, change and causal processes and events occur (Eilan *et al.*, 1993). The geometrical properties of a classroom, such as its length, width and volume, are joined together with the physical movements and routes of subjects and their velocity, acceleration and navigation throughout that geometrical space that in turn produces vectors, lines, axes and topological notions of the classroom space. The continuous spatio-temporal routes connecting places in the classroom through both visible and invisible lines depend on the individual subject's perspective, position, orientation and engagement with the spaces inside the classroom. Yet, each subject experiences this classroom space both differently and in the same way as others as well, once the classroom becomes a familiar terrain. Thus, space is a mode of conceptualization of the external, physical world of the classroom that students and teachers apprehend through their faculties of perception. As the school year progresses from day one, each classroom subject constructs her/his own routes from one place to another, and in turn, navigates herself/himself through the classroom space thereafter.

Furthermore, within the everyday classroom life, teachers and students use multiple tactics and strategies to manipulate their space through everyday rituals and operations such as the everyday practice of entering and exiting the classroom space. The constant composition and re-composition of space is thus multiform and fragmentary and the way this classroom space is used and how often it changes on an everyday basis. Spatial operations are put into place by subjects in the classroom who throughout the academic year come to orient, situate and temporalize their classroom space. The kind of subjectivity present in a classroom and the kind of space produced in the classroom create an interfacing relationship that is not only metaphorical, in which one can compare the mapping subject with the mapped classroom space, but also metonymic, in which the mapping subject is contiguous to the mapped classroom space. The classroom space in turn defines who the teachers and students are as subjective beings (Duncan, 1996).

However, even within the ordinary everyday classroom practices, there is the possibility for the revelation of hidden meaning discovered in the normalized everyday practices and their contingencies that can go unnoticed by the classroom subjects themselves. Oftentimes, in the everyday, we lose critical consciousness of underlying meanings and the signification of the daily habits and routines that we enact over and over as conditioned bodies-in-space; we become enmeshed in our daily habits and routines and forget what they might signify at a deeper, metaphysical level. For example, what meanings can one decode with the spatial production of perfect student lines marching in unison down the hallways in total silence? Is there a power differential produced between the teacher and student as they march? Yet, if this behavior is enacted on an everyday basis, do the classroom subjects lose consciousness of the underlying, hidden meanings within such synchronized routines?

Since the processes of spatial appropriation and reappropriation are related to the social situations in which they are set, power relationships are thus constantly determining the strategic manipulation of space and those power relationships are often expressed through both the use of language and through the movement of the body within that space. The suppression of student freedom, in terms of both the use of language and bodily actions and both inside and outside the classroom, can occur through the delimitation of student space and the subsequent confinement of student movement, since a power differential is produced regulating student freedom and agency. In turn, the everyday practices in a classroom, or its ways of operating, are constituted by what the teacher and students do regularly during their time within the classroom space and what normalized techniques and habits they use to organize and reappropriate their classroom space (de Certeau, 1984). In order to research the production of space in the classroom, one must observe what the teacher and students do during the day and observe what kinds of normalized techniques and habits are being produced to control that classroom space through both language use and bodily actions.

The researcher is the one who is able to see the classroom space as a totalizing whole from the vantage point of an outsider. S/he sees all the different places in the classroom coming together and how the teacher and students come to produce a framework for spatialities within their classroom. The scopic viewpoint of the classroom space to any outside observer presents this space as a multi-layered text before one's eyes that can be read and decoded for meaning and message by mapping the classroom space and examining its notions of situatedness, location and positionality. Researchers observe students and teachers moving back and forth within the classroom, often unaware of themselves situated within this space. Yet, the researcher's understandings of the classroom space emerge from the teacher and students' actions, positions and locations as bodies-in-space; it is through their bodies that the researcher experiences and perceives space and time (Merleau-Ponty, 1992). The space of the classroom is perceived experientially and phenomenologically by the researcher via the teacher and students' distinct spatial experiences in the classroom. Through both the actions and perceptions of the classroom subjects, the classroom space in its entirety gets actualized and subsequently analyzed by the researcher. The complexity of the classroom in turn becomes readable to the outside observer who carefully examines the daily behaviors and experiences of the classroom subjects as bodies-in-space and tries to map out and order how the everyday life of this classroom is actualized through the space-time-place continuum, for example, at what time is each place utilized in the classroom space and why. The physical paths that these subjects take become visible to the outside observer who is examining their lived experiences and how their moving, intersecting paths create fragmented trajectories and different positionalities and paths within that constantly moving classroom space: "All societies, even the smallest, can be analyzed as consisting of time-space zones, within which individuals trace out the recurrent paths of their day-to-day lives and which are structured through the very tracing of those paths" (Giddens, 1986: 148).

It is space that provides fixed positions and also permits circulations because space carves out individual segments within the classroom, establishes operational links between the segmented places, and marks places by indicating their value (Foucault, 1991). The outside observer records the multiple and heterogeneous places in which these subjects weave in and out, moving and mediating from one spatio-temporality to another, and transforming themselves in the process of spatialization. The vectors of direction, velocities and time variables come together in an ensemble and intersect with one another to actualize classroom space for the researcher. In turn, classroom space is produced through the multiple practices and operations of the classroom subjects who in turn define specific places within that space according to their value; places like the rug area, the desk area, the sink area, the closet area, etc. After a teacher geometrically constructs the places within a classroom, the space within that classroom is later actualized and defined by the spatial practices of all its subjects dwelling there.

Mapping the Space-Place Dynamic

The following description of Roberta's fifth-grade dual immersion classroom at PS 2000 narrates the places within the classroom space and this description serves as a textual map that provides a virtual tour of the physical classroom space investigated in this study. First of all, there were four main spatial zones within this classroom. A visitor can recognize immediately that when walking into the classroom it has a *fanned or branching spatial syntax* because a fan or branching movement structures and controls access to a range of other classroom spaces from a single segment of space that one encounters immediately (Dovey, 1999: 21). The cluster of student desks in the front of the classroom made up the single most influential segment of space in the classroom and then all the other spaces, such as the library corner, rug area and science center, branch out from this single segmented student desk area. The fan structure in turn gives access to the other segmented spaces in the classroom from this single segmented frontal area of student desks; the fanned structure controls the circulation of movement and social interaction within different spaces of the classroom by limiting the number of pathways through the entire classroom space.

When visitors are lead through the classroom, they often have to move around the student desk area and loop around to the other spaces where there are a smaller number of inhabitants. Since the dual immersion students are seated in clusters of four and these five clusters total make up the largest section of the classroom, the spatial narrative produced indicates that the students are not isolated in individual cells and can control for themselves the kind of access they have with the other students in their cooperative group clusters. Starting from when one enters the classroom, the next set of descriptions narrate the kind of spatial orien-

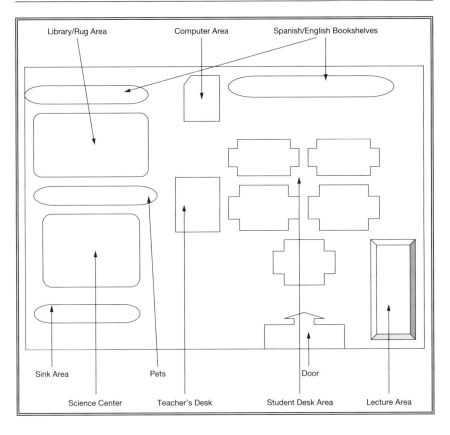

Library/Rug Area   Computer Area   Spanish/English Bookshelves

Sink Area   Pets   Door

Science Center   Teacher's Desk   Student Desk Area   Lecture Area

tations and techniques that go into producing a series of physical paths by which one moves around the fanned and branching classroom. The descriptions include the vectors or movements that one takes throughout the classroom by describing what is in front of the viewer, to the left, to the right, etc. The descriptions also move back and forth between a knowledge describing the order of places in the classroom and where one is going spatially in terms of those actions and movements that make up the changing vectors. The oscillating description between places and actions in turn produces a moving tableau of the dual immersion classroom. Yet, in addition to the tableau, the rules of social interactions and conventions that govern the places within the classroom also define how students are regulated within those shared collective spaces.

Nonetheless, it becomes readily apparent to the outside observer that the dual immersion model calls for a consistent, rational, stable classroom environment that enables the full separation of English and Spanish through the placement of clear and delimiting physical borders and boundaries. The large plastic sign hanging outside Roberta's classroom door states whether "Today we speak in English" or "*Hablamos en Español Hoy*" instead of the more common sign found in dual immersion programs "*Hableremos en Español Hoy*" or "We will speak in Spanish today." When you walk into Roberta's classroom, the physical space of the classroom, the three-dimensional space that both the teacher and students occupy on an everyday basis, becomes distinguishable as a setting for a dual immersion classroom. The physical space of the classroom is distinctively marked by the politics of language; English and Spanish exist within particular places, with identifiable physical coordinates, and distinct linguistic markers, borders, and boundaries. On the doors of the closets where the students keep their jackets and backpacks, immediately to the left of the main entrance, Roberta posts the class agenda for that day. If it is a Spanish day, then the agenda is written in Spanish and if it is an English day, then it is written in English:

Agenda for Monday, November 5
1. Class meeting
2. New Vocabulary in Spanish
3. Multicultural Education with Ms. Ayala
4. Character Education
5. Lunch
6. D.E.A.R.
7. Math
8. *Haroun and the Sea of Stories* by Salman Rushdie

Horario para el 6 de noviembre
1. Revisar el vocabulario
2. Español
3. Estudios Sociales
4. Compañeros de Lectura
5. Almuerzo
6. D.E.A.R.
7. Mathemáticas
8. *Haroun y El Mar de Cuentos* de Salman Rushdie
9. Limpieza

Agenda for Wednesday, November 7
1. Creative Writing Circle
2. Music
3. Project Time
4. Lunch
5. D.E.A.R.
6. Computers
7. The Chocolate Chip Experiment: Science
8. Independent Time
9. *Haroun and the Sea of Stories* by Salman Rushdie
10. Clean Up

Horario para el 8 de noviembre
1. Recreo
2. Español
3. Mathemáticas
4. Compañeros de Lectura
5. Investigaciones: Proyectos de Animales
6. Almuerzo
7. D.E.A.R.
8. Ciencia
9. *Haroun y El Mar de Cuentos* de Salman Rushdie
10. Limpieza

Agenda for Friday, November 9
1. Class Meeting
2. Spelling Test
3. Art-in-Action with Marta
4. Peace Education with Carol
5. Lunch
6. Drama with Mrs. Garland
7. Gym with Matt
8. Independent Time
9. *Haroun and the Sea of Stories* by Salman Rushdie
10. Clean Up

Next to the agenda, on the other four closet doors, she posts the "brain bogglers" or "*desafíos*" in Spanish, which are inquiry-based problems in mathematics, science, social studies and language arts that the students have to solve during the project time period. One week the inquiry-based problems are written in English as brain bogglers while the next week they are written in Spanish as *desafíos* so the children have to first understand what the Spanish problem is saying before they can even solve it:

Desafío Numero 8

Julio ha coleccionado 32 tarjetas de beisbol. Empezo a coleccionar las tarjetas cuando tenía 7 años y coleccionó cada año y el mismo numero de tarjetas. Tiene ahora 11 años. ¿Cuantas tarjetas coleccionó cada año?

* Ensenan todo el trabajo. Indica lo que significa la respuesta.

Brain Boggler # 9

A bologna sandwich is made with three slices of bologna and two pieces of bread.

Each package of bologna contains 12 slices and each loaf of bread contains 16 slices. What is the least number of packages of bologna and loaves of bread that must be bought to make sure neither bologna nor bread is left over after making sandwiches?

* Show your work. Label your answers!

The student chores or class jobs were also posted in both Spanish and English. Each week the students picked a chore or class job randomly from a box and placed their names within the pocket chart where the different names of the *oficios*/chores were posted:

Oficios/**Class jobs**

1. *Asistencia*/Attendance
2. *Aspiradora*/Vacuum
3. *Biblioteca*/Library
4. *Armario*/Closet
5. *Pizarron*/Chalkboard
6. *Materiales*/Materials
7. *Mascotas*/Animals
8. *Plantas*/Plants
9. *Puertas*/Door holders
10. *Lideres*/Line leaders

A student who walks into the classroom first thing in the morning will immediately see the agenda posted on the first closet door nearest the main entrance door. If it is a Spanish agenda, for example, then the posted agenda becomes a mechanism for locating the student in a particular social field for that day. The student will open her/his Spanish notebook, copy down the Spanish agenda, review notes from previous Spanish lessons and share answers from the previous homework in Spanish with other students in the cooperative group, etc. We can see here how the temporal plane of language overlaps with the material space of Spanish notebooks and homework sheets, the objective space of heterogeneous cooperative groups, and the social space of Spanish-dominant and English-dominant students discussing their Spanish homework. Each of these spaces, discursive, physical, material and social, help to construct the logic of a dual immersion classroom as students navigate and orient themselves in a fixed and demarcated classroom environment governed by a binary framework in which the two languages occupy separate spheres along a rigid and well-defined borderland.

The identifying characteristics of objects in this dual immersion classroom were also based on a binary spatialization according to languages. The two languages maintained their integrity as one walked and moved through a succession of places in the classroom and analyzed the objects within those places; the mutual dependence between spatial constructions and languages is fundamental to the character of many dual immersion classrooms. In the back corner of the classroom, next to the row of closets, there is a science center and all the supplies and materials are labeled in both Spanish and English: microscope/*microscopio*, aquarium/*acuario*, stones/*piedras*, chemicals/*químicos*, diagrams/*diagramas*, worms/*gusanos*. Adjacent to the science center, there is a semi-circular library corner that includes a blue rug area in the middle flanked by several bookcases and four computers. One bookcase is classified by a sign marking "*Libros en Español*" and the second bookcase is classified by a sign marking "English Books." In addition to the binary classification of bookshelves, bulletin boards, vocabulary charts, problem-solving question sheets, the student work displayed in the front of the classroom bulletin board, along the window sill and from clotheslines hanging from the ceiling and walls, also speaks of the fractured lines revealing the visible and highly irregular contours of Spanish and English lying beneath the physical surface of the classroom.

Vocabulary for the week of October 29	*Vocabulario para la semana 5 de noviembre*
1. coordinates	1. *hipothesis*
2. intersect	2. *experimento*
3. parallel	3. *agudo*
4. diagonal	4. *obtuso*
5. perpendicular	5. *recto*

6.	hypothesis	6.	*derecho*
7.	experiment	7.	*estimar*
8.	variable	8.	*circunferencia*
9.	criteria	9.	*diametro*
10.	consistent	10.	*medida*

In turn, the physical space of the dual immersion classroom mirrors its ideological and mental space by keeping the languages spatially apart but along the same axial line. Even the space that the students occupy when seated at their desks, the space of the body, is governed by a binary framework so that both languages seem much more present, more obvious, conscious and critical when two English-dominant students are interacting with two Spanish-dominant students and vice versa in their heterogeneous cooperative groups. Language and culture then center the students' bodily consciousness when they are seated in their hetero-geneous cooperative groups by language dominance, as well as culture.

Yet, language and culture also fragment or tear apart the students' subjectivity by weaving them into a larger ideological complex that might contradict the students' individual subjective spaces of personal belonging and identity. Different kinds of bodies, English-dominant and Spanish-dominant, are located in the abstract, mapped binary space of a dual immersion classroom that sets up borders and boundaries delimiting students' cooperative groups first and foremost by language dominance and cultural background as opposed to individual student choice. Dual immersion no longer remains an intangible word but signi-fies an imagined, utopian social community constructed by a conceptual space that operates in the physical, material spaces of the classroom by dividing up objects and subjects according to language and culture, thus objectifying even its subjects. Within this real space, English-dominant and Spanish-dominant bodies weave through a network of paths and places within the classroom and in turn traverse through both Spanish-dominant spaces and English-dominant spaces on a daily basis. The physical and material space of the classroom not only becomes a metaphor to compare to the dual immersion ideology but also a metonymic relationship in which the classroom space becomes a parallel adjunct to the language development process. The words *dual immersion* directly correspond to the materiality and objectivity of the dual immer-sion classroom space; the duality is in turn signified through the multiple signs and references that give a dual immersion classroom its binary shape. The objective and material production of the classroom space then becomes a formative device through which the dual immersion discourse affects the everyday reality of its classroom subjects and subsequently knowledge of its production (Kirby, 1996).

After examining the objective and material conceptualization of space in this dual immersion classroom, now let's turn our attention to the second dimension of Henri Lefebvre's spatial framework – spatial practices. Frames of spatial reference are produced when students are able to differentiate how to get to Place A in the classroom via a certain route, which might not be a straight line, and how to get to it from any other location in the classroom, all the while taking into account obstacles and barriers, since there are not many vast areas of empty space in most public school classrooms. Subjects in the classroom often move through a set of contiguous places that do not necessarily start at one place and end at another, thus deliberately producing gaps between places such as the gap between the students' desks and the teacher's desk. In addition, when we conceptualize space in relation to a framework of enunciation, we state that as we walk through a spatial plane we are enunciating a certain relationship through the path we take because our trajectory *speaks* of meaning as it changes from step to step (de Certeau, 1984). The discursive space of the classroom is thus verbalized when its subjects walk through this space from one place to another. Spatial practices are in turn signifying practices and the steps, paths and trajectories that students produce throughout the classroom space have symbolic meanings and significations that can be read as texts. The framing of space is thus a continuous, ongoing process that not only structures and shapes pathways in the classroom but it is also a process in which borders are constructed in order to enclose one spatial realm from another. Whenever there is a desire to create a sense of unity or wholeness, it is inevitable that borders will develop between places framed in the classroom space. By describing the discursive series of operations within each place marked on the classroom map, the chain of spatializing classroom operations and their local order, we are also marking the boundaries and gaps between these multiple places and marking the routes from one place to another. Even though the classroom plane juxtaposes several heterogeneous places, such as the rug area and the desk area, students are expected to move from one place to another throughout the day within this totalizing lived space. These heterogeneous places in the classroom may contain contradictory elements between them but come together to fill the homogeneous space of the classroom, forming a symbolic whole created by a collage of juxtaposed places.

In addition, in an elementary classroom, there are often distinct boundaries constructed between different places so that each one is defined in counter-position to another beyond its bounded space; for example, the open rug area acts in counter-position to the closed desk area. Thus, by placing borders around the room, the teacher is securing the identity of places throughout the space-time continuum by distinguishing between bounded, enclosed spaces such as the student desk area as directly counterposed to spaces of flows such as the fluid space of the rug area. When a dual immersion teacher walks into the physical space of the classroom, s/he begins to conceptually map out how the two languages will be anchored within the objective space of the real classroom situated before her/him. By placing borders between distinct yet juxtaposing places, the dual immersion teacher is giving each language a material weight and body. Fredric Jameson (1991) defines this practice as *cognitive mapping*, a process in which the educator uses categories of space to constitute the classroom. In this classroom, the students never contested Roberta's cognitive mapping of the classroom according to languages; however, the students often did make comments and suggestions regarding how the classroom should be rearranged perhaps for greater spatial mobility.

However, even though each place in the classroom was saturated with signification, at the same time, signifying practices invented and created new imaginative spaces within the classroom. For example, the sink area near the science center was a functional space where students went to wash science instruments and materials, collect water to feed the plants and animals and hang their drinking mugs above the sink where they drank filtered water from the tap. Yet, since it was a high-traffic, student-centered space, due to the fact that students were entirely responsible for the watering chores and spent much time in the science center, the signifying practices centered around the sink area led to the production of a playful and imaginative space. Here students met informally and had conversations amongst themselves, but it was also an area for spontaneous free play, since it was located in a secluded, unsupervised corner of the classroom, away from the teacher's totalizing gaze. The students in turn produced a *space of injunction* at the sink area in which they acted as initiators to invent a private and secluded place for themselves; yet, the sink area was not a radical space where students challenged teacher authority, rather it was a space of their own (de Certeau, 1984). Thus, the fragmented places in a classroom sometimes come together in a makeshift fashion but are also marked by the subjects' boundary-making footpaths that determine the borders and gaps between places.

Furthermore, in his book *Non-places* (1995), Marc Auge states that there are also *non-places* that compose spaces of transit and temporal occupation such as the space between the closets and between the desks where students were always in transit. The corridor space in front of the closets was a fleeting, momentary space in which students were found moving through during different times of the day and in a relatively discontinuous manner from one moment to the next. The mobile space in the corridor allowed for dispersed positionalities so individual students decided for themselves what they wanted to do there and where they wanted to go within that non-place. Even though the students nonetheless moved from one site to another in the classroom, connected by well-beaten paths, they had the freedom to choose which pathways and sites they wanted to situate themselves in during that specific time period. When they walked into the classroom in the morning, they found themselves in these non-places of transition as they moved about in a hurried fashion to first put away their coats and backpacks; to take out all the necessary materials from the backpacks; to place all the necessary materials in their desks; to find out what chore they have been assigned to that morning; and to complete that chore before the school day formally begins and then be seated at their desks quietly while the teacher reviewed the agenda for the day – all within the first fifteen minutes of the school day.

There were also several moments in the day, in addition to the morning routine of getting acclimated, during which the students found themselves in non-places of transit and transition. Project time occurred in the afternoon when students were given time to work on group research projects in either science or social studies and here students were given the freedom to move about the classroom as they desired. Independent time was another bracketed time slot that occurred right before lunch in which the students grabbed their journals from the bin and completed the English brain bogglers or Spanish *desafíos* in their journals either as a group or individually, but they could sit where they wanted and moved about the room when they desired. During D.E.A.R. time (Drop Everything And Read), students were also given the choice as to what they wanted to read and where they wanted to read it. The mobile space of independent time or project time thus allowed students to become metaphorically *lost* and emerge as a different kind of a subject: a diffracted self immersed in a moving and somewhat chaotic classroom environment following an unpredictable logic of its own that is very different from the structured and ordered space of seatwork. At the same time, individual students often aligned themselves according to race, gender and language dominance during this "free time" when students were given choices as to how they wanted to situate themselves in the classroom space and with whom. For example, the female students were more likely to stay put in one place, such as at their desks, during free time until they finished the task at hand. Meanwhile, the male students were much more likely to travel along the pathways in the classroom from here to there with their male friends, thereby endangering the hermetically sealed spaces of the female students as they moved back and forth. Thus, the dimensions of the classroom, the orientation from one place to another and the affinity of different places in the classroom all come together to simultaneously partition the classroom space into different parts and at the same time to structure it as a whole.

Mapping the Space-Power Dynamic

The isolation and interplay of the different places in the classroom also perform a decisive role in terms of the power relations between the students and the teacher. Oftentimes, spatial practices are regulated and controlled within a classroom by the teacher who determines the procedures that will organize them due to her/his power as the sole authority figure. The teacher often authorizes the establishment of certain disciplinary limits in terms of what kinds of movements are permitted from the students within the different partitioned places in the classroom. Authority from the teacher is what initially categorizes and operationalizes the space in the classroom. For example, a teacher often determines the rules of behavior for students when they are sitting on the rug area versus when they are sitting at their desks. The differentiation and redistribution of classroom space is determined as well by the teacher who has the power to invert, displace and accumulate a network of places. The organizational shifts in room arrangement that a teacher makes throughout the academic year alter the existing spatial relations in the classroom and new relations between places are constructed. Oftentimes, the construction of places in the classroom is based on an a priori decision that is determined beforehand by the teacher. Sometimes the teacher brings a mental representation of what s/he imagines the classroom should look like and feel like based a map-like or *allocentric* conception of the multiple places that are detached from each other but come together visually to compose the objective classroom space (Eilan *et al.*, 1993).

For Roberta, who had been working at PS 2000 for over eight years, there was an investment already put into the development of places in the classroom that ensured the permanence of ordered places such as the rug area and science center over several years of teaching. Yet, at the beginning of every school year, there is always the tension between the place-bound fixity a veteran teacher like Roberta appreciates and the spatial mobility of new places that allows for the reshaping and reorganization of the classroom's physical infrastructure. New learning centers, for example, might be put into place in order to signify a new form of knowledge production within the dual immersion curriculum. However, the reshaping of classroom space is at the expense of the dissolution of extant places, and then, this process of reshaping sometimes leads to a loss of identity that differentiates one classroom year from another, from one year to another.

Places in the classroom are also individuated by their spatial relations to certain objects such as a floor rug or sink basin in the classroom. These objects provide a frame of reference for the spatial representation of the classroom by allowing the teacher to divide it into parts according to the location of certain objects and materials. Roberta first individuated the parts of the classroom by both objects and by languages such as the need for the science center to be located near the sink area. Then she coordinated what events were to take place in which spatial positions, thus anchoring the spatial representation within a taxonomy based on relations of sameness and difference amongst the various places. Since the rug area produced an open space of inclusion, as opposed to the structured student desk area, the whole class decided that the rug area was where the class community meetings should be held; where students could read independently during D.E.A.R. time; where students could sprawl across during independent time and project time; where they could hold their creative writing circle discussions; where they could sing songs when the Spanish music teacher came to the classroom; and where they could go to play when needed.

Roberta coded such spatial information not only in relation to her personal conception of the classroom, which was based largely on the progressive philosophy she acquired as a graduate student at a local school of education known throughout the city for its student-centered practices, but also according to her situated place in it. Many places in this classroom were coordinated in relation to a centroid space, composed of her desk situated in the exact center of the classroom, with the other spaces sloping from this centroid space, forming a geometric center of power distribution in which her desk was centralized and the students' desks branched out from this center (Eilan *et al.*, 1993). According to Foucault (1991), the center is where all gazes turn toward because nothing can escape the eye found in the center of the space. By having the administrative position located in the center of a room, the policing functions of student surveillance from the center encourages the checking and control of student behavior at their desks and subsequently obedience and work from them. Oftentimes, Roberta did monitor student behavior from her desk, yet there were also moments and times when multiple students came to her desk to discuss questions and concerns, thus blocking her power of maintaining student surveillance. However, Roberta never stayed at this center of power very often and instead was quite mobile and moved around the classroom.

The spatial representation of places in the classroom is thus determined by the teacher who initially *frames* the classroom space, both literally and discursively, even before the students arrive in August. Subsequently her/his spatial representation determines the students' navigational abilities between these multiple places. Even if students soon after frame the classroom space through their own subjective navigations and routes, the teacher is often given sole responsibility for representing places and spatial relations in the classroom before anyone else and sole responsibility for generating connections between the multiple places in the classroom. Thus, it is the teacher who determines the conceptual representation of the classroom while the students often solely perceive these predetermined spatial representations when they first enter the classroom. The taxonomizing ways of representing places in the classroom and the relations between them are devised by the teacher who in turn keeps in mind the navigational abilities of the students and what kinds of limits and conditions need to be placed between places in the classroom.

Furthermore, the spatial representation of the classroom and the display of its physical objects are often guided by the teacher's philosophy toward education, and her/his beliefs and values toward how students should act and move throughout the classroom. The kinds of experiences the teacher wants the students to gain in her/his classroom are closely tied to the spatial representations of the classroom and the placement and display of the physical objects within it. Student movement may be structured and shaped by walls, doors and windows, but their movement is often first framed and shaped by the teacher's conceptualizations of classroom space. Thus, the teacher's spatial representation of the classroom has significations and implications for the students' actions and navigational abilities in the classroom, their interactions with the external classroom world and the connectedness of places in the classroom; it is a spatial representation that is both ontological and epistemological.

Closed and Open Spaces: Examining Teacher and Student Agency

In *Framing Places* (1999), Kim Dovey states that power can be lodged in many diverse forms of everyday spatial practice and is mediated by places in the spatial layout. In the classroom, for example, the way spaces and places are used can produce power differentials in which some spaces and places might be more student-powered versus teacher-powered, more fluid than rigid, more open than closed. There are multiple dimensions of place-power mediations that can be used to analyze classrooms in terms of how power operates in different places and what kind of pathways, borders and boundaries are constructed between places. The spatial syntax of a classroom in turn becomes a methodological framework for analyzing power relations in the classroom through the space-place-power dynamic. According to Dovey (1999), these compounded and dynamic space-place-power mediations in turn have several dimensions along which the dialectics of power in places and spaces are played out: (1) orientation/disorientation; (2) public/private; (3) segregation/access; (4) stability/change; (5) authentic/fake; (6) nature/history; (7) identity/difference; (8) dominant/docile; and (9) place/ideology. These multiple dimensions of space-place-power mediations allow us to analyze how the built form of a classroom can orient, disorient and reorient its subjects through the spatial framings of it everyday life; how it can segment space so that students act under conditions of surveillance; how it can create boundaries and pathways that segregate places by language, race, gender, class, etc.; how it can use teacher authority to naturalize certain places and not others; how it can instill the appearance of permanence in some places to create social order and avoid dynamism, change and innovation in those places; how it can authenticate some places over others; how it can use spatial representation to produce symbolic places; how it can sanction the domination of certain places over others; and how it can allow some places to be appropriated by strict dual immersion ideology. These dimensions of space-place-power mediations will be used in the following section to carefully examine and analyze how power was appropriated and reappropriated in this classroom.

Both the physical and social structure of a classroom can either enable or constrain different forms of student agency, depending on the rules of behavior enforced in the different classroom spaces that then determine and regulate the students' activities within different places. The interaction between structure and agency has been examined by many eminent sociologists and anthropologists such as Pierre Bourdieu (1977). His theory of the *habitus* stated that ideology is inscribed and embedded in our everyday habits and thus this cultural *habitus* constructs the sense of one's place in the social and physical structure of society. Agency then can be used to voice dissent and change the structure of our sociocultural *habitus*, either through major revolutions or through small challenges to the conventional thinking found in *habitus* and hope it gradually transforms the social values found in greater society. However, there is a continued need to address student agency in the classroom and its ability to transform both the physical and social structure of the classroom through the changing transformation of its lived space. In this section, we will also examine how student agency relates to the space-place-power mediations listed in Dovey's definition and whether student agency was able to transform the cultural and structural *habitus* of this classroom: (1) What kinds of student agency is enabled and constrained by particular places in the classroom?; (2) How does the spatial layout of the classroom frame power relations?; and (3) How can student agents change the form, use and meaning of the classroom's physical and social space?

Furthermore, in *Discipline and Punish* (1991), Michel Foucault states that when social institutions such as schools, hospitals and prisons frame their space by isolating and alienating the subject within confining places they are in turn producing a disciplinary form of power that controls the subject through the body. By limiting the body's movement in the space-time continuum, these institutions are inevitably also limiting the subject's agency. According to Foucault, discipline requires the enclosure of a closed space that protects the *disciplinary monotony* regulated within that confined space. Every minute during the school day, for example, is regulated through specific rules of behavior, inspections of those behaviors, the meticulous observation of behavioral details and constant student supervision. The architectural design of public schools uses a set of micro-practices that confine the space of the subject through the centralized power of the school administration overseeing the discipline within each individual, isolated classroom. In the classroom, the student desk area is often coded as that space of disciplinary monotony because it partitions the students individually so each student has her/his own place. Their individual cells are often laid out in a serial grid pattern that then becomes a technique of power and a procedure for disseminating knowledge efficiently to students without agency. They become actors and not agents.

Disciplinary power also operates through the normalizing, panoptic gaze of teacher surveillance, which disciplines the students' bodies by making them docile and subjects them to a confined regulated space throughout the school day. The control over the timing and spacing of classroom activities by the classroom teacher is yet another organizational technique that attempts to dissolve the agency exhibited by young children through the school-mandated machinery of disciplinary power:

> The organization of a serial space was one of the great technical mutations of elementary education. It made it possible to supersede the traditional system (a pupil working for a few minutes with the master, while the rest of the heterogeneous group remained idle and unattended). By assigning individual places it made possible the supervision of each individual and the simultaneous work of all. It organized a new economy of the time of apprenticeship. It made the educational space function like a learning machine, but also as a machine for supervising, hierarchizing, rewarding. (Foucault, 1991: 147)

By seating students in straight rows of individual desks so that they cannot communicate with each other, schools turn students into docile bodies and control any form of student agency that might challenge the normalized social and spatial practices in this classroom.

The panoptic gaze of the teacher, who is often standing in front of the rows of student desks, also produces a form of disciplinary power. The gaze is used as a surveillance instrument over students who never know when the teacher is watching over her/him, thus producing asymmetrical power relations between the teacher and the students. Furthermore, there is a hierarchical organization in which the students are dispersed across the room and distributed in relation to each other while the teacher who stands in the center of the panoptic space uses her/his disposition to channel in pedagogical power. S/he subsequently uses this power to discipline the students and normalize their behaviors by arresting any deviant actions such as talking out of turn and daydreaming. Also, in this panoptic space, the lecture method of instruction embodies a kind of disciplinary power that has the ability to circumvent any counter-argument from the students because the teacher is the one who is solely framing the terms of discussion and has the power to deter conflicts (Goffman, 1981). Thus, through its geometric and architectural design and schema, the panoptic space becomes an apparatus of power that economizes, centralizes and disciplines spatial relations, subjects, knowledge, materials and time. The type of discipline found in a panoptic space is identified by Foucault as a modality for the exercise of power that comprises a whole set of actions, techniques, instruments, procedures, levels of application and targets. A disciplinary panoptic space thus has "a physics or an anatomy of power, a technology" (Foucault, 1991: 215). In turn, no agitations, revolts, spontaneous organizations, coalitions and horizontal conjunctions can be formed in the panoptic space of a classroom. Historically, the geometric design of American classrooms and their constricted design have often restricted the movement and behavior of its students through the use of solid lines that are still today rigidly controlled:

> Everywhere one looks there are lines – generally straight lines that bend around corners before entering the auditorium, cafeteria, or the shop. The linear pattern of parallel rows reinforces the lines. The straight rows tell the student to look ahead and ignore everyone but the teacher; the students are jammed so tightly together that psychological escape, much less physical separation, is impossible. The teacher has 50 times more free space than the students with the mobility to move about. (Sommer, 1969: 99)

Moreover, the segmentation within the panoptic space is essentially defined by a divisible homogenous space where one can find a center and a periphery: the teacher is situated in the center and the students are situated in the periphery. However, even within a panoptic space with a central authoritative power, there are zones within that panoptic space that are not necessarily homogeneous, contrary to what is proposed by Foucault. According to Deleuze and Guattari in *A Thousand Plateaus* (1987), there are three zones within a panoptic space: (1) a zone of power that is created through solid rigid lines; (2) a zone of indiscernability where its power is diffused; and (3) a zone of impotence where it cannot control lines of flight and their subsequent flows. Even within a panoptic space where the teacher appropriates centralized power, there are zones where power escapes and dissipates, thus a chain or web of power ebbs and flows in and out of the panoptic space. For example, even if a teacher is giving a lecture within the center, the space below a student's desk is often a zone of impotence because the teacher sometimes cannot control the students' actions underneath the desk where her/his actions escape the teacher's gaze, such as the folding of paper airplanes and the writing of personal notes underneath the desk. In turn, even within the panoptic space, there is a zone of resistance that can challenge the authority of centralized power through everyday subversive acts that often remain hidden from the teacher's powerful gaze of surveillance.

Students can also use their agency to reappropriate spatial practices by "acting-out" spatially within certain places in the classroom and reappropriating how they walk and talk through certain places in order to perhaps enunciate a form of spatio-linguistic resistance – a zone of indiscernability (de Certeau, 1984). Sometimes these acts of spatial resistance transform what the signification of a particular place within the classroom means so that it signifies something else instead of its original signification. By defying the fixed construction of classroom space, multiple possibilities can open up when limits and prohibitions are lifted by the students through agency and voice. The classroom library, for example, can be reappropriated by students when they begin to act-out in this space and transform the meaning of what a classroom library should signify.

Nevertheless, in this particular study, Roberta, the classroom teacher, did utilize a panoptic space when the students were seated at their desks while she delivered her lectures. During these lectures, she exercised a pervasive form of authority, as well as produce a stable, reliable and productive form of power that was legitimized through such forms of teacher-centered discourse (Dovey, 1999). In order to resist the teacher authority, the students needed to expose conflicts and contradictions by voicing them through language, while at the same facing the risks for further marginalization of student agency and the subsequent repression of conflicts. Oftentimes, students remained docile and invisible during teacher-centered lectures, thus confirming their cooperation in this totalizing power of teacher authority. Their marginalization in this grid-like, panoptic setting produced a space that was no longer subjective; instead, it was an objective space of adult calculations and non-negotiations. Thus, for classroom conflicts to be voiced, they had to be perceived in a space that allowed such conflicts to come effectively into play, but in a grid space, social relations were no longer operative between the students and between the teacher and the students. The following field notes depict how, during Roberta's lectures within the panoptic space, the discourse often moved rapidly from a teacher question to a student response. The students rarely were able to respond to each other, unlike other classroom spaces where there was more student freedom to do so:

> When they came into the classroom and sat down at their desks, Roberta began by admonishing them for their poor behavior during music class. She is speaking to them in Spanish and is using phrases like *"no me gusta"* [I don't like it], *"controlar"* [control yourself], and *"calmada"* [stay calm]. Then Roberta has the students take out their Spanish notebooks for her Spanish lesson. Roberta begins her lesson on *verbos* [verbs]. She asks the class what are *verbos*. Mary raises her

hand and replies that they are *"una palabra de accion"* [an action word]. Roberta congratulates Mary on her use of Spanish and then continues with the lesson. She asks if everyone is on task, *"¿Estan listos?"* [Are you ready?]. She writes a list of Spanish words on the chalkboard: *cantar* [sing], *parar* [stand up and stop], *caminar* [walk], *sentar* [sit], *hablar* [talk], and *viajar* [travel]. Then Roberta has the students act out the verbs with their bodies. When she says *"parar"*, only Julia, Lisa, Maria, Jose, and Scott stood up from their desks. Then Roberta mentions that *parar* has two definitions: one is to stop and the other definition is to stand up. Next Roberta asks the whole class, *"¿Cómo saben que estan palabras que indican acción?"* [How do you know that these words indicate action?]. Anjelica raises her hand and replies that all the words end in "ar." Then Roberta asks, *"Cuál es el nombre de esta forma del verbo?"* [What is the name of this kind of verb?]. Javier raises his hand and says *"infinitivo"* [the infinitive]. Roberta then transitions to the next section of the lesson and says, *"Todos idiomas tienen reglas."* [All languages have rules.] She then begins going over the grammatical rules for the infinitive Spanish verb form.

The concrete grid, formed from a unidirectional teacher-centered discourse in which the students are passive recipients of knowledge, never became a theatre of conflict and contradictions, unlike the circular rug area where contending dialectical forces were often deployed. The concept of a grid, like concepts of a code and system, is itself above reproach because the grid space eliminates contradictions in order to produce a coherent space using its specific strategic aims of removing all that is not homogeneous and pure: "The removal of every obstacle in the way of the total elimination of what is different" (Lefebvre, 1991: 371). The forces of homogenization in a grid space absorb all differences, especially when the teacher-centered discourse retains a defensive posture against counter discourse from students contained within the grid space. When Roberta alluded to their poor behavior in music class as reported by the music teacher, none of the students contested her judgments of their behavior even though she was not there. Centrality and normality are thus bound to a grid space in order to destroy whatever has transgressed in relation to discursive boundaries. In contrast to the grid space, the rug area opened up a chasm for generating differences and for openly talking about them.

Unlike the confining panoptic space of the desk area, the rug area provided an alternative space for student-centered dialogue and student empowerment. The rug area or *alfombra* was a place located in the back corner of the dual immersion classroom and covered one-fourth of the entire classroom space. The rug area was literally a blue, square office rug that was set off on three sides by bookshelves alternating between Spanish and English books. The fourth side of the rug area opened up into the larger classroom space composed of the teacher and students desks. The rug area was used primarily on Monday and Friday mornings for the class meetings; on Wednesday mornings for the sharing of creative writing stories; and on a daily basis for reading, project and independent work.

The difference between the lived space of the rug area versus the lived space of the panoptic desk area lies in how these spaces are socially and spatially segmented. Deleuze and Guattari (1987) state that the way in which space is segmented determines the kind of social spaces produced within that segmented space. For example, the panoptic space is segmented in a linear form with student desks moving from the teacher's space in the center along a straight line, thus encompassing all students in its ordered subsystem. Yet, even within the linear space, Deleuze and Guattari clarify that there are differences between supple lines that allow for cross over from one space to another, thus eluding totalization and centralization, and rigid lines that separate and distinguish spaces into highly structured cells and seal, plug and block lines of flight.

Supple lines lead to the molecular organization of spaces whereas rigid lines lead to a molar organization of space. Molecular organizations work in flux and fluidity and allow for the reshuffling of segmented spaces that can operate in small groups, as opposed to individual cells, since they are complementary and coexist in a space where the barriers between the small groups are dissolved and fluid. Furthermore, a molecular organization reveals gaps and voids within its structure and shows "holes in fullness, nebulas in form, and flutter in lines" (Deleuze & Guattari, 1987: 228). Meanwhile, the molar organization contains a totalizing and centralizing force that micromanages individual cells within the entire organization and overcodes them. When the center focuses on a single absolute point of accumulation and power, such as the teacher's body, rigid lines break the student desks, located in the periphery, into units of measurement and mark and divide the desks by strict linear borders. However, the lines in-between the student desks are more likely to be supple lines that are less restricting and confining and allow for a greater flow of movements and words between students situated within the same cluster. Thus, there is an inevitable and inherent overlap between rigid and supple lines within both the desk area and the rug area, since both come to constitute the classroom space and are in turn relational to each other in the classroom space. However, overall, the summation of rigid lines is much higher in the molar space of the desk area while the summation of supple lines is much higher in the rug area where a molecular organization of space is produced.

Furthermore, the openness of the rug area also symbolized a sense of liberty that was missing from the student desk area, where there was a greater degree of physical enclosure and social constraint. The contradictory relationship between a theater of action such as the rug area and an area of displaced student agency such as the desk area produced tensions as students transitioned daily from the rug area back to their desks and as they moved from one activity to the next. Oftentimes, the students' bodies collided into one another as they moved from the flow of the rug area to their stationed seats and sometimes their physical contacts and collisions lead to little skirmishes between them, predominantly amongst the male students. In turn, a paradox was produced as students moved between a point of conjunction at the rug area to a point of disjunction at the desk area, producing a border as the students passed through the space of conjunction to get to the space of disjunction and vice versa. Even though there was not an actual physical line dividing the two places in the classroom, this in-between space also took on a mediating role as well since students continued their discussions, exchanges and encounters as they crossed from the rug area to the desk area, where their dynamic interactions would inevitably end. The bridged space between these two classroom places both welded the rug area and the desk area together and also kept them apart as students practiced their movements from one place to the other on nearly an everyday basis.

During the class meetings on the rug area, the students discussed issues that were listed on the class agenda, which was posted near the rug area so each student had the opportunity during the week to list any issue or concern, along with her/his name, that s/he wanted to discuss and share with the rest of the class. The student council members ran the meeting, took minutes and held voting practices at the end of the class meetings if decisions needed to be made as a whole group. However, depending on which student council members were running the class meetings, the student teacher and classroom teacher sometimes played a more central role in regulating these meetings. When a particular student council president was not able to delegate time restrictions and move the meeting along as quickly as possible, the teachers intervened. Some of the concerns and issues that were listed on the agenda throughout the academic year included the monitoring of closet space, the choice of class pets, class rules and regulations, field trips, homework woes, class celebrations and parties and even issues related to language use such as the Spanish spelling bee, which will be discussed later in this chapter.

In the Monday and Friday meetings, the students took on ownership of the democratic process while the student teacher and classroom teacher often positioned themselves along the side of the rug space, away from the student circle. They wanted to give the students the power to decide on what concerned them the most and subsequently make important decisions as a collective group. Thus, the rug area produced a space of narrativity in which students constantly practiced the need to narrate the real to each other in the class meetings and thus construct their own local epistemology of the classroom and its inner workings. Furthermore, the circular structure of the rug area pedagogically came to symbolize an open and inclusive space in the classroom where the dual immersion students conferred to talk about their subjective experiences and also to divide up their social responsibilities. The circular forum also functioned as a place of political assembly where decisions were made based on majority consensus. The following transcript is from a student council meeting in which the issue being discussed is the actual rug space and its parameters. The student council president running the meeting is Lisa, and Trisha is the student teacher from the spring semester. Here we can see Trisha controlling the meeting, as opposed to Lisa, who was not able to move the meeting along as quickly as possible:

Lisa: Yolanda has a comment.

Yolanda: Oh yeah . . . the rug . . . in every meeting that we've been having . . . whoever sits here is really annoying [Yolanda points to some students who are sitting in that bridged space between the rug area and the desk area] because they're blocking the entrance to the circle.

Maria: So, have you heard of walking around? [Maria is one of the students who is situated in that in-between space.]

Scott: That's blocking the entrance!

Trisha: You mean right here?

Yolanda: Yeah.

Trisha: Okay that I'll do . . . so . . . what would be the solution?

Yolanda: If there is space on the rug elsewhere, go to that space. [Yolanda points to pockets of empty space between students.] Over there and there . . .

Claudio: Right here! [Claudio points to the spot next to him.]

Trisha: I think that's a good point . . . this seems . . . this seems like as if they're on the outside . . . being in a circle . . . [Trisha uses her fingers to show a connecting circle] you can't get out . . . you can't get into a circle . . . a circle . . . it's not like a square where there is an angle . . . or a point at which you can . . . actually enter or puncture it . . . and that's why . . . a circle . . . actually did you know . . . that's why the symbol for a wedding is a circle . . . for eternal love . . . eternal . . . because it can't be broken . . . a circle cannot be broken and so . . . uh . . . uh . . . that's an interesting comment Yolanda. So for this Friday's meeting, we will have everyone on the rug in a complete circle . . . okay.

The telling and retelling of incidents and dilemmas from the past weeks, the dialogic exchanges between the students about issues such as the construction of a circle at the rug area, and the call for democratic action to resolve such dilemmas by the student government officers at the end of the morning meetings, were storehouses for the local ways of talking and ways of doing things in this dual immersion classroom. For the most part, when the class as a whole came to the rug area, the students situated themselves in a circle and acted as active participants, with the classroom teacher sitting in her chair overlooking their participation, ensuring that the links were properly maintained between the various discussions. Since the students always sat in a circular form on the rug area, the objective, geometric figure of this circle represented a space that symbolized the subjective. Here the dual immersion students presented an expressiveness on the rug area bound with emotions and feelings of the subjective kind that was not found in any other place. Within the molecular organization of the rug area, there was no totalitarian form of molar organization. All the students had the liberty to speak up and voice their opinions, thus upholding a strong measure of democracy. The essence of the rug area was in its interior dispositions since it was clearly a common area that allowed for the organic development of student-centered knowledge in comparison to other occupied spaces in the classroom. The following transcript is from another class meeting held at the rug area but we now notice how the student teacher, Trisha, shifts authority back to Lisa:

Trisha: Yolanda . . . can the president have the agenda because that's the way we run the class meetings. [Yolanda is busy trying to add an item to the agenda. Lisa takes the agenda from Yolanda.] What's the first item on the agenda?
Lisa: Animals.
Trisha: Who wrote that?

Yolanda: I wrote it. I wrote it because I want to know what we're going to do with the animals and who's going to take the hamster?

Scott: Yeah . . . who's going to take the hamster?

Joshua: Who decided to take the hamster? [Students are talking out of turn.]

Students: Shhh!!

Trisha: Do you want to talk about who's going to take him home? . . . [The noise level increases.] Excuse me . . . excuse me . . . in this discussion circle . . . in this discussion circle . . . if you have a comment or question please raise your hand . . . Jose is bringing up . . . raising his hand . . . why don't you explain what your ideas are.

Jose: We need somebody to take the pets home for the summer . . . uh . . . so who can take them home?

Yolanda: We don't know . . . what Roberta is going to do. We don't know anything yet.

Trisha: Roberta said yes. It's been decided. [Students begin talking out of turn.] Student council? Lisa? Excuse me . . . excuse me . . .

Joshua: For the hamster, Roberta says not to use the gloves because Roberta says he needs to get used to human hands and that's why he bites . . .

Trisha: From the scent?

Joshua: He doesn't bite me but with other people sometimes he bites so they still need the gloves.

Trisha: Uh . . . uh . . . I noticed how . . . did you notice this before the science fair or after the science fair?

Joshua: I think before but then after also.

Trisha: I know more so during . . . because I can only imagine how exhausted and how traumatized he was from . . . from seeing everyone. But that makes perfect sense and I never would have thought of it that way . . . it's very difficult to go from the gloves to the scent . . . right . . . and feel the skin.

Jose: He looks like he's giving you the evil look.

Trisha: Does he bite you?

Joshua: Maybe when he stands on his hind legs . . . that's the reason why . . . and he goes like that maybe because he thinks we're going to attack and that's why.

Scott: Maybe he does that because that's his territory.

Joshua: I know . . . I don't think hamsters are that cute.

Trisha: What would that be? What is the word that Roberta uses to show when we give human characteristics to animals?

Scott: Anthromorphizing.

Jose: Joshua showed me how to use my hands. At the science fair, I put him in a little box that he has and I picked him up but then he bit me.

Yolanda: He bit me too.

Trisha: You know what . . . at the science fair though . . . let's give Nibbles a little leeway . . . because he . . . without . . . not only is he nocturnal and that for him it was like 3 o'clock in the morning when he should be asleep and then he's surrounded by numerous people and their hands, fingers and eyes.

Joshua: Yeah . . . but like Brian . . . he did not get bitten like other people . . . because I always use my hands and if you use your hands you won't get into trouble and if you use your hands . . . he'll get used to you and that's why a lot of times dogs will sniff you to see who you are and it's the same thing with the hamster. He won't bite you if you use your hands.

Trisha: Your final statement is . . . your final point . . . use your hands. Jose give him a little time to feel you out and not bite you but give him a little more time to sense who you are.

Jose: I didn't know if I would get infected when I put my hand in the box . . . so I put him in there and then he bit me when I picked him up.

Trisha: Joshua . . . Joshua since you have a good rapport with Nibbles . . . maybe you and Jose can go over there later on today and you can show Jose before he brings him home.

Jose: I don't want to take him home.

Trisha: So wait . . . you brought this up to see who can take him home . . . for the summer . . . raise your hand if you are interested in taking Nibbles home for the summer. [Joshua quickly raises his hand.] Mary would you write that down in the minutes? That Juana, Joshua and Alicia are interested in taking him home. Claudio? Are you raising your hand to take Nibbles home? Yeah . . . okay . . . and that they are going to ask their parents for permission . . . if that would be possible.

Juana: Can I take home the plant?

Yolanda: I don't know . . . that's Roberta's plant.

Trisha: Actually . . . why don't we . . . we'll go through it . . . [Noise level goes up.]

Yolanda: Can you please be quiet?

Mary: Can I have the avocado plant?

Trisha: Mary . . . Sunny . . . and Juana want to take the avocado plant home . . .

Yolanda: No! That's Roberta's plant!

Juana: Calm down Yolanda!
Trisha: Goodness gracious . . . okay . . . what other animals do we have left?
Yolanda: The fish and frogs.
Trisha: Lisa, could you please ask your classmates who might be interested in taking home the fish and frogs?
Lisa: Who wants to take home the fish?

Furthermore, the rug area was one of the places in the classroom where there was no single, fixed center point of accumulation and power; instead, there were multiple focal points of power that were constantly in motion and shared by many students. On Wednesday mornings, during the creative writing period, the rug area created a circular space of interpretation in which students shared stories from their creative writing journals and critiqued each other's stories, as well as offering further suggestions for story development. The discussions during the creative writing circle often mirrored this kinetic motion of shared, networked power by never allowing one topic or student to take center attention. The rug space, unlike the panoptic space of the desk area, was in many ways a utopian space where there was a free exchange of ideas between students. The intersubjective space produced in the rug area allowed for the initiation of interactive dialogue through this metaphysical medium of connective space between the students. The rug area invited students to perform, to respond and to speak in relation to each other. Since the circular design of the rug area had students sit in a round circle, it allowed them to face each other and engage in face-to-face dialogue that did not have restrictive borders and boundaries. Yet, the interpretive space of storytelling during the creative writing circle did not really allow for the possibility of mediations and transgressions because there were no extended diacritical discussions surrounding the stories. Instead, storytelling was an objectified process that was centered and grounded on the texts being read by the students. However, the students were given the freedom to write about themes and topics that might not have been appropriate to discuss in other classroom spaces and places. Also, since many students wanted to share their creative writing stories, there was hardly any time for digressions and interruptions either and thus the creative writing sessions moved forward in a steady, fluid stream.

The following transcript is of a creative writing circle discussion that alludes to the imaginative space that was produced on the rug floor where students offered each other critique and feedback on their stories. The

student teacher and classroom teacher also offered their feedback and
guided the discussion of student stories. There is also a greater degree of
playfulness in this transcript in comparison to an earlier transcript when
the students were at their desks listening to Roberta's lesson on Spanish
verbs:

Trisha: Juana can you sit in the circle so we can start the discussion?
In the circle . . . Juana. [Juana who was initially sitting in the center of
the rug moves back into the circle.] . . . Let's see who is going to share
today . . . [Trisha reads the roster of students who have signed up to
share their creative writing stories.] The order is Yolanda, Jose,
Anjelica, Alice and Scott.
Students: Can I read? Can I read please?
Trisha: Absolutely. Let's see . . . [Trisha adds names to the roster.]
Claudio . . . Shakima. I'll add you two on . . . Yolanda, you are up my
love.
Yolanda: Me?
Trisha: Yes.
Yolanda: I'm starting with the same story and the last sentence was
"'Okay, I'll tell you but of course we want to know the truth.'" Okay
I'm starting. [Yolanda reads from her journal and continues from
where she left off.] "'The reason I am crying is uh . . . uh . . . uh . . .
because I miss all the kids,' said Roberta. 'Wait . . . no . . . I'm sorry
that's not the reason why. The reason is because uh . . . uh . . . uh . . .'
Roberta kept on saying, 'Uh . . . uh . . . uh . . .' But Trisha knew that it
had to do with the kidnapping. But Trisha did not say anything. So
Roberta said, 'You know . . . just forget it. It's okay. I'm fine now.' Then
Roberta got a napkin and wet it to wipe her face. Then Roberta got up
and finally . . ." That's where I ended.
Students: No! You have more! Can you please read some more?
[Alice and Maria try to peek into her journal to see if she has written
some more. Yolanda is smiling and blushing.] Read! Read! Read!
Trisha: Yolanda . . . what happened . . . "and finally" and then what
. . .
Yolanda: I stopped at "finally."
Trisha: And finally . . .
Students: Read! Read! Read!
Trisha: Would you like to read some more? [Yolanda is blushing and
looking down at her journal.] Going once . . . going twice . . . okay
thank you Yolanda.
Scott: Read some more!

Alice: Please!

Yolanda: Okay . . . fine . . . I'll read some more.

Students: She's reading . . . she's reading . . . shh . . . shh . . . shh

Yolanda: "Then Roberta got up and finally she said, 'There's something I have to tell you about what I've been doing okay.' Trisha said, 'Okay.' Right when Roberta finished saying what she said, Trisha said to herself, 'It might be that she might tell me she kidnapped the other kids. Who knows?' But . . ." That's all.

Students: More.

Maria: That's all she wrote.

Alice: She has nothing else to read. [Roberta now joins the students on the floor and sits next to the students on the rug circle.]

Trisha: We still have a little bit of school left my darling . . . for you to finish this product of yours.

Maria: Can you finish writing it and then type it up for the whole class?

Joshua: That would take a long time.

Jose: How many pages long is it?

Yolanda: Twenty-seven pages.

Roberta: Please remember that what makes a story good is not necessarily its length . . . it's not how long the story is but it is the what . . . think about the Italo Calvino stories we read.

[   ]

Brian: Even Scott's stories.

Roberta: Those stories were nowhere near twenty-seven pages. Don't let length be the thing that determines the quality of something.

Trisha: Jose you're next.

Jose: I'm continuing with the same story even though I changed the name of the title . . . it's called "The End of Days" now.

Roberta: It's called what?

Jose: "The End of Days" . . . uh . . . [Jose begins reading from his journal.] "Scott and Julia continued to walk into the tunnel. Scott saw a statue and decided to lean on it. The hand on the statue kicked back and a block on the wall slid open. Then all of a sudden arrows popped out of the opening . . . shot out of the opening . . . all the arrows missed except for one . . . which hit Julia in the head. She said, 'Whatever' and fell to the floor and died. All the boys clapped except for Scott who was reading his science history book. But then the block from the wall fell to the ground and crushed Scott." [Students started laughing at this last part.]

Scott: But you forgot a part!

Jose: Okay I'll say it. "Scott fell to the floor and looked like a turtle on the floor because his arms, legs and his head are sticking out . . . [Jose makes a turtle motion with his body.] Then he says, 'Julius Caesar died 2000 years ago.' And then everyone said, 'Die faster!' and started kicking him." [Students start laughing at this imagery.]

Roberta: Are you accompanying your stories with illustrations?

Jose: I haven't thought about that.

Roberta: You might want to think about that . . . that image that you just created . . . you can write it with words or you can draw it.

Jose: Okay. [Claudio raises his hand and Trisha calls on him.]

Claudio: I have a comment . . . did you write "drop out" because it's better if you write "shot out" because it pops out . . .

Roberta: Claudio, what do you think is the difference between "drop out" and "shot out"?

Claudio: "Popped out" means it went up but "shot out" means that it keeps on going.

Roberta: Very interesting subtle difference he's pointing out. Something that's popping out is short lived because it just goes "pop" . . . and yes it's an onomatopoeia Brian . . . thank you for bringing that up . . . but something that shoots out in some people's minds . . . have a longer distance to travel . . . very subtle and interesting point.

Maria: I like your story. It's really good.

Roberta: What makes it good?

Maria: The way everything changes so quickly.

Roberta: The way he actually puts his words together? Nice compliment.

Scott: Funny story.

Jose: Why?

Alice: I like the part where Julia gets shot in the head with an arrow and says, "Whatever." [Alice shakes her head to show the dizziness of the character.]

Students: Whatever . . .

Alice: It's like . . . whatever . . . [Alice makes the same Valley Girl head motions.]

Brian: Who says that?

Students: Julia!

Brian: Valley Girl!

Alice: Like whatever . . . [Alice makes the same Valley Girl head motions.]

Jose: Then she falls to the ground and dies.

Alice: I liked the way Scott also dies because he kept repeating, "Julius Caesar died 2000 years ago."

Roberta: It's hard to keep track of what's being said because so many people have so many interesting things to say . . . too bad that it's happening all at once and I'm missing some things.

From the reading of the transcript, it is evident that the rug area allowed for a greater degree of playfulness. In fact, it was Roberta who authorized the rug area as an area of free play since it was a practice she sanctioned based on her progressive education philosophy. Play is a large part of most elementary school classrooms given the well-argued fact that the freedom of play nurtures early childhood development, especially in a rug area where play is securely protected behind its temporal and spatial walls. In *Playing and Reality* (1971), D. W. Winnicott states it is only through playing that children are able to be creative and thus come to discover their individual selves. Spaces that allow for the freedom of play, in which play is non-obligatory and non-functional, allow students to set themselves apart from the normal, everyday, proper ways of behaving. The space of play is where subjects come together, interact and occasionally transform the way borders and boundaries get drawn, erased, shifted and re-inscribed in those places. When borders and boundaries are shifted in places of play, they subsequently shift the bounds of the categories that contain them – race, class, language, gender – so that children from different sociocultural backgrounds interact much more freely in spaces of play.

In addition to the rug area, play had its place in the music class, drama class, on the playground, in the lunchroom, during the transition period from one activity to another and in informal meeting places such as the closet area and the sink area. It was only when play spilled over into unmarked areas such as during a lecture or in the structured line en route to a different part of the school that the teacher interfered to regulate the temporal and spatial boundaries of free play. Thus, informal play is often isolated and confined within the everyday life of the elementary classroom so that it does not affect or disturb the formal curriculum. Classroom rules often help clearly define the borders of free play and reality so students can instantly detach themselves and transition from one frame of reference to another. Furthermore, there is a degree of meta-play even within play since students are often made conscious of when, where, what and how play is allowed within the classroom. There is a degree of *as-ifness* in play because it can be restarted and repeated and each end to play clears the way for another beginning of play, creating a continuous flow of time in which play is never a cumulative process in an elementary classroom (Bauman, 1993). Rather, play is an element that is woven continuously throughout the elementary classroom curriculum. Moreover, the rug area was also a migrational space in which students could drift back and forth during independent times of free play from the rug area to other formal places in the classroom.

Places of play can also become sites of transgressions since they allow students to step outside of the classroom structure through both their imaginative powers and the boundary-loosening, open, fluid social and physical space surrounding them. The playfulness of places such as the rug area and the music class allowed the dual immersion students in this classroom to act with spontaneity and gaze at each other directly and openly in a physical and social space that was often fluid, non-confining and only semi-controlled. The flow of language increased in these fluid, open spaces of play where the speech act was not so scripted, expert-made and staged. In terms of power relations, negotiations between the students occurred through an ongoing dialectical process in which students often mediated their differences and the messiness of their conflicts in these fluid, non-confining and only semi-controlled spaces. If there were no rug area within this classroom, then perhaps the students would have found or created an alternative space in the class that was also fluid, non-confining and only semi-controlled – perhaps voicing their conflicts on the crowded and divided school playground and not in the classroom. However, the research in this study clearly points to the importance of places of play like the rug area for student growth.

Furthermore, the kinds of experiences students have in specific places and locales determine the degree of *ontological security* felt by them through face-to-face interactions, bodily experiences and the childhood development of a sense of home (Giddens, 1990). The rug area often provided ontological security for the dual immersion students because it was in many ways a metaphorical cocoon that allowed students to develop their own self-identities in a safe and comfortable space of play. Thus, the spatial structure of a specific place in the classroom can construct a certain experience of place, time and self by connecting the spatial representation of a place with the lived experiences of its subjects. Subsequently, due to its ontological security, the rug area in this dual immersion classroom was also a place where students' motivating desires could be articulated, and it gave way to modes of address and contestation within this space of social encounter. Such talk of student desires and contestation also reflected the power relations within the classroom and the struggle of forces that were enacted in the classroom. The rug area was one of those places in the classroom that played a primary role in terms of defining and redefining the power relations between the students and teacher. In many ways, it became a theater for practical actions and became a field that authorized risk-taking, social actions from the students. The rug area produced a discursive site for opening up and reopening discussions and dialogue regarding several topics of concern for the students during their morning meetings, including the boundaries between the Spanish and English languages. The rug area was a decentered and unbounded place that became an allegory for the possibilities of opening up gaps in the order of things and giving license for students to be themselves during these meetings. Places like the rug area allow teachers and students to approach the clash of epistemologies between them and to use the rug area to open up discussions citing gaps or slippages within the classroom discourse. These discussions show how the constitution of the classroom can be tense, contradictory, dialectical, dialogic, texted, textured and filled with desires.

In turn, the rug area can be seen as a *space on the side of the road* that gives itself up to "digressions, deflections, displacements, deferrals, and difference" and thus allows for the construction of a counter discourse and a critique of coherence in the dual immersion classroom (Stewart, 1996: 6). It is a place where there is always something more to be said. It is a place where students not only set their stories straight but also open up gaps within them, gaps that reflect things that cannot be contained and bounded. It is a place where they can imagine possibilities for their classroom and the spaces in it. It is a place where speech acts from the students often moved to student action and agency; it is a polyphonic space where multiple positions, voices and registers existed together within a poetics of encounter (Bakhtin, 1981).

The rug area recorded interruptions, evoked student voices and their ruminations and even gave way to the voicing of tensions between the Spanish and English languages in this classroom. During the school year, there was one particular metalinguistic conflict concerning the Spanish spelling bee that was situated entirely on the rug area, a conflict revolving around how this dual immersion classroom positioned the Spanish spelling bee in relation to its English counterpart. The focus of this book is grounded in metalinguistic discussions concerning the subjective nature of language, and the following section in particular examines how the organic composition of the circular rug area allowed the dual immersion students to use metalanguage in order to critically discuss the unequal treatment of the Spanish spelling bee in relation to the English spelling bee and to identify politically with the consequences of those inequalities. Thus, the students used metalanguage to point out the contradictions between the two spelling bees and to voice their resistance on the rug.

The Spanish Spelling Bee

When the Spanish spelling bee made its appearance as an item on the agenda during a class meeting in December, a few English-dominant, white students kept questioning the teacher, Roberta, as to why the Spanish spelling bee was not given equal importance in comparison to the English spelling bee. They also questioned whether or not they could have a temporary extension so that they could have more time to prepare for the Spanish words. The teacher responded to their requests by stating that the Spanish words on the list were too difficult to comprehend and thus she did not want to make the Spanish spelling bee "a big thing." In addition, she said that they did not have enough time to practice the words, since the district determined the deadline beforehand. Perhaps another reason could have been the fact that spelling bees are not a common school practice in the Spanish-speaking world and here the American discourse of spelling competitions was imposing itself onto the Spanish language.

Nevertheless, a dialectical discussion soon ensued in which a few dual immersion students pointed out the contradictions in the classroom teacher's distinctions and differences between the two spelling bees. In this situated context, the students seated themselves on the rug area in a complete circle as usual, their bodies facing each other. However, the central eye and gaze of the classroom teacher was monitoring the English and Spanish borders during the Spanish spelling bee discussions and subsequently Roberta used her teacher authority to direct the class meeting here instead of the students:

Scott: First thing on the agenda is the spelling bee. But I don't know who wrote it. [Students debate as to who wrote the item onto the agenda.]

Roberta: It doesn't matter. I asked the person to write Spanish spelling bee because of what happened yesterday. Something interesting happened today. Jose returned the words ... and so did Yolanda. That means I have two ... Jose and Yolanda have decided not to do it. So I know ... that's a huge task ... that we're asking you to do ... and I was going to make copies for everybody but I think we have to go about it differently ... [Roberta is fumbling with the Spanish spelling bee lists in her hand] because I know that Anjelica and Alicia wound up being the two people left yesterday. But I also know that ... we do not spend a whole lot of time in this room spelling Spanish words.

Joshua: Yeah . . . we only do it . . . during . . . for certain words . . . like science and social studies.

Roberta: That's right darling. So if you need to participate . . . if you really want to participate in the Spanish spelling bee, you have to study this [Roberta points to the spelling lists in her hand]. And I don't know how many of you really want to do this . . . I only want you to do it if you really want to do it.

Scott: I didn't get one of those lists because I was not in school.

Roberta: You didn't get it? [Roberta's response indicates a sense of loss because Scott has the highest degree of Spanish proficiency in relation to other English-dominant, white students]. You didn't get one of those because I didn't have enough to hand out yesterday to those people who thought they were interested . . . and you're right. You weren't here and at some part of the day . . . at any rate . . . how many of you . . . after . . . how many of you after taking this home last night or not taking it home thought about the spelling bee and have something you want to say . . . yes dear.

Alice: I think that . . . uh . . . that we weren't prepared for it and it wasn't exactly a fair thing. So the kids who don't speak Spanish didn't have the words ready.

Roberta: Insightful and thank you for your comment. Do you have a suggestion?

Alice: Umm . . . Maybe we can have like . . . maybe study more words . . . study it and redo it.

Roberta: Thank you for your suggestion. [Roberta looks for students who are raising their hands.] Alicia?

Alicia: I know how to spell the words but I don't know what they mean.

Roberta: I know . . . the meanings . . . uh . . . you're not the only one. The meanings elude many of us. Some of these words I've never heard of before. So, if you need the meanings, we have to hit the dictionary.

Scott: I think we should redo it Monday so that . . . we . . . others can try out.

Roberta: Yes . . . thank you . . . I'm glad you added that. I think it should go to the people who really want to do it . . . how many of you sitting in this room . . . right here . . . right now . . . really want to do it? [Half the class raises its hands.] How many of you got this yesterday? You got it . . . you got it . . . you got it . . . okay . . . put your hands down. How many of you did not get it who want it? [Roberta takes a tally.] One . . . two . . . three . . . Alice?

Alice: I'm not sure.

Roberta: You want to think about it some more? Well then ... I'm going to ... did you decide if you're going to do it? [Roberta looks at Javier.] Do you need a copy?

Javier: No.

Roberta: You're not going to do it? Let me have it back my love ... and so here ... here ... who else had a hand up? [Roberta distributes lists to those who want to participate and collects lists from those who do not want to participate.] You want to do it? [Roberta looks at Shakima.] Shakima, are you going to do it or not?

Shakima: Not.

Roberta: So give me your copy sweetie ... look ... I don't want to put any extra pressure on you. [Sunny raises her hand.] Yes, sweetie?

Sunny: I kinda want to try it ... to see if I'm good at it ... but I don't want it to be a big thing.

Roberta: I don't want it to be a big thing either. Shakima ... Pierre ... anyone else who is not going to do it? If you're not going to do it, le me have it ... and I'll make some more copies today ... So what are you going to do? Study these words over the weekend?

Students: Yes.

Roberta: Study these words over the weekend and on Tuesday of next week ... we'll have another run-off with the children who want to it.

Joshua: If the district contest is in April ... then why don't we do it later? So we get more time.

Roberta: Because ... I was supposed to hand in the names of the children who want to participate in November ... by November 15. It is now December 10. We are almost a month late for the district. That's why we need to do it ... How about if we gave you until Thursday? It's a huge list.

Scott: I think that would be good because I know that ... kids who care can maybe study harder. It's that ... we can study A one day ... B another day ... the other day C ...

Shakima: That's so ... you're not going to be finished by Monday.

Scott: Exactly!

Joshua: Yeah ... but if you do that ... if you don't really care much about the spelling bee you're not going to look up just A ...

　　　　[　　　　　　　　　　　　　　]

Scott: I'm not saying that idea ....

Joshua: I'm not saying you would ... but if you did do that you wouldn't care about it that much so ... if you would do that then you shouldn't join.

Sunny: What if you just want to try it?

Alice: I want to try it.

Roberta: So that's three copies I have to make.

Alice: It seems like it's going to be a big thing.

Roberta: It's not going to be a big thing. [Roberta shakes her head to indicate the negative.] If you want to try it, I appreciate it so very much . . . I'm going to make three copies. How about you Belinda? You don't want to do it? You got one?

Belinda: I don't want to do it.

Roberta: Alicia . . . you definitely want to do it . . . Anjelica . . . you definitely want to do it. Don't you? [Anjelica and Alicia nod their heads to indicate the positive.] Maria? Lisa? If you're interested, you have to have a list. Lisa, you look a little hesitant. Tell me the truth. Remember we're not making a big thing out of it but we will give you until Thursday to study. How do you feel about that?

Lisa: No.

Roberta: Claudio you have a list. Julio, I'm making you a list. So I'm making three copies. Fair enough. Settled. Next Thursday we'll have a run-off.

The ambiguous directions for the Spanish spelling bee by the classroom teacher reflected the precarious balance of languages in this dual immersion classroom. When the students looked outward and gazed toward the English-dominant world by pointing out the lack of emphasis on the Spanish spelling bee, they looked more closely at Spanish subjectivity and how the Spanish language became the Other within the classroom discourse, especially in relation to English subjectivity (Silverman, 1983). The gaze of the classroom subjects became a projectile vision when it reflected back what was occurring to the use of the Spanish language from an outward position, such as by noting the marginalization of the Spanish spelling bee, the delimiting time spent on the Spanish spelling bee and how much space it occupied in the formal curriculum. It was only when the gaze of the Spanish Other returned to the subjects in the classroom that English dominance was questioned and the dual immersion classroom tried to go back to its proper balance of languages. Thus, an honest and realistic gaze upon the subject of Spanish and how it is being actualized versus being marginalized must occur often in the dual immersion classroom so that the classroom subjects could reflect outwardly upon language use and linguistic borders and boundaries in order to determine when Spanish is annexed too much and conversely owning up to too little Spanish in the curriculum. The gaze upon the

Spanish language can help describe both its limits as it has been formed in the dual immersion discourse as well as help reconstruct and reshape the classroom curriculum due to the insights the outward gaze can provide into the linguistic dynamic between Spanish and English. The analysis of the gaze also allows us to examine the divisions of power between the two languages because it is a medium in which the differences between the two languages can be observed by the subjects themselves.

Yet, the direction and quality of the gaze is determined by whoever has the power to wield the gaze. In this dual immersion classroom, when both the English-dominant and Spanish-dominant students took on the gaze of the Spanish language, they simply reversed the binary so the differential power structure moved toward a greater dominance of the Spanish language. Thus more time was allotted to the Spanish spelling bee at the end of several dialectical discussions surrounding its marginalization. Even though perhaps some goal-orientated students were motivated to resituate the position of the Spanish spelling bee for academic reasons as opposed to sociolinguistic reasons, the agency available to the students in this rug space nonetheless allowed them to take the position of a desiring subject, regardless of their motivations for such desires. The use of the gaze by an agent has the power to challenge the traditional linguistic borders and boundaries and reform both their form and the relations between them. The gaze can also be defined metaphorically as an in-between space that constitutes the flexible medium in which the subject is able to navigate between the bounded space separating the English and Spanish language. Yet, the gaze is also a medium for effecting change in the shape of the Other and within the classroom discourse (Kirby, 1996). The structuration of the gaze in a classroom borrows from and reinforces patterns of viewing from mainstream society but disturbing the gaze's symmetry can also disturb the smooth reproductions of the two languages. In other words, a disturbance of the visual field through the gaze can destabilize the borders and boundaries between the two languages because it allows bilingual classroom subjects to see how the two languages are parceled and arranged within the physical, social, metaphorical and epistemological classroom spaces.

One could also propose that Spanish and English are affected not just by the divergent physical space of the classroom and their social and epistemological positioning but also by the distinctive and different psychological formation, or psychic spaces, that shape the consciousness of the bilingual subjects. The interior world of the bilingual students and teacher qualitatively shapes the psychic space of the two languages as linguistic ideology comes to define the subjects' consciousness in relation to who they are as individuals and in relation to the two languages. Are they really a dual immersion classroom that produces a balanced relationship between the two languages or are they like any other bilingual program in which Spanish is once again marginalized? Questions such as these often remain residual in the consciousness of bilingual classroom subjects. Yet, oftentimes the space afforded to English within the psychic space of a dual immersion subject is derived from a space that is assumed to be increasingly expansive, rigid and intrusive while the space for Spanish often connotes a space that is penetrable, susceptible, passive, submissive, imploding and collapsible (Kirby, 1996). Within the binary of subjective constitutions, English occupied a dilating psychic space that was always expanding its frontiers outward in this dual immersion classroom. Spanish occupied a psychic space that was always cringing, shrinking and was forever vulnerable to the dominance of English, especially for fifth-grade students who faced pressures from American popular culture.

Thus, when English and Spanish are made to be *different* in a dual immersion classroom, then a disparity of representation can be produced in the psychic spaces of its classroom subjects. These psychic spaces are also marked by borders, boundaries and separations, just like the markers of separation in the physical space of the classroom and the cognitive space of the bilingual brain. Furthermore, the subjective constitution of the students' psychic space for the two languages is complemented by the psychic space of the teacher's whose beliefs and values toward the two languages will be picked up by the students themselves as part of their own psychic structure. If the teacher sees the Spanish language as different from the English language and sets up this difference in her/his words and actions and thus in her/his psyche, then a much deeper schism can occur between the two languages within the students' psychic spaces as well. The students can internalize this Otherness from the teacher, the idea of the Spanish language as the Other, and return this attitude. In this particular classroom, the Othering of the Spanish language disrupted borders, unsettled boundaries and threw into crisis the certitude of a binary model in which both languages were to be treated equally.

One of the main forces for creating shifts in borders and boundaries is the capacity for students to occupy positions of desire and power that can lead to the subsequent reformations of the psychic space so that Spanish can become something more than the Other. When the classroom subjects reclaim a space for Spanish within the dual immersion discourse, they in turn reforming the psychic space. By crossing the threshold and preempting the teacher's strategic move to eliminate the Spanish spelling bee, a select group of dual immersion students confronted the dynamic tension between knowledge and power and acted as agents to keep the Spanish spelling bee intact. They also stabilized the rug area as a subjective space governed by students and far removed from the objective knowledge of classroom reality. The contradiction between the Spanish and English spelling bee finally achieved resolution when the class eventually held a second competition to see who will represent them at the district Spanish spelling bee contest. The second round of competition allowed English-dominant students more time to memorize the orthography of the Spanish words in the list and in turn many more English-dominant students made it to the final round. In the end, two Spanish-dominant females, both from the Dominican Republic, represented the class in the district-wide Spanish spelling bee contest. Thus, the dual immersion students maintained a representation of the rug area as a space bound to notions of resistance/counter discourse, as evident in the other classroom episodes recorded and narrated in this book.

It is also important to note that the teacher constructed such a space of resistance to exist in the classroom. Even though at times the students were disempowered subjects situated in a panoptic space, there were also certain places and times when they were empowered social agents who could use their voices for social action. As a teacher, Roberta was consistent in terms of providing multiple ways for students to make comments and critiques that can lead to changes in the physical, social, epistemological and psychic design of the classroom. Student agency in the classroom was allowed at times to challenge the rules of behavior that determined the overall physical and social structure of the classroom, leading to a student-led change in classroom design. In this particular classroom, the rug area became a place where student agency did challenge the physical and social structure of the classroom. By bracketing the language generated at the rug area, one can see that the time-slot for rug use and its spatial layout allowed students to assume the role of social agents as opposed to disempowered social actors.

Furthermore, the students used the space of resistance at the rug area to create a psychic space of fortitude for the Spanish language through the repeated defense of the Spanish spelling bee and other such acts of resistance. Yet, in addition to being a site of alterity where contradictions were identified, the rug area also produced a mediating space that opened up the possibility for a metaphorical *third space*. It is a space that attempts to mediate and resolve the contradictions, tensions, digressions, deflections, displacements, deferrals and differences between the two languages because the third space is more like a strategic space that becomes a standpoint of resistance. The third space is an open, expressive, in-between space in which there is room to maneuver back and forth between problematic binaries of language so the mediation of their meaning and moments of transgression beyond structural binaries can become possible: "The third space is where the negotiation of incommensurable differences creates a tension peculiar to borderline existence" (Bhabha, 1994: 218). The transgressions within the metaphorical third space have the power to disrupt the order of things in the classroom, such as the allocation of time and space for the Spanish spelling bee. These transgressions also have the power to transform the Otherness and marginality of the Spanish language, as well as to intensify latent topics and concerns regarding other forms of language use by forcing them to the point of their visibility, making countervailing possibilities and alternatives tangible by playing them out (Stewart, 1996).

By introducing discontinuities within the natural order of things, the third space allows for the denaturalization of borders and boundaries that may have seemed concrete and structurally rigid, so in the face of critique, borders and boundaries can become shifting, fluid and no longer binding. Old boundaries soon are transgressed and disrupted and finally replaced by new divisions. Once boundaries have been transgressed, the transgressions then create *a spatial lacuna* that permits the reconstruction of those very same boundaries and an expansion out beyond the boundaries of structural enclosures and boundedness (McDowell, 1996: 138). The discussions on the rug area around the Spanish spelling bee created a third space when students shifted the boundary between the two languages and produced a spatial lacuna that allowed the Spanish spelling bee to move beyond its present threshold in the classroom and regain greater time and attention. The construction of identity in a dual immersion classroom is somewhat regulated by these *dialectics of boundary control*, who controls which boundaries and where the threshold points are located (Dovey, 1999: 27). Furthermore, equalizing binary pairs, leveling hierarchies and destabilizing fragile boundaries are needed in order to promote equality between the two languages, thus pushing back the frontiers of the dominant, English-dominant psychic space and reforming classroom reality. Subsequently, by transforming the position of the Spanish spelling bee, the students were transforming how the knowledge of Spanish is represented in the dual immersion classroom's composition of conceptual space. The conceptual space for each language is determined by the kinds of knowledge and epistemologies one wants to form and implement for that language in the curriculum. Thus, by becoming advocates for the Spanish spelling bee, the students were able to reconceptualize the knowledge and positioning of Spanish words, their meanings and their spellings.

However, the dissipation of linguistic borders and boundaries between the Spanish and English language may seem far too progressive for those who still want to reify the closed binary structure and not allow for the continual renegotiation of languages, especially given the time constraints imposed by the school district. There is also a great degree of anxiety produced in the in-between spaces of linguistic negotiation because the subject is fragmented and decentered in the in-between space due to a series of ruptures and gaps within the extant webs of knowledge and power (Bhabha, 1994: 216). The Spanish spelling bee discussions did produce a great deal of anxiety amongst the students, teachers and parents, as evident in the continued discussions surrounding the Spanish spelling bee and its temporal and spatial location in the formal curriculum.

In addition to the Spanish spelling bee, there were several other dialectical discussions that occurred on the rug area where the dual immersion students disturbed dominant language tendencies through their critical analysis of linguistic borders and boundaries.

Reading in Spanish: Changing the Margins

In another school-based program, titled *Compañeros de Lectura* or "Reading Buddies," the fifth-grade dual immersion students were required to read books in Spanish and write in Spanish as well with the second-grade dual immersion students who came to their classroom an hour before lunch every Tuesday, a Spanish day. However, during this weekly time period, many students began to see the *Compañeros de Lectura*/Reading Buddies time period as free time and subsequently did not read or write in Spanish with the younger students. Eventually, Roberta brought her concerns to a classroom meeting about the students' lack of focus on the Spanish language during this time period. Here she was arguing for more student-initiated Spanish reading and writing, which was a different stance from her earlier view on lessening the focus on the Spanish spelling bee versus the English spelling bee. In the end, the class as a whole decided to create a list of rules of behavior during the *Compañeros de Lectura*/Reading Buddies time period so that the teacher does not have to always patrol the borders to make sure that Spanish was indeed in full use:

Reading Buddy Rules	*Reglas para Compañeros de Lectura*
1. Read a book in Spanish.	1. *Leer en español.*
2. Practice words in Spanish that you do not know.	2. *Practicar palabras que tu no conoces.*
3. Work first, then drawing.	3. *Palabras primero, entonces puedes dibujar.*
4. Read a book in Spanish, then write about it in Spanish.	4. *Leer el libro en español despues escribes en español.*
5. If you need more space, go into the hallway.	5. *Si necesitas más espacio, puedes ir al pasillo.*
6. Spend more time reading and writing, instead of drawing.	6. *Pase más tiempo leyendo y escribiendo nada más.*
7. Create an activity box.	7. *Hagan una canasta para las actividades.*
8. All games must be made before we meet with our Reading Buddy.	8. *Tiene que ser su juego antes que compañeros de lectura.*
9. Make a chart to keep track of the books that you read.	9. *Hagas una lista de libros tu leiste.*
10. Stay with your Reading Buddy.	10. *Quedas con tu compañero de lectura.*
11. Translations are allowed. Spanish first!	11. *Puedes traducir—Español Primero!*
12. Bring your Spanish books. Read old books, but bring new, challenging books too.	12. *Trajo tus libros en español y tambien puedes leer libros más difícil.*

Specifically, when they created the *Compañeros de Lectura*/Reading Buddies rules in both languages during several class meetings held on the rug area, the teacher and students began talking about language with language as the object of their critical discussions. Thus, they were using metalanguage to articulate the conflicting development between Spanish and English during the *Compañeros de Lectura*/Reading Buddies time period. This bringing to the fore of a binary opposition between Spanish and English, and of its conflicting dialectical character, specifically implied both the subordination of Spanish to English and the centrality of English, both in the classroom reality and in the conceptual realm. In the desire to abolish unequal borders and boundaries between the two languages and promote a model of harmonious development, six dual immersion students throughout the school year in particular took on a greater leadership position during the dialectical discussions: Jose, Yolanda, Alice, Scott, Shakima and Claudio. They wanted to deconstruct the contradictions between the two languages when they sensed that Spanish was not equally valued or recognized. When they examined the psychic space between the two languages, the distancing of Spanish led them to the awareness that Spanish is the Other. If the psychic space afforded to the Spanish language could be projected onto a curricular map, then it would look most like an archipelago of blots of knowledge dispersed throughout the curriculum rather than a compact and continuous landmass. These six students who contested the devaluation of Spanish more often than others will be referred to frequently in later chapters as the *border crossers* because they were able to critically analyze when and where there was an asymmetrical relationship between Spanish and English.

Social Segregation: Redefining the Utopian Rug Space

The counter discourse produced in the rug area made it seem quite often like an all-empowering space because it allowed student voices from the margins to be heard and provided a critical space for students to challenge the dominant discourse. The rug area became the locus of student agency that eventually came to resist the organizing forces of the dominant discourse. However, the rug area became a third space mostly during the class meeting times on Monday and Friday mornings as opposed to the other times of rug use. The rug area also came into view as a third space when something happened to interrupt the ordinary, naturalized flow of events, leaving the students to react by writing down on the morning meeting agenda clipboard what issues and concerns they wanted to talk about at the next class meeting. The items on the agenda were then dramatized to the classroom by the student who listed that item on the agenda. Yet, the morning meetings were mediated by the student council representatives, as well as by the student teacher and classroom teacher, so everyone was given equal time to say what s/he wanted. The other students then joined in the dialogue, all hoping to contribute views and opinions that might lead to a resolution in the end. During the morning meetings, there were moments of dramatized, embodied spectacle and moments of the *mimetic excess* when students were watching to see what happened next in the dialogic encounters and assessed their unforeseen consequences, which were sometimes subject to intense eruptions resulting from the tension of things and a contest of claims and counterclaims (Stewart, 1996). The morning meetings became an intermeshed place where the ways of acting, seeing and talking flowed together in a rhythm of continuous student action. So while one student was acting and talking, the other students were seeing and listening to what was said and sometimes they raised their hands to make something of what was just said, thus, the fluid space produced during the morning meetings was constituted by continuous student engagement and encounter. The bi-weekly morning meetings held on the rug area had a great capacity for transformative activity and gave students the possibility to exercise some kind of agency for change even within limited situations. The rug area became *the place of struggle* where challenges to hegemonic practices were waged through voiced words (Harvey, 1996: 82).

The countervailing tendencies of the students situated on the rug area were also a step toward recapturing power from those who controlled it, the classroom teacher and the student teacher, as well as other peers. A dialectic of power and control was produced at the rug area and eventually lead to the students escaping the strict, rigid surveillance of the teachers and the direct and constant gaze of student supervision (Giddens, 1986). Rather, there was a balance of authority flowing from the supervised to the supervisor. The solidarity and democracy practiced in the rug area during morning meetings, creative writing circles and independent free time all demonstrated that the emancipating spatial syntax of openness can increase the visibility and recognition of student agency. Foucault (1991) defines a space of liberty where students have control as a *heterotopia* because it is a space outside of social authority and power-laden processes. A heterotopia is also where subjects try to build an alternative social order by trying to reshape the objective qualities of that space and by making it a non-hierarchical and communitarian space.

However, we must also be cautious of fixing the meaning of particular places such as the rug area with liberty and openness, and as a fixed heterotopia, so that we do not enclose them and essentialize their identities (Massey, 1994). The identities of places can be unfixed, contested and multiple since the meaning of places is often fluid, contextual and sometimes dissolute. For example, even though the utopian aim of the dual immersion program is to break down the sociolinguistic barriers between the Spanish-dominant and English-dominant students, it seemed that more often these two sociocultural groups were neither neighbors nor strangers when seated on the rug area, as well as in other spaces of alterity such as the music and drama class. Thus, before we can fix the rug area as a utopian space, we need to make a distinction between physical space and social space, since there is a dialectical relationship between these two forms of spacing (Bauman, 1993).

Physical objective space is measurable and quantifiable in terms of proximity and distance; however, social space is a subjective space made by human interactions and is non-objective. The social space is where we live with other human beings while the physical space constitutes the parameters in which the shared social space is defined and set, as well as the defined and set physical objects within this physical space. Our knowledge of the world is based upon our perceptions of both the physical and social space of our external reality. The spatial arrangements within a social space are based on the differentiating social notions of intimacy and anonymity, strangeness and familiarity. The concept of the Other is an awareness of the distance and social remoteness between human beings that occurs within a social space (Bauman, 1993). Even when human beings inhabit the same physical space, the distancing of one from the Other creates clear identity borders and boundaries between different social groups and also between different individuals.

When seated on the rug, the students created definitions of place by sitting alongside peers from the same sociocultural group and thus territorializing that space through their bodily practices. The exclusionary practice of *saving places* on the rug for their friends created place-based identities that were conflated with race, language and gender. Oftentimes, even before they arrived at the rug area, the students talked amongst themselves at their desks and strategically decided beforehand who was going to sit next to whom and determined their subsequent locations and positions on the rug. "Save me a space next to you" was a common phrase said right before any communal meeting on the rug area. The positions mapped out by students when they sat down on the rug area for their communal meetings were often aligned with their socially constructed subject positions. The Hispanic, lower-middle-class, Spanish-dominant students often sat along one side of the rug area while the white, upperclass, English-dominant students sat along the other side. There were of course some students who sat in-between these two sociocultural groups and thus occupied in-between spaces along the semi-circular seating arrangement.

One can also state that the rug space became an organic model of subjectivity in which students created walled areas of belonging and acceptance that were different from the desk area subjectivity. The unity amongst the Spanish-dominant and English-dominant students in this dual immersion classroom was not necessarily a given based just on the notion of a linguistic commonality. Yet, the dual immersion classroom was always attempting to work toward and struggle for that unity, regardless of differences in class, language, culture and gender. Even though on the rug area the students aligned themselves on top of an ontological terrain of identity, these same students can be located in alternative subject positions in other places and during other moments in the school year that did not correlate with their race, culture, gender, class and language. However, on the rug area, the ontological subject positions were often reproduced over and over. One group did not necessarily prompt the other group to keep its distance as outsiders, but the social encounters between the two groups did not either lead to long-lasting friendships between students from different sociocultural groups.

Though there was informal, subconscious boundary drawing between the two sociocultural student groups, especially in informal spaces such as the rug area and the special activity classes, this sedimentary social figuration never led to a continuous warfare of sociocultural boundary drawing and boundary defense. The power relations between the two sociocultural groups were predominantly symmetrical, even though the power relations between the languages within the classroom space were asymmetrical. Moreover, Roberta regulated the social space to make sure that each student had a voice in the classroom's decision-making power and that neither the Spanish-dominant nor the English-dominant students were being marginalized. Roberta was nonetheless aware that there was a degree of distance and strangerhood between the two sociocultural groups and was hoping that the heterogeneous seating at the desk area would remove the sentiment that they were strangers even when seated as neighbors. It is often the teacher who defines the rules of proximity and social distance between and amongst the students through the careful examination, comparison, calculation and evaluation of social space in the classroom. Roberta often changed the students' seating every few weeks and did not remain oblivious to the social interactions amongst the students, stating that it was a pedagogical concern to taper off any form of estrangement and uneasy coexistence between the distinct sociocultural and sociolinguistic student groups.

Even though the dual immersion model attempts to eradicate the sense of Otherness that often occurs in mainstream classrooms where different student groups are not obligated to interact with one another, there are still moments and places when and where a metaphorical unity cannot be produced. Obdurate distances can remain between English-dominant and Spanish-dominant students. Sometimes the two different sociocultural groups live in different worlds within the same physical classroom and these worlds converge occasionally during the day but one can also say that the two different sociocultural groups live in different sociocultural spaces. The boundaries between these two different sociocultural groups were more than arbitrary; their borders illustrate the tangible differences in interests and tastes that emerge across race, culture, language, gender and class. The following transcript from an interview with Alice highlights how and why there were divisions between the two student groups:

Author: Do you think there is a division between the Spanish-dominant students and the English-dominant students? Do you hang around together?

Alice: Well it depends . . . I mean in class . . . definitely not. Roberta treats us all equally but . . . there is not actually fighting or hatred . . . it's just . . . you sort of drift over to your best friends . . . whether they are Latino or not.

Author: Do you hang around the Spanish-dominant students?

Alice: Well . . . not really . . . there are sort of groups . . . we talk to each other . . . like I'm friends with Yolanda and some people like that . . . but it's sort of like groups . . . Scott, Sunny and I . . . Lisa and Mary . . . Yolanda and her gang which is like Shakima, Jose, Javier and Jorge . . . people like that . . . and then there is the rest of the totally American boys like Brian, Joshua and Pierre . . . they hang out together a lot.

Author: Well what about Claudio? [A reference to a student who goes in-between.]

Alice: It depends . . . he's best friends with Scott and hangs out with the American boys and the boy clique . . . but when the boys are not around he once in a while goes with Yolanda and her group as a backup . . . because they know him . . . I don't know how to describe it . . . they are sort of like him . . . Sunny and I . . . we are sort of strange . . . we like disgusting things and we're kind of funny . . . and we're sort of strange and we sort of drift together.

Author: Do you think it's about color? Do the white kids hang around with just the white kids . . . ?

Alice: I don't know . . . I hang around with Yolanda and her group sometimes . . . not much . . . no . . . I don't know . . . even when I go to their group . . . I sort of feel a transition. I say things to Sunny and do things with Sunny and feel like one person but then I become a totally different person with Yolanda and her group . . .

Author: What kind of a person?
Alice: I don't know how to explain it . . . I feel like . . . like . . . almost like . . . almost like . . . I was more mature because Sunny and I . . . we do silly things and we make fun of each other . . . but with Yolanda . . . it's just different. She's much more mature . . . and the kids that hang around her and stuff . . . are really mature as well . . . and as soon as I go in with them . . . I don't even do it intentionally . . . I stop acting silly. But . . . not serious . . . but I don't say things like *poopy face* which Sunny and I joke about.

Thus, on one hand, the rug area was an empowering communal place where students were endowed with power and agency. On the other hand, the rug area was also where exclusionary politics were taking place informally because the students were simultaneously defining themselves in opposition to one another's social identity even within this communal space.

Yet, Bauman (1993) states that the categories of neighbor and stranger are too polar and produce a neither/nor relationship between human subjects and thus we must push aside this all-embracing dichotomy. Rather, we must conclude that there were moments and places when the two sociocultural groups came together as a whole, but there were also moments and places where there was a disjuncture between the two sociocultural groups that led to separation and division. Even though both sociocultural student groups and their parents knew that the dual immersion model promotes cultural and linguistic diversity, the following chapters in this book closely analyze the real conditions for the solidarity between the two distinct sociocultural and sociolinguistic groups.

Conclusion: Mapping Language, Space and Power

When using a language-space-power theoretical framework in a dual immersion classroom, one has to pay close attention to how the two languages are constituted in the classroom discourse, where one language begins and the other ends and where the linguistic borders are located. In terms of the spatialization of the two languages, the centrality of the English language versus the marginalization of the Spanish language in this chapter showed us where the distinctions, rifts and disjunctions between Spanish and English existed in this dual immersion classroom (Lefebvre, 1991). Yet, the internal split, or gap, between the Spanish and English boundary within this dual immersion classroom also created the possibility for complex appropriations and resistance toward the linguistic centrality of English through unexpected eruptions of student agency. The gaps and slippages between the two languages also posited the possibility of different student voices and points of view questioning what seemed natural in the order of things and questioning how borders were patrolled in this dual immersion classroom. Thus, discursive space and power, defined here as a set of positionalities, a network of power relations and a domain of material and discursive effects, also became disrupted when students in this dual immersion program challenged the conventional associations between the two languages and disrupted their naturalizing norms (Duncan, 1996). The reactions toward the Spanish spelling bee and *Companeros de Lectura* / Reading Buddy regulations reflect how human agents in a bilingual classroom can change the symbolic configuration of languages in order to imagine their bilingual classrooms differently.

The stark contrast between the use of Spanish and English in this classroom was voiced most often in the rug area where spatio-linguistic differences gave way to the dialectical transgressions of borders and boundaries. The rug area created the optimal conditions under which a centrality of English could be questioned – where it ruptured, exploded, or was rent apart through the student-led metalinguistic discussions, which supported the increased presence of Spanish but were nonetheless conducted in English. In doing so, the select border-crossing students eventually spurned the dialectics in order to expel the centrality of English and bring the peripheral elements of Spanish to the center. Yet, even though the rug area offered a different positionality and conferred a new subjectivity, the transactions that took place on the rug area neither maintained Spanish in its normative marginalized role nor catapulted it as an aggressive subject of debate. Nor was there a reversal of the Spanish language's position in the original dichotomy. Nonetheless, we can see how transforming the form of Spanish in the classroom discourse can in turn transform the class' subjectivity and lived experiences.

Next, in the language-space-power framework, power was a relation and outcome of negotiations at the rug area where it was produced and reproduced. By offering students choices and the space-time possibilities to negotiate, power was no longer imposed from a hierarchical model in which the teacher evoked a desired response from the students. Situations like the classroom meetings, in which there was an equal and symmetrical power layout, allowed for the reformation of linguistic parameters. In addition to the rug area, other spaces of negotiation and renegotiation included the drama class, the music class, the hallways, the playground, the gym class and the lunchroom. These spaces gave students more freedom to redraw boundaries of language, as well as other areas of subjectivity such as race and gender. They offered the students sites of power and resistance not analogous to the powerless space found in the traditional seating arrangement of the students' desks. In fact, it was rare for students to challenge the teacher within the panoptic space produced during lectures and discussions that were teacher-led, with the teacher in the front of the room and the students seated at their respective desks. Unlike the panoptic spaces of disciplinary control, spaces of play like the rug area allowed for the students' continual negotiation with their external reality and allowed them to deviate from external reality through this process of continual negotiation and recreation. A space of play can also be seen as a space where we encounter one another and interact with one another in a subjective space that can be continuously transformed by our imaginative and empowering experiences (Kirby, 1996).

Yet, the geometry of power and its signification and meaning are always shifting in places such as the rug area so power can exist simultaneously in multiple spaces and in a network of social relations that are always fluid and fleeting. Even though the geometry of the classroom space can have power over the students by shaping both their perceptions and conceptions, this power nonetheless also shifts. Throughout the academic year, once the students acquired self-consciousness or awareness of themselves within the dual immersion classroom space, students took on more initiative to re-identify places in the classroom relative to themselves, thus producing an alternative frame of reference for spatial representation within the classroom geometry. Some students became social agents who wanted to create change without themselves being influenced by external forces, and in doing so, some places were re-identified over time as their use-value began to change as well. For a place, such as the desk arrangement, to function the same way, however, it had to stay in the same place and manner over a long period of time. The student desk area became a constant feature of the classroom and became an enduring part of the panoptic space (Eilan *et al.*, 1993). Thus, the spatial layout of the classroom constantly plays upon the students' desires. However, instead of eradicating such seductive places such as the rug area, the students in this classroom came to understand the seductive capacities of the rug area where they often engaged in free play, imaginative productions and critical discussions.

Furthermore, the language-space-power framework can also be used to examine social relations between classroom subjects, the margins between subjects and the external reality between subject and subject

(Kirby, 1996). There are radical possibilities for space in which it can blur the boundary between subjects and negate any difference or redesign borders to maintain a sense of difference between subjects. Most educators are not indifferent to the manipulation of classroom space; yet, many might not be aware of how the classroom space affects the social structure. Classroom space can be symbolic and conceptual but one needs to observe how the space divides subjects and objects from one another, the gaps separating material objects, the rifts between subjects, and in turn how that space can be reconstructed differently. In addition, the spatial organization of the classroom also reflects how the teacher wants to lay out the curriculum and pedagogy, thus it is necessary for a teacher to examine the patterns and mediations of the classroom space before it becomes immutable. The organizational control over classroom space also needs to be seen as a form of power that a teacher possesses; the teacher's organization of classroom time and space determines what kinds of social interactions are put into effect in the classroom. In this classroom, Roberta used her authority and power to cognitively map the classroom's environment, and by determining what kind of programmed student action should occur in which places, Roberta created boundaries between places and drew borders in order to avoid certain student behaviors in certain places throughout the classroom. Yet, Roberta's surveillance and control over the classroom space was not always coercive since the students were also given the freedom to express their intentions of changing the order of things in their classroom.

In conclusion, space provides the ideal medium for linking the many dimensions of the classroom. It brings together the physical space of subjects and bodies as they circulate inside and outside the classroom, and it examines how these movements affect the social categories of that space. The conceptual framework for a classroom is also very much dependent upon the multiple dimensions of space: the division of classroom space, the separation of classroom space, the conflation of classroom space, the opposition of classroom space, etc. However, the application of space also allows one to examine power relations as well in the dual immersion classroom through multiple frames: the fluidity of the third space, the linguistic divisions between Spanish and English, the space of the gaze, the positionality of Spanish in the dual immersion discourse and social practices and the division of social spaces between the two sociocultural student groups. The register of space in turn becomes a three-dimensional lens that a researcher uses to explore not only the material and physical space of a classroom, but also the abstract and metaphorical spaces.

The spatiality of boundaries, gaps and thresholds in the next three chapters will continue to show the complex contradictions and disjunctions within this dual immersion classroom and its uneven development of the Spanish language. Contradictions allow conflicts and struggles to become evident and hopefully these conflicts can be mediated and the contradictions less frequent. However, the process of resolving contradictions is an ongoing process that goes through a continuous cycle of identifying contradictions and then using agency to resolve contradictions. The following three chapters continue to show similar conflicts and contradictions of language use and linguistic borders and boundaries. Instead of characterizing dual immersion classrooms through an absolute structural binary, the following chapters examine how a dual immersion classroom can also be characterized by complex episodes of uncertainty that provide bilingual subjects with radical possibilities for reforming the schema of language representation. In Chapter 3, we will examine how the teacher and students discussed and debated over how they should define their dual immersion classroom identity through the development of pep rally cheers. In Chapter 4, we will examine how language was consumed and produced in a bilingual Cuban play, and Chapter 5 examines how Spanish folk music provided that ideal third space of fluidity and hybridity.

The Cheers: The Ethics of Making Aesthetic Judgments

Rituals and Taboos: Examining the Racial Politics of Cheerleading

Barbara Rodriguez is a school aide at PS 2000 and is responsible for the daily monitoring of student behavior in unregulated school spaces such as the overcrowded cafeteria, playground, hallways and stairwells. However, Barbara has also informally taken on the role of a counselor and is often seen talking to the students, getting to know them individually and understanding their perspectives and feelings toward life outside of school. In November 1999, Barbara took on the initiative to increase school spirit at PS 2000 by asking all the fifth-grade classrooms to design a classroom cheer that would best represent who they are as a class to the rest of the school in an upcoming pep rally. Since the fifth-graders are the oldest group of students at the school, Barbara was hoping to foster role models and increase communication amongst students across the different grade levels. The fifth-grade students were given a three-month time period to complete their cheers and perform them in front of a peer audience; however, in the end, the fifth-grade classes performed their cheers four months later since many classrooms needed more production time for the cheers. Yet, even before they began designing their cheers, Barbara invited the Lady Knight cheerleaders from nearby King High School to perform their cheers in front of all fifth-grade students at PS 2000 so that the fifth-grade students would have a model-image of what a cheer should encompass in design.

The cheerleaders from King High School were all black female students, minus the captain who was a Puerto Rican female student; however, the captain did state that they also have male cheerleaders on the squad who were unable to perform that day. Nonetheless, their gender-specific cheerleading motto stated that "To Be a Lady Knight It Takes Femininity."

After presenting a series of cheers they often perform at basketball games, the Lady Knight cheerleaders encouraged verbal crowd participation from the fifth-grade students by calling out individual room numbers and having the students from each class yell as loud as they could to demonstrate their class spirit. All of the cheers the Lady Knights performed were based on the African step-dance movements and were not traditional acrobatic and athletic American cheers often found in suburban high school settings. In mainly black school communities, cheerleaders perform step dances that are characterized by loose ankle movements that cause the sole of the shoe to make multiple sounds during the cheer. Step dances use the foot to make beating sounds and are a feature of the sophisticated rhythms of West African dances and have become a part of African-American history since slavery. The step dance is a musical genre and style found throughout the African diaspora and is often performed at black fraternity and sorority social functions in the United States. Step dance movements have continued over from the African slave experience and have subsequently formed a relationship between musical genres and a memory of the past (Gilroy, 1993).

In addition to the step movements, the language in the Lady Knights cheers also reflected the current pop culture vernacular, as well as the local school culture at King High School. One cheer in particular resembled a *novelty cheer* since it involved audience actions in its words (Hanson, 1995):

We're going to turn around
Touch the ground
Shake our booty
And get, get, get down

Even though the style in this particular cheer created an overwhelming audience response by using short, simple phrasing and measured delivery in its step dance movements, the content of the words in this cheer reflected the cultural characteristics of an urban and minority high school, and thus, alienated the audience at PS 2000, which was composed mostly of middle-aged, white, middle-class teachers and administrators and students from a diverse range of races and ethnicities as well as various socioeconomic backgrounds. Some of the students responded negatively with a visceral "ooh" to signify that the language and actions in this cheer were unorthodox to them and therefore taboo. Yet, others cheered them on with claps and mimicked their movements.

The perception of the taboo in this cheer can relate to both the sensual nature of its physical form and its choice of words. The distaste toward the labeled "booty cheer" by the teachers, who exclusively expressed rejection, was accompanied by pitying or indignant remarks such as "I can't understand how anyone can call that a cheer." After performing their cheers, Barbara Rodriguez came up to Roberta, the fifth-grade dual immersion classroom teacher in this study, and asked her if she liked the King High School cheerleading. Roberta replied with a negative response: "These are not cheers. When I was a cheerleader, we used to jump up in the air and do stunts and acrobatics. These girls don't look like that they can do that." In her reply, Barbara emphasized to Roberta that the Lady Knights are therefore good role models for the students at PS 2000 because they are setting a positive example by being high school cheerleaders, even though they are not traditional icons of American beauty.

However, for Roberta, these cheers were not acrobatic and athletic enough, and she strongly felt as if the Lady Knight cheers were unauthentic. In addition, the Lady Knight cheerleaders did not physically match the image of cheerleaders represented most often in the American media. Since most of the black and Puerto Rican cheerleaders at King High School had dark complexions and were not thin like suburban cheerleaders, they might have conformed to their black and Hispanic peer standards of physical attractiveness, but they did not conform to the pervasive, white middle-class cultural images of thin, blonde, white cheerleaders often seen in advertising and the entertainment media. Physical criteria for being cheerleaders are often expressed in general terms that imply thinness and an overall desirable appearance. However, in the 1920s, the early prescriptive literature on cheerleading stressed character as well as personality and physical attributes. Today, however, the emphasis is placed solely on physical attributes.

Moreover, since Roberta was a cheerleader herself during a generation in which cheerleading became formalized and uniforms became a conspicuous aspect of the cheerleading performance, the Lady Knights' semi-uniforms, consisting of mid-thigh black miniskirts of various shades and a mix-matched group of white shirts, did not conform to the standardized image of cheerleaders wearing the same matching color-coordinated clothes. In her youth, the cheerleaders' matching uniforms created an appearance of unity that helped focus the crowd's attention and therefore did not distract the crowd's attention. Furthermore, the cheerleaders from King High School did not use the emblematic pompoms and megaphones, which are used often for decorative and ceremonial purposes in cheering. Yet, Roberta did not acknowledge that significant aesthetic changes in the style and performance of cheerleading had occurred since her original days of cheerleading in the 1950s. Roberta's insistence that cheerleading should still be a rigidly feminized spectacle ignored the contemporary cultural perceptions recognizing the fluidity and variety of gender roles emerging in our postmodern society. Changes in the socio-economic status of cheerleaders and their cultural backgrounds has also led to conceptual changes in the structure, style and content of contemporary cheering since its transformation to mass culture status during the post-World War II era.

The reaction of the teachers to this Lady Knight cheer also reflects the teachers' unconscious or conscious expectations of what cheerleaders should look like and act like. Their aesthetic orientation toward the Lady Knight cheer was defined by both race and class values brought into and reinforced by PS 2000 as the larger school institution. Even though the school advocated a multicultural philosophy and even created a multicultural parent group, the daily practices and norms of appropriate behavior in the school reinforced a white, middle-class sense of ethics. In turn, the cultural practices of PS 2000 contradicted with the Lady Knight cheer and subsequently the school audience assigned a taboo status to their cheers. The types of behavior and practices that the school rewards and the sociocultural positions of the teachers themselves did not give a legitimate disposition to the Lady Knights cheers. In many ways, the cheers that these girls presented seemed less legitimate and were perceived by most teachers as not worthy of admiration in themselves. The teachers were not able to recognize in the Lady Knights cheers something that was already known to them – they were middle-class white female teachers who did not recognize any of the stylistic characteristics familiar to them in the bygone years of cheerleading. As a group, the teachers were armed with a set of perceptual and evaluative schemes defining their aesthetic dispositions toward cheering, which were then generally applied to other artistic productions of cheering. In determining the worthiness of the cheers performed by the Lady Knights, most of the teachers came together informally after the performance to classify the legitimacy of the cheers through their collective words while walking back to their respective fifth-grade classrooms: "Did you hear that cheer? Do those girls look like cheerleaders?"

Aesthetic dispositions often impose legitimacy upon artistic productions such as cheerleading. The norms of our own perceptions oftentimes become an essentialized aesthetic disposition, which we then use to objectively measure other artistic productions. Thus, the essentialization of aesthetic dispositions leads to accepting only one right way of approaching aesthetic objects and artistic productions. The specific aesthetic intentions and points of views we use to recognize and constitute aesthetic objects and artistic productions refuse to take into account the collective and individual genesis of this specific product and its *raison d'etre*. Since the Lady Knight cheers did not follow the caveats of developing a traditional suburban American cheer, the King High School cheerleaders instead presented original cheers that did not replicate authorized cheers adopted from standardized cheerleading manuals. Their cheerleading style was influenced by the current popular culture in black and Hispanic school communities and whose origins can be traced to the soul music of the 1960s and 1970s. Most of their cheers were based in a black, rhythm and blues style, which has since gained a wide appeal in mainstream pop music, contemporary rap and hip hop, and dance club culture.

A Brief History of Cheerleading: Changing Aesthetics and Changing Racial Politics

The influence of black culture extended into cheerleading during the 1960s and 1970s when the increasing presence of black male and female cheerleaders led to the integration of *soul yells and soul dancing* in both all-white and integrated high school and college cheerleading (Hanson, 1995). By 1972, cheer entrepreneur Lawrence Herkimer incorporated "Rhythm and Soul Cheers and Chants" into the material taught at his nationally recognized cheerleading camps. Yet, the dancing, jiving rhythm and motion of soul cheerleading differed drastically from the straight-arm style and standardized cadence of mainstream American cheerleading from the 1950s. Although cheerleading began as an essentially all-male activity in the 1920s to promote athleticism and school spirit in colleges and universities, today's cheerleader is often portrayed as highly feminized and eroticized and less athletic than the classic modern male cheerleader. Contemporary cheerleading is now an icon of popular culture whose images have been proliferated throughout juvenile and adult literature, movies, television, dramas, commercials, cartoons and the general mass media. The recent 2000 Hollywood movie *Bring It On* highlights a brooding racial and cultural rivalry between a white, suburban acrobatic cheerleading squad who steals the more "racy" cheers from a black, inner-city, soul cheerleading squad in order to win the state cheerleading competition.

As cheering styles evolve to maximize mass entertainment value for the popular audience, they will become more performance orientated and will continue to heighten the visual and verbal appeal of feminized cheerleading, and thus, cheers will become less subordinate to the male athletic events that provide their original context. However, traces of gender specific binaries between male athletes and female cheerleaders and binaries between the positive cheerleading stereotype and the negative cheerleading stereotype can still be found even within the new cheering styles:

> The cheerleader is a recognized symbol of youthful prestige, wholesale attractiveness, peer leadership, and popularity. At the same time, the cheerleader has also been recognized as a symbol of mindless enthusiasm, shallow boosterism, objectified sexuality, and promiscuousness. (Hanson, 1995: 2)

In turn, cheerleading has come to represent both a higher echelon of social success and the target of social scorn as well, thus both positive and negative stereotypes prevail in newer, modified forms of cheerleading.

Cheerleading also creates a dichotomy between the Good Girl and Bad Girl image. During the modernist 1950s era, the wholesome Good Girl cheerleading image was maintained by institutional and parental definitions of appropriate feminine behavior. The Good Girl cheerleader was a young female who was attractive, cute, socially popular, intelligent, well behaved and influential as a role model. In the modernist era, being selected as a cheerleader was defined as a positive achievement of civic duty: "In 1955, the desirable traits for cheerleaders included good manners, responsibility, dependability, leadership ability, scholarship in good standing, and citizenship of high standing, as well as good personal appearance, coordination, and voice" (Hanson, 1995: 32). The ritualistic value of cheerleading in high schools contributed to the *civic identity* of the 1950s Eisenhower era; spectacles like football games and cheerleading squads played a large role in modern American life by influencing the masses as well as the elite. In addition, being a cheerleader in the 1950s was everything a girl dreamed of because there were not many other extracurricular options available for female students.

Furthermore, the school cheers and the school song kept up the school morale and created a ritualized pageantry within the everyday life of the American high school. The school communities maintained these rituals through the financial support of their local teams. By the 1950s, middle- and working-class cheerleaders in public and private schools outnumbered college cheerleaders. Now cheerleading was a part of the public school culture at all socioeconomic levels and with most sociocultural backgrounds. Elementary and secondary schools created activities such as booster sections, drill teams, cheerleading teams and dance teams to promote male athletic events such as football and basketball games. The national commodification of cheerleading developed soon after with fundraising, financial liability, scholarships and cheerleading camps, classes and gymnasiums across the country. However, the female cheerleader always maintained a subordinate role in relation to the prized male athlete and thus created a popular metaphor for traditional male and female relationships in which the ideal heterosexual couple is a male athlete and a female cheerleader. From a spatio-temporal perspective, the cheerleaders maintained a subordinate position by performing only during the game's half-time and occupying marginal spaces along the sidelines of the playing field.

With the Civil Rights Movement in the 1960s, racial representation in cheerleading and other school activities became a controversial issue in newly integrated public schools. Oftentimes, black male athletes protested until the public schools appointed black cheerleaders on the predominantly white female cheerleading squads. However, in the 1970s, the passage of the Title IX law gave girls additional opportunities to compete in athletics since female students were no longer restricted to cheerleading and drill teams. Today, in the midst of challenging structural binaries, educators question whether cheerleaders are the *living dinosaur* of a bygone modern era in which men and women held sexually divided, conventional roles (Hartoonian, 2002). Others believe that the cheerleader role has not evolved much since the 1950s and still produces the same cultural perceptions of women as prized trophies of male accomplishments. However, unlike the Good Girl image of the 1950s, the contemporary cheerleader has also acquired a prized Bad Girl image defined in negative qualities such as vanity, promiscuity, exhibitionism, eroticized femininity, acquiescence and a lack of intelligence. Thus, within the *changing but somewhat same* definition of cheerleading, the cheerleader icon reveals both the conflicts and consensus in cultural values concerning social status, youth, aesthetics, gender, race and sexuality: "As a stock character, the cheerleader embodies both positive and negative stereotypes, reflecting contradictions and ambiguities in the social construction of gender roles and social ideals" (Hanson, 1995: 100).

Beyond its binary representation of gender roles, cheerleading also personifies fundamental themes of American mythology such as individualism, celebrity status, democratic cooperation idealized in teamwork and a competitive work ethic. Cheerleading is a quintessential American invention that has become an integral part of national sports teams and national education. The cheerleader is a pervasive, enduring icon that reflects and reinforces the national culture and its values and institutions. Cheerleading also portrays aspects of modern systemization with its stress on disciplined, unified performance in the ritualized arena of organized sport. It also reflects corporate capitalism and entrepreneur interests in advertising and merchandising through cheerleader toy figures, athletic insurance and summer camps. In turn, the iconographic significance of cheerleading functions in many contexts, serves many different agendas and appeals to a broad social and demographic spectrum. The reality of cheerleading as an American invention is greatly magnified by its symbolic power in American culture: "Cheerleading is one of the few purely American phenomena, both in its inception and in its development. We gave the cheerleaders birth, and we pioneered and nurtured their growth. In a word, they are ours" (Hatton & Hatton, 1978: 39).

Yet, since cheerleading moves away from the more scholastic and classical areas of the American school curriculum, it is perceived as a less legitimate area of artistic production and a more outlandish area in extra-curricular school culture. The status of cheerleading is a highly popular yet contested phenomenon because it sits at the crossroads of competing discourses about gender, sexuality, spectacle and sport (Grindstaff & West, 2000). Since cheerleading relies on more feminine qualities such as aesthetics and performance, it is often seen as a less legitimate cultural form than male sports that emphasize masculine qualities such as athleticism and aggressiveness. In order to gain cultural legitimacy in American high schools, cheerleading needs to be seen as an artistic form of expression that can produce equally valid aesthetic effects. By combining verse, music and dance movements, the development of cheers has become a part of our popular culture, and it is also a significant social ritual in American high school culture, perhaps even moving toward an art form. In *Art as Experience* (1934), John Dewey defines art as the experience of creating something with physical material, the body or something outside the body, with or without the use of intervening tools and with a view to production of something visible, audible, or tangible. Using Dewey's definition of art, one can define cheerleading as an art form that involves the singing of songs and chants, the playing of instruments or music in the background, enacting roles on stage or the field and going through rhythmic movements in a dance. The production of cheers then can be seen as an artistic production that can be judged by its aesthetic properties.

The Aesthetics of Cheerleading: What Makes a Good Cheer?

Aesthetics is the analysis of values, attitudes, tastes and standards involved in our experiences of and judgments about what we consider beautiful. The philosophical dimension of aesthetics and the ethical disclosure of defining what is beautiful emerge in the classroom discourse when teachers and students begin to openly discuss the material form and function of both aesthetic objects and artistic productions. When the class reflects upon the objective form of a student's artistic production, for example, and judges the degree of pleasure it emotes, the class subjects are using their faculty of taste to qualify whether it is aesthetically pleasing to them. They attend to the objective features of the student's artistic production and determine its aesthetic value by judging its formal properties, design elements, representation of concepts, method of expression and symbolic content. At the same time, their aesthetic perception should lead them to *feel* what the student's artistic production means and thus develop an affective reaction to the artistic production at the same time they are using their cognitive faculties to judge it. Oftentimes, the immediacy of the appeal for making aesthetic judgments relies on the classroom subjects' intuitive understandings of what they first notice and then the teacher moves the students to the awareness of what is not immediate (Parsons & Blocker, 1993).

The distinction between these two types of aesthetic judgments, both objective and subjective understandings, provides the ground for different accounts of what we consider to be beautiful and for thinking about the assumptions we are making about what is beautiful versus ugly. However, teleological judgments of aesthetics are judgments that refer solely to the objective form of the artistic production and the cognition of that artistic production in relation to a given concept, and thus, have nothing to do with the feeling of pleasure, intuitive understandings or the subjective apprehension of the artistic production. Here teleological judgments serve mainly to determine the purposiveness of a student's artistic production and are always set alongside the objective representation of its artistic concepts. In *Critique of Judgment* (1951: 83), philosopher Immanuel Kant distinguishes aesthetic judgments of the beautiful from the sublime. Beauty is inherent in the form of the object and is discovered through its quiet contemplation by the observer. In contrast, the sublime is formless and purposeless and thus is apprehended only in a state of excitation. Furthermore, Kant defines the sublime as a momentary checking of the vital powers and a consequent stronger overflow of them. Judgments of sublimity, in contrast to teleological judgments, exhibit solely subjective purposiveness and emotion and are not contingent upon the form and concept.

In turn, our reflective aesthetic judgments attempt to determine an equal ground between the teleological objective and the subjective sublime. The kinds of affects and pleasures a student's artistic production creates determine the subjective judgments, but when judged objectively, the harmony of the student's artistic concept with its form determines the teleological judgment of that artistic production. In apprehending the aesthetic value of a student's artistic production, we can privately determine if it provides us pleasure; however, when such judgments need to be valid for all members of the classroom community, there needs to be an intersubjective common ground for making aesthetic judgments. Aesthetic judgments are in turn problematized in the classroom when teachers and students intersubjectively begin to codify and systematize the features of students' artistic productions and come to a universal decision of its aesthetic value.

Immanuel Kant further states that our aesthetic judgments and our understandings of what is beautiful are bound to a juxtaposing paradox in which aesthetic judgments are at once subjective and universal, meaning that the subjective maxims that guide our individual aesthetic judgments must be subjected sooner or later to the test of universality. The subjective judgments of students and teachers regarding other students' artistic productions must be applicable to all members of the classroom community in order to sustain a sense of aesthetic universality. However, even within aesthetic universality, there is the possibility of a discursive space for alterity to open up in the classroom discourse so that essentialized categories of aesthetics are challenged. The heterogeneous will of the classroom subjects can take on a collective agency that attempts to dispense categorical aesthetic imperatives defined by the universal classroom community. If there is to be a heteronomic ethics in aesthetics, the pressures of alterity emanate from subjective judgments that cannot be contained in the aesthetic metanarrative, which attempts to dissolve aesthetic differences and assimilate them into a universal form. In *Truth and Method* (1975), Hans-Georg Gadamer states that the aesthetic consciousness is of fundamental importance because it allows for the inner contradictions in the aesthetic judgments to be voiced and experienced so that the aesthetic norm must go beyond its metanarrative and move toward an alterity that offers a heterogeneous framework for judging aesthetic objects and artistic productions. In turn, the ethics of making aesthetic judgments are tied to the concept of the aesthetic consciousness and how this consciousness is utilized to make fair and ethical judgments about the production of artistic student work.

However, in order to first determine the aesthetic validity of an artistic production's beauty and pleasure, there needs to be a court of appeals that can provide the social space for determining the common understanding and value of students' artistic productions and for raising aesthetic consciousness. In *Rules of the Art* (1992), Pierre Bourdieu states that the places of exhibition, the institutions of consecration, the institutions of reproduction and the specialized agents within the artistic field are all endowed with the ability to use specific categories of perception and appreciation to objectively measure the value of artistic productions. In the context of schooling, the language used by the students and teachers to talk about their artistic productions, their use of descriptive words, such as pairs of adjectives like good and bad and their mode of remunerating artistic products, all play a determining role in the disclosure of aesthetic value, meaning and its consciousness. In the artistic field of the classroom, subjects confront each other and engage in a competitive struggle over the definition of the meaning and value of students' artistic productions through an aesthetic court of appeals. Their discursive struggles often pertain to the concepts used to think about the students' artistic productions, the judgment and classification of the students' artistic productions and the characterization of the students' artistic productions as defined by their relation to a certain genre, form, style and movement. The different points of view presented within the contesting struggles to define aesthetic value are often irreconcilable with the dominant position-takings in the center of the aesthetic debate and the marginal position-takings on the periphery that are constantly resisting the dominant discourse and pushing the peripheral counter discourse to the center. Thus, the aesthetic judgments that are made regarding students' artistic productions and the ethics of those aesthetic judgments are situated in the discourses of language, space and power – the ways in which students and teachers use language to describe aesthetic productions and judge aesthetic productions play a pervasive political role in the social space of the classroom and are an instrument of aesthetic domination. At the same time, a physical space must exist within the classroom where such critical discussions of aesthetics can take place often so that an aesthetic consciousness develops within the classroom discourse.

In the first section of this chapter, we saw how the student and teacher audience aesthetically judged the performance of the Lady Knights cheers when they made comments aloud about the objective form of the cheers and their subjective meanings. The judgments that they made about the Lady Knights cheers closely followed the mainstream criteria determining the aesthetic metanarrative of what makes a good cheer. Yet, Barbara Rodriguez did try to bring forth a court of appeals with the teachers when she contested their universal and essentialized aesthetic judgments and then attempted to propose an alternative heteronomic ethics that wanted to validate the Lady Knights cheers. However, it was only when the students and teachers were walking back to their classrooms that Barbara Rodriguez was able to speak with some of the teachers but was not able to open up a larger discussion as to what constitutes a good cheer. As she was walking through the crowded hallways, she could not find the physical space needed to present a counter discourse and thus felt disempowered by their negative comments.

The following sections of this chapter will continue to focus on the development of class cheers at PS 2000 that originally began with the Lady Knights cheering event. Over a span of four months starting from fall semester to the beginning of spring semester, contesting struggles ensued over the aesthetic value and meaning within the students' own artistic productions of class cheers, just as they had during and after the performance of the Lady Knights cheers. However, along with issues related to aesthetic judgments, issues related to race, gender and language also surfaced within the classroom discussions surrounding the production and performance of the class cheer. In addition, the following sections also examine the relationship between teacher authority and student agency throughout the development of this dual immersion classroom's cheer.

The Three Class Cheers: Judgments of Aesthetics, Authenticity and Ethics

After watching the performance of the Lady Knights cheerleaders, the fifth-grade students at PS 2000 returned to their classrooms and developed their own cheers over a four-month period, and at the end of that period, each fifth-grade class performed its cheer in front of a peer audience. The objective of the cheer was to create a performance that best represents the identity of the class as a whole. Yet, the greater purpose of the cheer was to increase school spirit amongst the fifth-grade classes. Throughout the artistic production of the cheers, each fifth-grade classroom at PS 2000 was involved in using dance movements, music and material objects to create a visible, tangible and audible cheer that best represented their classroom identity. Their identity formation emerged as a construct of the cheers, and thus, as a kind of aesthetic production that entangled students in the complex interplay of *differences* and *sameness* with oneself and between oneself and others in the classroom – as well as differences and sameness with other fifth-grade classrooms. The concept of aesthetics was strongly embedded in this cheerleading episode because students were required to create an artistic production that had formal properties, design elements, representations of concepts, methods of expression and symbolic content. Thus, the processes by which the students in this dual immersion classroom developed their cheers and the experiences that came to be represented from the cheers will be analyzed in the context of the aesthetic conflicts, encounters and struggles that ensued in the production and performance of the class cheers.

In Roberta's classroom, students were initially given free time during their music and drama classes to develop their class cheers. Roberta stated at the very beginning that there was not enough time in the formal curriculum for the students to work on their cheers, thus the cheers were developed mostly in informal spaces and times and with little teacher direction. Since the drama and music classes consist of open spaces in which students do not have to sit in formalized seating arrangements and often work together in circles on the rug floor, the students in Roberta's class naturally divided themselves up during one particular music class into three distinct sociocultural groups, separated according to race, gender, ethnicity, cultural tastes and friendship ties. That day the music teacher allowed the students to work in separate spaces with their group members, develop a cheer and present their initial cheer to their fellow classmates at the end of class time. The students initially decided not to be with each other as a whole in a homogenous class group and instead formed three separate sociocultural groups. In turn, the collective agency of the class soon divided itself up into its respective multiplicities, even though the challenge was to create one cheer to best represent the entire class.

One sociocultural group consisted of predominantly white male students (Brian, Pierre, John, Joshua, Scott), with the exception of two Hispanic males: one a second-generation Hispanic male from Central America (Julio) and one adopted from Central America (Claudio) but who lives with white parents. This group's cheer was a parody of Will Smith's movie theme pop song, "Men in Black", which was a very popular blockbuster sci-fi movie that was released in summer 1997. Using the same beat and rhythm, but with different lyrics, the boys used the chalkboard in the music room and first wrote out the satirical lyrics to their parody of "Men in Black." Initially, their cheer did not mention that they were a dual immersion class; however, after Roberta discussed the importance of representing their bilingual and multicultural identity during a class meeting, the boys changed the lyrics to signify that they are a dual immersion class:

We are the ducks in black!
308 defenders
We are the ducks in black!
We speak Spanish
Don't forget about that!

Quiz me
Just quiz me
Everybody just quiz me

We are the ducks in black!
The dual immersion class!

It is interesting to note that the boys initially spelled "immersion" as "amersan", but they were not the only group to misspell words in their cheers. The second sociocultural group consisted of students who were all ethnic minority male and female students: black (Shakima), Puerto Rican (Yolanda, Javier) and Dominican (Jose, Anjelica). This second group's cheer was initially written entirely in Spanish and also incorporated African step-dance movements. The type of cheering found in the Spanish cheer reflected a cheering style found in predominantly black urban high schools like King High School, which was more of a stomp-clap, soul-swing cheer. Jose, the group leader, stood in the center of a circle and shouted the following Spanish words while the other students came onto the floor in a spiraling motion one after the other using step-dance movements and then formed a circle around Jose who was still in the center:

Ono, tows, tres!
Osotros somo la clase de Roberta
Te Vomo senayl algo o tow

Osotros somos la clase numero uno
Nate lo quede ganal a osotros!

After showing Roberta their cheer written on paper, this second group of mostly Spanish-dominant students corrected the numerous Spanish spelling errors in the original written text and finalized a revised version of the original Spanish cheer with no mistakes:

Uno, dos, tres!
Nosotros somos la clase de Roberta

Te vamos ensenar algo o dos
Nosotros somos la clase numero uno
Nadie le puede ganar a nosotros!

Since the other students in the dual immersion class felt as if an all-Spanish cheer would alienate the monolingual peer audience, this second group went back and translated their Spanish cheer into English. Now, they were going to begin their cheer first in Spanish and then transition into the English version toward the end of the spiral motion:

One, two, three!
We are Roberta's class
We are going to show you something
We are number one
Nobody could beat us!

There were also a few students who were disinterested, detached and indifferent to the cheers' production. The refusal to invest oneself in the cheer and not take the cheers seriously was evident in two minority female students, Juana (Dominican) and Maria (Hondurian), who remained at odds from the very beginning due to a brewing contention with the Puerto Rican-led Spanish cheer group. The third sociocultural group consisted of predominantly white female students (Lisa, Mary, Sunny, Alice, Susanna), with the exception of two Hispanic female students: one from the Dominican Republic (Julia) and one from Puerto Rico (Belinda). Their cheer resembled a traditional all-American cheer found in the modernist era of the 1950s. Using student-made paper pompoms, the girls stood in a linear row, jumped and shouted to the following cheer that consisted of simple phrases that were repeated three times with a fast moving rah-rah style:

Stand up!
Shout out!
We are class 308!

It is also interesting to note that the three different student groups divided themselves into different physical spaces while they were working on their cheers in both the music and drama classes: (1) the Ducks in Black cheer group stayed and worked in the occupied classroom; (2) the Spanish cheer group worked under the main stairwell; and (3) the Valley Girl cheer group worked in the hallways.

The three different cheers, developed by three different sociocultural groups, also represent three different contradictory styles of cheering. In *Performing Rites* (1996), Simon Firth makes formal distinctions between various musical productions and classifies these distinctions into three aesthetic discourses: a pop culture discourse, a folk discourse and an art discourse. The Ducks in Black cheer was rooted in a pop culture discourse since it incorporated the production and consumption of mass culture (Strinati, 1995). If it is through consumption that culture is lived, then the process of developing the Ducks in Black cheer locates the consumption of contemporary cultural values with this group. The all-male cheer reflected a satiric mimicry of pop culture styles that revolve around the contemporary music industry and its values around what pop songs qualify as best-selling commodities. Similarly, the values of cultural goods can be equated with the values of the group consuming them. In turn, the boys' parody of "Men in Black" attempts to create a commercialization of the cheers event in which the identity of being a dual immersion student is represented as "fun" and "cool" and an escape from the everyday life of the classroom through the laughter of figuratively being referred to as "ducks in black." Furthermore, when the boys performed their parodic cheer, they were also imitating the physical gestures of performer Will Smith in his blockbuster "Men in Black" music video; they were learning by doing, learning through imitation and listening carefully to the original song at home in order to reproduce the exact sounds and movements during rehearsals. Thus, the boys saw themselves in the place of the person being imitated and were mimicking Will Smith's black hip-hop mannerisms.

In contrast to the commercial influences in Ducks in Black, the Spanish cheer was rooted in a folk discourse that was fully aware of developing an aesthetic and authentic sound focused on oral, immediate, traditional, idiomatic, communal and centrist beliefs (Firth, 1996). The Spanish cheer fulfilled the cultural necessity of creating a cheer that represented the dual immersion identity. Thus, appreciation of the Spanish cheer is tied to its social function of representing the class's *truthful* bilingual identity. Their use of an African step-dance style also incorporates folk values of the natural in their performance and moves it away from an overly stylized pop culture performance. By also supporting an unchanging truth about their identity as a bilingual and multicultural class, the Spanish cheer takes on an anti-modernist ideology. However, by taking an anti-modernist stance, the Spanish cheer creates a distance between the Spanish-dominant performers and their hypothetical English-only peer audience. Due to the audience's incomprehensibility of Spanish, the

Spanish cheer becomes completely introspective and self-satisfying at the expense of not being communicative with the monolingual audience.

The third cheer presented by the all-female group was rooted in an art discourse that placed greater emphasis on the cheerleading canon. Their cheer reflected a cheering style found in white suburban high schools, which was more of a traditional, straight-arm motion style. On the rug floor, the formal arrangement of all the girls standing in a row and performing their cheers with pompoms and uniforms also used an operative definition of cheerleading that is reflective of professional cheerleading today. The fixed stages of development, starting with the girls kneeling on the floor with their heads down, then jumping up and shouting out the words from the cheer and finally finishing off with cartwheels and splits, gives the all-girls cheer a sense of credence, as if it could be sanctioned and authorized by an academy of cheerleading specialists who can easily recognize the formalized steps and drills, unlike the African step-dance movements from the Spanish cheer. In addition, the girls' tightly controlled kinaesthetic composition and its linear-aesthetic narrative could be readily accepted by the English-dominant mass culture audience. However, when the form of a cheer rules over its content, there is an inevitable sense of emptiness because the all-girl cheer had nothing to say about their bilingual and multicultural class identity and merely displayed its technicality as a modernist cheer.

When the class had to decide which cheer to pick as the representative cheer, questions related to their collective class identity and its specific subjectivities led to face-to-face, conflict-ridden class discussions, which were rooted in the cultural landscape of making aesthetic judgments, assessing measures of true and false consciousness, the ethics of authenticity, the politics of authority and the necessities of linguistic interpretation. By choosing which cheer they would perform in front of an English-dominant audience, the students began the discussions by discriminating between the three different cheers and by exercising their aesthetic tastes and judgments. Therefore, by constructing cultural concepts of what is a good cheer versus a bad cheer, the students' aesthetic judgments rested on criteria that were based on both the cheer's musical and sociocultural characteristics such as language-based criteria and gender-based criteria. Since social relations are often constituted in cultural practices, the students' sense of a collective identity and a sense of individual difference were actualized in the process of discriminating between the three contradictory cheers. The formation of the three sociocultural cheer groups and its relationship to making aesthetic judgments about the three cheers is crucial to understanding the multiple discourses in which these judgments were cast and the circumstances in which they were made.

Discursive clashes regarding which cheer best represented their class was rooted in their aesthetics effects, by referring to their beauty, craft and spectacle, and assessing their differences in relation to the essence of what was best represented in each cheer and whom it represented. At times, the discursive clashes between the three groups of students created unbridgeable tensions and gaps among the students, since each individual group's authorship of its cheer was challenged during the listening of and performance of the cheers, which then added other layers of aesthetic value to the original compositions. Overall, the class discussions surrounding the interpretations, judgments, distinctions and choices of the cheers focused on one's own opinion about the cheers, one's own opinion about other people's opinions about the cheers, and the kinds of understandings wrought from the cheers.

The initial discussions on the cheers focused on the differences between each individual cheer's degree of aesthetic validity and its degree of functionalism in relation to the projected monolingual peer audience. Firth (1996) further states that aesthetic discussions often revolve around the following axes: (1) believability; (2) coherence; (3) familiarity; (4) usefulness; and (5) spiritual uplift. During the dual immersion students' discussions of the class cheers, aesthetic and functional judgments centered mostly within their believability, coherence, familiarity and usefulness. However, the kinds of questions they brought about in reference to believability, coherence, familiarity and usefulness, were different for each group's cheer. The questions surrounding the Ducks in Black cheer included whether or not the students were really ducks and whether or not it coherently and truthfully represented their collective multicultural identity in terms of both form and content:

Shakima: For me . . . even though it has the Spanish stuff in it . . . it's still . . . its still . . . even though we're not ducks!
Brian: Yes we are!
Alice: Shakima . . . Shakima . . . some of us are . . . [Alice turns around and points to the boys in the back.]
Brian: [Brian stands up, flaps his arms and makes duck noises.] Quack . . . quack . . . quack . . . .
Alice: Some of us . . . some of us . . . are ducks.
Brian and Joshua: Quack . . . quack . . . quack . . . .
Shakima: But we're not ducks!
Jose: And the only person who is black in this class is Shakima!

The parodic intentions of the Ducks in Black cheer seemed to be an aggression against the bilingual representation of the class, and it was perceived by many of the students, especially the minority students in the Spanish cheer, as an affront to common sense and sensible people. The protest against the parodic experimentation in this cheer stemmed from a need to create a cheer from the logic of a field of production excluding linguistic games being played with words and their meanings. Thus, a sort of censorship of the expressive content in this parodic cheer developed and was most evident in the informal conversations amongst the minority students: "Do you find the Ducks in Black cheer funny? I just don't like it. It's stupid." Many of the minority students rejected the triviality of the other two cheers and based their aesthetic judgments on tangible, informative representations of their bilingual identity; issues over language representation thus led to the rejection of the other two cheers. The minority students' aesthetic judgments were based more so on the expressive adequacy of the signifier, the cheers, to the signified – a fifth-grade Spanish/English dual immersion classroom. For them, the cheer needed to convey the signification of a meaning tied to the object of representation – their bilingual classroom. Thus, many of the minority students provoked judgments of the two other cheers in response to the empirical reality being represented in the cheers and to the representation of their collective identity as a class.

On the other hand, the overarching question surrounding the Spanish cheer included whether or not their monolingual peer audience would be familiar with the Spanish words and their meanings. However, in relation to the other two cheers, discussions surrounding the degree of authenticity and believability within the Spanish cheer was also brought up during a music class with Michael the music teacher:

Joshua: Do the other classrooms . . . they probably have . . . do their cheers have to do with their class?
Michael (Music Teacher):   You know what . . . you're the only class that has done any stuff with the cheers. I haven't heard anybody else's.
Yolanda: You know what . . . that's because we . . .
         [   ]
Brian: What does the Spanish cheer mean?
Anjelica and Yolanda: Oh my god!
Yolanda: That's because we . . . in our class we had a meeting . . . a class meeting . . . Lisa and Pierre said theirs but it didn't have to do anything with our class. Then Roberta came up with an idea that we should make cheers that have to do with our class.
Claudio: But our new one has to do with our class.

Yolanda: The Spanish one?
Claudio: No our new one.
Anjelica: The Ducks in Black?
Yolanda: I don't know about that. [She shrugs her shoulders.]
Joshua: Like it sounds better . . . our old version of Ducks in Black sounds better than the new one.
Yolanda: My opinion is that . . . I think the new one is better than the old one.
Michael: Maybe it's more . . .
    [   ]
Brian: Because it has to do with the class.
Michael: It is more appropriate.
Yolanda: It has Spanish words and dual immersion stuff in it.

Lastly, the overarching question surrounding the all-girls cheer included whether or not its form was too feminized for the boys to perform alongside the girls on stage in front of their coed peers. The degree of believability and spiritual uplift were both questioned as well by some of the dual immersion students during class discussions:

Scott: I switched groups because I wanted to be in Pierre's group and not Lisa's group.
Yolanda: Why?
Scott: Because Lisa's cheer is all girly.
Yolanda: I know what you mean.
Scott: It's like all Valley Girl like . . . you know . . . Valley Girl. [He flails his arms up and down in the air and raises his voice to a higher pitch in order to sound overtly feminine.]

Thus, the students reacted differently to each cheer and asked different aesthetic and identity questions. Nonetheless, at the end of their discussions, how well a cheer served the function of entertaining the English-only peer audience and fulfilling its pleasure was the category most valued. The aesthetic gaze divided the peer audience into two opposing groups – those who understood Spanish and those who did not understand Spanish. Since everyone in the audience could not understand the Spanish cheer, the legitimization of the Spanish cheer was limited, and it lost cultural legitimacy decreased during the consensus.

Being faithful to the dual immersion class' bilingual identity was a category that received value only from a few vocal English-dominant students such as Scott and Shakima and a few vocal Spanish-dominant students such as Yolanda and Jose. The Spanish cheer took itself to be a utopian cheer and thus negated the existence of the class reality as it was now, especially in terms of it not being a truly dual immersion class in which both languages were treated equally and given equal weight. Yet, however perfectly the minority students performed the Spanish cheer and its representative function, the cheer itself was only seen as fully justified if the Spanish language and culture represented was worthy of being represented to the English-only peer audience. Thus, even though the Valley Girl cheer did not cut across gender and race boundaries, the populist assumption was that the Valley Girl cheer would allow everyone to universally participate in it since it was not based entirely in Spanish and since it didn't parody the students as singing ducks. In fact, the Valley Girl cheer did not depend on issues related to language identity and was seen as a cheer without language barriers. By keeping the audience in mind, the Valley Girl cheer was seen as the best-selling cheer for empowering the audience, even though it was not able to transcend over the race and gender based boundaries developing in the dual immersion classroom and the linguistic boundaries developing between Spanish and English. It was also rare for the students to analyze the cheers in terms of their complexity, their philosophical content and their degree of creativity and form. Furthermore, at no point did anyone question who the audience really is and the ambiguity inherent in not really knowing who are the future consumers of their cheer. Thus, the romanticization of the audience and treating its tastes and choices as the evaluating measure to judge all three cheers created a performance in which innovation, artistic effort and student motivation were no longer prized. Instead, the Oz-like, groomed image of the dual immersion students standing in rows, jumping and shouting a traditional cheer written entirely in English, imitated the modernist images of cheerleaders in the post-World War II era, cheering to imitate a formula of homogeneity.

Yet, the question still remains whether the judgment to choose the Valley Girl cheer was an ethical judgment. Was the Valley Girl cheer suitable to represent a dual immersion classroom? Was the use value of this cheer able to define the class identity and sense of self? Truth-to-self concerns such as the ability to identify with the cheer as a collective, the degree of authenticity and sincerity and the value of content over form all needed to be recognized by the entire class. In fact, there was one moment during the class discussions when a few students brought forth the possibility of combining all three contradictory cheers to create a *postmodern pastiche* amalgamating all three cheers into one. In *The Cultural Turn* (1998), Fredric Jameson defines the pastiche as the moment when stylistic diversity and heterogeneity appears in the aesthetic representations of our current experiences. Instead of parodying a traditional cheer, some of the students suggested combining all three cheers at certain nodal points to best represent their class in its totality, with each sociocultural group having ownership of the final product by weaving the three cheers together. Unlike a parody, which uses satire and laughter to mock the original style and character, Jameson states that a pastiche is able to reinvent a picture of the past identity through a new lived totality. However, since the fusion of these three cheers would inevitably be dictated by problems of content, the degree of reflexivity surrounding the possibility of producing a pastiche was not thoroughly exacted by enough principal subjects in the class to create structural changes during the development of the cheers. Even though class discussions during music class, drama class and weekly class meetings opened up spaces for critical reflexivity and alterity, not enough students were interested in spending their free time to experiment with the cheers in order to create a new lived totality from all three cheers. Also, since the students were not given instructional class time everyday to work on the cheers, the lack of alternative, extracurricular time deterred the possibility of producing a totally new cheer combining the original three cheers to create a postmodern pastiche.

Moreover, since the classroom teacher often has the ultimate authority to sanction more artistic time and space for student production, Roberta decided to use her authority as a teacher to instead explain why the Valley Girl cheer was an authentic cheer. Thus, she helped deter the possibility of the students producing a pastiche from all three cheers and the possibility of mediating differences amongst the three cheers to create a heterogeneous cheer. In turn, one must assess the ideological implications behind Roberta's decision to use her teacher authority to influence the students' final decision about the cheers and to steer the students toward the Valley Girl cheer. Even though the students were given freedom from the beginning of the developmental process to come-into-their-own-being and become active interpreters of the cheers, and since the onus was to represent their collective identity, why then did Roberta intervene and redirect the performance of the cheers toward the end of the production process? Why did she here renege the importance of a bilingual cheer? What does her appropriation of the cheers in turn disguise? Why didn't the students resist her demands to reorganize the cheers?

Nostalgia: Recuperating Meaning from the Past

The turning point in the production of the cheers occurred when one day Roberta decided to demonstrate to the students on the rug floor, during one of their class meetings, what cheerleading was like for her as an American teenager at Hanover High School during the 1950s. By jumping up and down with her arms criss-crossing each other, as if they were holding imaginary pompoms, Roberta provided a historical model of cheerleading to the students that eventually eliminated any discrepancies and resistance toward the Valley Girl cheer. On that day, her impulse to entertain the students with her tumbling and acrobatic moves as a high school cheerleader created a spectral moment or phantasm – defined as the gesture toward the displaced origins of the past that the invocation of tradition calls up. To return to the nostalgic past, one must return to that *spectral moment of originary loss*, just as Roberta had returned to her past as a cheerleader (Ivy, 1995).

After sharing the cheers from her past during that class meeting, Roberta came in the very next day and shared a black and white photograph of her with her cheerleading squad at Hanover High School, which was located in a suburban area outside of the city. She was kneeling in a row with other cheerleaders who all had on the same uniform – full pleated skirts below knee-length, sweaters with the school's monogram and ankle socks with saddle shoes. In comparison to the contemporary cheerleading uniforms, which usually consist of a white, short-sleeve polo shirt, athletic shoes and a dark, mid-thigh, pleated miniskirt, the cheerleaders of Roberta's era stressed propriety, uniformity and conservative values through their lengthened, inconspicuous clothes. Because the cheerleading uniforms represented the school as an institution, the behavior of the cheerleaders while in uniform seemed regulated as well. Furthermore, the cheerleaders in the photograph were presented as icons of beauty and symbols of school pride. Their uniforms represented their school's conformist identity and signified the cheerleaders' status as leaders within the high school's social hierarchy. The uniform was a totem that revealed the Hanover High School's cheerleader status and certified their legitimacy as group members set apart from the general crowd and masses of the school.

The black and white photograph of Roberta as a cheerleader presented an image of what was perfect in Roberta in what seemed to be the most perfect moment in time. Even though she was the only minority student in the photograph and one of a few minority students total at suburban Hanover High School in the 1950s, her ethnic marker as a light-skinned Puerto Rican seemed to have disappeared in the photograph because of the perception that Roberta at one point perhaps desired to *become white* by joining the all-white cheerleading squad (Britzman, 1998: 106). The desire to become invisible at Hanover High School and lose one's ethnic and racial markers may be connoted with Roberta's desire to join the cheerleading squad. In fact, Roberta's ethnic identity as a Puerto Rican female almost seems invisible in the photo. The photograph in turn can be seen as an ocular witness that presented a great moment in Roberta's life, as well as contextualizing deeper issues related to her gender, race and ethnicity.

Yet, the photograph did more than just present Roberta's past. The authenticity of the black and white image of pristine, predominantly white, middle-class, high school cheerleaders poised in straight rows was authoritative as well. The image of Roberta as a cheerleader seemed so real and existed not only as a record of a past time, but it also existed in the present moment of projection. The temporal depth sensed by the students as they gazed at the black and white photograph provided a reality to Roberta's past. This moment of the students' gaze on the photograph, which was being passed around the group circle on the rug, was dominated by the spectral immediacy of Roberta's cheerleader image. The striking image of Roberta kneeling on the gymnasium floor with her long skirt and monogrammed sweater provided a memory of past events for the students. It also helped Roberta shape recollections of cheerleading to the extent that she wanted the students to replicate this image in their present-day class cheers as well. With its ability to capture and collapse time, the photograph was a modern marker for Roberta's *accelerated memory*, a relentless telescoping of time in which the boundaries between the past and the present appear to dissolve, and all time and space are rendered apparently simultaneous in the present spectral moment (Huyssen, 1993). The photograph was not only able to represent an image of Roberta in the past, but it also had the power to preserve a visual reality of the past. Furthermore, the photograph not only framed space but also stopped and captured time; by imprinting images on celluloid bands, the photograph preserved the image of Roberta as a cheerleader in temporal suspension. The photograph allowed Roberta's past to be almost instantly displaced in the present. At the same time, the quickness of its presentation and its astonishing directness annihilated not only temporal and spatial distance, but it also annihilated critical reflection on the part of the students, since they were unable to analyze the photograph outside of this group viewing (Ivy, 1995).

Furthermore, the photograph provided a point in memory that strengthened her longing to keep the image of herself as a suburban high school cheerleader alive. Since Roberta was turning fifty years old that year, perhaps in some ways she was hoping to recapture and preserve pristine moments from her past through the students' own cheers. In order to recover her past and deny the losses of old traditions, Roberta's modernist nostalgia was an attempt to perhaps preserve a sense of what was absent in the students' cheers, thus displaying Roberta's fetish for the past as well as her nostalgia as a cheerleader.

Her disavowal of the students' hybrid cheers thus can be possibly seen as an attempt to replace what was missing in the students' cheers through its replacement with a *substitute presence* of her own past as a cheerleader (Ivy, 1995: 10). However, this replacement inevitably conveyed to me the feeling of covering up the students' cheers. Even though I did not interview Roberta about the events within the cheers episode, her disavowal of the students' cheers seemed to create a *splitting of the subject* because Roberta knew something was missing in the students' cheers but was bent on replacing what was absent in their cheers with her own false consciousness of her youth. Her anxiety over the students' cheers appears as a symptomatic effect of her initially allowing the students to create a bilingual cheer that was to be uniquely their own and then retracting her initial supposition by replicating their cheers with her ideal cheer. The movement toward self-fashioning a class cheer based purely on acrobatic, athletic steps and drills was indicative of Roberta's own fetishistic investment in the cheers. In order to improve the status of the students' cheers as aesthetic icons of cheerleading, Roberta wanted to literally embody the essentially traditional cheer and its contingent discourses and practices, thus creating a moment of fetishistic disavowal in which the students' cheer creations are rejected for the teacher's own fetishistic investment in the cheers.

In some ways perhaps Roberta was working through the personal loss of her youth through the cheers. The rhetoric of loss and recovery and the narcissism of nostalgia perhaps carried over into the classroom discourse on the class cheers. Her search for an authentic cheer might have been symbolic of the search for her own youth as she turned fifty years old. The preoccupation with her own increasing age, which she often stated aloud in class, might have led to complex reconfigurations of the students' cheers, which originally reminded Roberta of what cheers used to signify for her as a teenager. Sometimes a little nostalgia goes a long way, as it was evident here when Roberta's deeper identifications with loss were perhaps not conducive to creating authentic student cheers.

Roberta's modernist appeal for unity, precision, repetition, synchronization, multiple bodily formations, tumbling, lifts, accentuated arm motions, drill choreography, cadence and pyramid building in the students' production of the cheers reflected the extremely complex and sophisticated style of feminized cheerleading in the 1950s. The stylized routines of cheerleading that were developed during that era, mostly in California, embodied the modern values of America after World War II. For example, in the drill team routines, the cheerleaders shift in and out of lines, break into smaller groups and recombine into the full group in a highly polished, self-contained performance. Furthermore, during the modern era, urbanization, mass transit, the emergence of mass print and radio media and increased leisure time all helped to foster game and cheerleading spectatorship as a means of promoting communal affiliation, mass entertainment and leisure from the daily grind of work (Lefebvre, 1999). The phenomena of organized cheering and uniform cheerleaders added validity to the stereotype of 1950s Americans as highly organized individuals who even organized youthful ebullitions to a fine point. The class cheer produced and performed in this classroom greatly embodied the ethos of 1950s America.

Moreover, Roberta later suggested that the female students do the verbal "Stand up! Shout out!" chant while the male students build a three-tier pyramid, in which several boys mount on top of each other to achieve a structured formation, thus establishing further gender boundaries in the modernist class cheer. The assumption was that the male students can build the pyramid so that they do not appear too *feminine* if they performed the verbal chant. The male students agreed with Roberta's suggestion; however, one of the white female students, Alice, challenged the gender boundaries by choosing to join the male students in the pyramid formation instead of singing and dancing the Valley Girl cheer. While the male students and Alice were mounting and dismounting off the pyramid, they were susceptible to physical injuries, however, the female students cheering were susceptible to vocal injures caused by the compression of their voices. Meanwhile, Lisa, the most popular girl in class, was chosen to lead this formalized group cheer. Lisa was also a student who often followed conventional gender behavior and was often compared to a famous movie star who embodied the American sweet heart persona. She assumed the position of a class icon of beauty that could lead the cheer along with the other female students and then move aside for the boys to build their pyramid, with Alice as the sole female student supporting the base of the pyramid.

By invoking the notion of a traditional cheer, Roberta gestured toward the historical origins of modernist cheerleading in the students' cheers. Roberta's newly found preoccupation with an essential, classroom identity and with a singular cheer that maintained a self-sameness also exposed her denial of sociocultural differences – race, ethnicity, language, class and gender – in the production of the class cheers. Even though

Roberta generally favored heterogeneity at most levels of classroom life, her insistence on a singular, totalizing cheer negated *differences* by adhering to a powerfully normalizing and standardizing method of cheerleading. Thus, this new modernist cheer and its reductive singularity threatened the heterogeneity of the students' original three cheers and the possibility of creating a pastiche of cheers. To a certain extent, the students' original three cheers were disrupted and marginalized by that trajectory of homogenization projected by Roberta's nostalgia. The modernist cheer, with the girls shouting and the boys building a pyramid, became spectacularized as the singularly representative cheer of the dual immersion classroom culture in Room 208 at PS 2000. However, the enactment of this now-singularized cheer and its theatricalization on stage never reassured their peer spectators, composed of five other fifth-grade classrooms, of their dual immersion class identity.

Even though the cheer itself lasted less than five minutes, the competitive nature of performing the class cheer in front of an audience composed of fifth-grade early adolescent peers provoked anxiety amongst the students, as well as the subjective nature of judging each other's performances and whether or not the other cheers were "cooler." In some ways, the competitive nature of the cheers eclipsed the possibility of creating a heterogeneous cheer to better represent and mirror the heterogeneous class identity. Furthermore, this new modern cheer, driven partly by Roberta's nostalgia, was not able to eliminate residues that were left over from earlier discussions regarding the fact that Spanish was being displaced and marginalized within the classroom, as evident in episodes such as the Spanish spelling bee. Thus, anxieties increased as the performance date came closer and closer to actuality. Accompanying those anxieties came the students' failed attempts to recover the earlier forms of their three original class cheers.

Surviving the Spectacle: The Day of the Performance

On the day of the performance, the fifth-grade classes came down to the auditorium along with their teachers. Barbara Rodriguez, the person responsible for promoting the cheer event, introduced each class before they performed on stage. Since they were the last group to perform, Roberta's class watched in amazement and embarrassment as all the other classrooms presented a pastiche of cheers composed of improvised rap songs, break dancing routines, drill team cheers, pyramids, stand up comedy and synchronized dancing. Even though the other monolingual fifth-grade classrooms did not have to represent their language identity, since they were comprised of homogenous language groups, the cheers themselves represented a diversity of discourse styles that included a heterogeneous mix of black urban youth culture and the more traditional forms of cheering found in white suburbs. However, when it was their turn to perform, many students in Roberta's dual immersion classroom were hesitant to come onto stage because they realized that their homogenous cheer was not "cool enough" in comparison to the other heterogeneous class cheers and because it was "too girly" and had nothing to do with being "dual immersion." Once on stage, the girls stood in the front of the stage and began their Valley Girl cheer; however, several girls were stage struck and looked at each other for the next step in this synchronized cheer. Meanwhile, the boys stood in the back trying to create their tiered pyramid, but after two failed attempts, many of the boys ran off stage and then back to their seats in the auditorium before the girls even finished cheering from the front of the stage. Soon, the girls also ran off the stage and slumped back into their seats. Roberta was watching from the doorway and left the auditorium before the students returned to their seats from their evanescent performance.

Unlike the other fifth-grade classrooms that seemed to have made their cheers into an art form by creating a pastiche of contemporary cheers that crossed cultural borders, one can posit that this dual immersion classroom's final performance turned the cheer into a spectacle rather than an art form. In *The Society of the Spectacle* (1994: 14), Guy Debord, a French sociologist, defines the spectacle as a societal event in which "the spectacle proclaims the predominance of appearances and asserts that all human life, which is to say all social life, is mere appearance." When the students walked onto the stage, the audience members were given the appearance that they are about to perform a cheer that reflected their class identity. However, since they were unable to even complete the performance of the cheers in its entirety, the cheer appeared more as a spectacle and showed the physical and social separateness among the students on stage. This kind of self-cleavage and self-contradictoriness in the spectacle, according to Debord, is also a portrait of power in which the spectacle is overpowered with its fetishistic appearance of pure objectivity and scripted emotions, thus failing to address the true character of the cheers as the relationship between students in the same class, the relationship between students in different classes, the relationship between all the classrooms, and school spirit. The spectacle also freezes itself as an image and thus the image of the students fleeing the stage and hurriedly returning to their seats becomes frozen in their unconscious memory as a moment of failure and embarrassment.

The sense of alienation felt afterwards by the dual immersion class is yet another effect generated by spectacle performances in which isolation is purposefully maintained amongst individuals – a spectacle in turn unites people superficially but also maintains their dividing separateness. Spectacles are thus contradictory in nature because they attempt to create a totalizing experience ascribed by a feeling of wholeness amongst the participants while also maintaining a sense of fragmentation amongst the individual participants. In comparison to the other fifth-grade cheers, a sense of fragmentation and alienation was strongly evident in the dual immersion cheer. Furthermore, the strange juxtapositions and contradictions inherent in the performance of the spectacle subsequently masquerade the sensations of alienation and fragmentation by proclaiming that the participants originally had the freedom of choice to participate in the spectacle. The pseudo-gratification gained from the experience of the spectacle nonetheless cannot hide the lasting sense of embodied repression that an individual participant feels after experiencing the spectacle as a whole. Thus, sometimes the dissatisfaction from a spectacle experience can lead to a form of rebelliousness against the spectacle itself.

In order to survive the embarrassing aftermath of their cheer performance, several students used imaginary reconstitution to postulate what the reaction of their peers would have been if they had returned to their original three cheers and combined them together into a pastiche as the other classes had done. At the same time, as they were walking back to their classroom, many of the dual immersion students tangentially talked about their own feelings of isolation from the other monolingual fifth-grade classrooms during such school-wide events. In addition, some students talked about how they noticed that Roberta had left the auditorium before they even finished their cheer. Javier remarked, "Did you see Roberta? She walked right out of the auditorium. She didn't watch all of our cheer." Roberta's vanishing from the auditorium midway through their cheer performance disclosed even further anxiety about their cheer. When they returned to the classroom, there was no discussion of what had occurred on stage; instead, the cheer event was repressed, and through-out the school year, most members of the class evaded discussing the topic of the cheers. Within five minutes of their return, Roberta asked the students to open up their notebooks so they can begin the Spanish vocabulary lesson and thus she failed to recognize the poignancy of what had occurred just a few minutes ago in the auditorium. Even though Roberta had functioned earlier in the episode as the cultural broker and cultural insider who shared her own understandings of the culture of cheerleading with the students and how to reproduce that dominating culture in their own cheer, Roberta now seemed to be passing judgment onto the students' failure to produce a successful cheer by remaining silent after the event. She failed to become a cultural mediator who instigates discussions around what they had just experienced and why they felt that the cheer failed. By adopting the posture of the everyday, the class was able to avoid discussing the aftermath of the cheer event; students opened up their backpacks, sharpened their pencils and started writing down the Spanish vocabulary words that Roberta dictated to them. Soon, they were immersed in using the Spanish dictionaries to look up word definitions; all traces of the cheer event disappeared and remained hidden in the daily life of the dual immersion classroom, far removed from the unsettling remains of any dialectical discussion concerning the representation of their true class identity.

Hidden Desires and Blocked Happiness

From a psychoanalytical perspective, the blocked student praxis in the development of the cheers can be seen as a block to student happiness due to the force of negativity that overtook the students after their final performance in the auditorium. The level of unhappiness that followed the final performance, along with the level of shock and disgust, led to the resting of the cheers in a final state of disinterestedness in which they were never mentioned again. The shock the dual immersion students felt was from finding out during the performance that the other fifth-grade classes created a "cooler" pastiche in which they performed multiple cheers that were strung together into a totality. The disgust they felt was also from examining themselves after the performance and questioning why and how they allowed themselves to get on stage and perform a not-so-cool Valley Girl cheer. Perhaps the dual immersion students realized that the other classrooms had taken pleasure in both developing their cheers and presenting them, as evidenced by their liberating form and vivaciousness, and because they were particular to their classroom identity and not to universal norms. In many ways, the traditional modernist cheer exercised ideological power over the dual immersion subjects as it increasingly became autonomous of what it should represent. Instead of standing firm and creating a heterogeneous cheer, which would have instilled some degree of happiness into the final performance of the cheers, the students became beings-for-others and lost substantiality in the performance of the class cheer.

In *The Sublime Object of Ideology* (1989), Slavoj Zizek states that when a subject imitates a *model-image* of what it should be then the question to ask is for whom is the subject enacting this role and which *gaze* is being considered when the subject identifies herself with a certain image. If a subject is preventing her success by humiliating herself and organizing her failure, then the crucial question is how to locate the *superego gaze* that is procuring the subject's pleasure. According to Zizek (1989: 106), this *jouissance* (happiness) gap can be best articulated with the Hegelian identification binary of a *being-for-others* versus a *being-for-itself*. Since the dual immersion students were performing their cheer as *beings-for-the-teacher*, the majority of the dual immersion students accepted what was happening in its development as the only way of performing cheers, thus the Valley Girl cheer held an ideological hegemony over its subjects. Hegemony in this sense might be defined as an *organizing principle* that is diffused into every area of classroom daily life but without questioning (Gramsci, 1971). This prevailing consciousness is internalized by the student population and becomes part of what is generally called class-room *common sense* so that the philosophy, culture and morality of those subjects in power, such as the teacher, come to appear as the natural order of things. In the cheers episode, the dual immersion students internalized the teacher's desire for a traditional model-image cheer because her orga-nizing principles for the cheer appeared as the natural order of things in the everyday life of their classroom.

Furthermore, ideological hegemony places a dark veil over *real* rela-tionships through its power relations. The ideological hegemony of the cheers episode functions to disguise and blur the real relations between the Spanish and English languages, between the teacher and students, and between the different sociocultural student groups:

> If thought is in any way to gain a relation to art it must be on the basis of something in reality, something back of the veil spun by the play of institutions and false needs, objectively demands art, and it demands an art that speaks for what the veil hides. (Adorno, 1998: 18)

Here the veil was hiding concerns regarding the marginalization of the Spanish-speaking identity, the lack of multicultural awareness and the reproduction of gender divisions within the production of the classroom cheers.

However, ideological hegemony must be first understood in its contra-dictions, and then, by the removal of the contradictions, it can be revo-lutionized in practice (Marx, 1947). Here the contradiction between the uneven development of Spanish and English in the cheers, between student autonomy and teacher authority, and the differential perception of the three cheers, were never fully realized. For example, the false appearance of student autonomy in the development of the cheers can be explained by internal contradictions between Roberta's hegemonic role in the development of the cheers, which she initially expressed objectively as a student-driven product, and the students' lack of resistance toward her interference in this development. These contradictions were never transformed and removed by either the teacher or students, and thus, the problem of authenticity was never resolved, leading to the students' false consciousness of the cheers as their own. The displacement of the Spanish cheer, for example, needed to lead the dual immersion students to further deconstruct the greater binary signification between Spanish and English in their larger classroom discourse: the presence and representation of Spanish; the disguising and unveiling of Spanish; the truth about and false consciousness of the dual immersion classroom; the unconscious and conscious decisions affecting the marginalization of the Spanish language; and the obscurity and transparency of language use and linguistic borders and boundaries. But this counter-hegemonic deconstruction never happened in this episode. Nonetheless, even within these dialectical discussions over the value and use of Spanish, there is an irretrievable *residue*, something that will never have access to consciousness and continues to stay repressed in the *originary* moment of the class event that led to such discussions over language use – a *residue* that remains in the subconscious.

Moreover, the psychoanalytical framework can also be used to examine the gender boundaries in this dual immersion classroom, in addition to its linguistic boundaries. We can posit that the boys' initial resistance toward the feminized Valley Girl cheer can be interpreted as the repression of the gendered Other, as a thing that is not a part of their essential heterosexual, male selves (Lacan, 1997). During the final performance of the cheer, the opposing dualism between a male dual immersion Self and a female dual immersion Other created gender-specific borders and situated gender-based student positionings in the final performance of the cheers. In order to overcome the problematics of appearing "too girly" in front of a coed peer audience, the teacher positioned the boys behind the girls on stage in order for the boys to create a structural three-tier pyramid while the girls did acrobatics and voiced the chants in the front of the stage. Thus, during the cheers, the boys and girls were told to behave differently and occupy places of different value on stage during the final performance. However, the gender-specific cheer was critiqued by Alice, the sole subject who decided to challenge gender norms and join the boys on the pyramid instead of the girls.

The Self/Other dualism can also be used to analyze the act of repressing the Spanish language within the final cheer by certain individual students and also by the teacher who does not reveal her fear of appearing as the "Other" in front of the gaze of the English-only audience. The aesthetic judgment of the omnipotent audience gaze changed the pure pleasure one can receive from creating a student-driven cheer to instead focus on the classical norms of cheers. The aesthetic gaze of the audience in turn brought about a rupture in the relationship between the ethical disposition and aesthetic disposition of the cheers episode in which a total conversion of the cheering style had occurred for aesthetic purposes alone, thus questioning the ethics of such aesthetic decisions. The powerful aesthetic gaze of the English-only audience asserted its power over form and function and even power over the students as subjects of the cheers, because in the end, it was the monolingual fifth-grade peer audience that was apprehending each other's artistic productions. By creating a popular English-only cheer that used traditional acrobatics and chants, the dual immersion class was hoping to secure their peer spectators' participation in the cheer and their collective participation in the overall festivity, which was to increase school spirit. Regardless of whether one is not quite sure who will actually be in the audience during the performance, the pure gaze of the popular audience is inseparable from the production process: "The popular aesthetic and the popular audience delights in plots that proceed logically and chronologically toward a happy end, and identifies better with simply drawn situations and characters than with ambiguous and symbolic figures and actions" (Bourdieu, 1987: 32). Yet, the traditional Valley Girl cheer did not satisfy the taste and fulfill the sense of revelry in this fifth-grade school event, which was attempting to overturn conventions and proprieties by setting an alternative time and space for the students to liberate themselves from the daily grind and express their artistic ideas, regardless of appearing as the Other in front of their peers.

Furthermore, the language the students and teachers used to talk about the production of the cheers also contains underlying unconscious symbolism of the hidden meanings of the cheers episode (Lacan, 1997). The unconscious functions in many ways like language and uses language to express what has been repressed in the unconscious. Word play, puns, metaphors, Freudian slips, silence, gaps, word associations and other speech patterns allow us to better understand the repressed contents of the unconscious by understanding the structure of the language used to talk about that content. The following interview between Yolanda and Scott, two of the border-crossing students who challenged the hegemonic development of a homogeneous cheer, highlights the unconscious symbolism of the cheers. The two students reveal the inconsistency in the cheers development by enunciating structural gaps, pauses and places of rest in their use of language during the interview to mirror the structural gaps in the cheers production:

Yolanda: We've been talking about the cheers and the way we started . . . uh . . . the way we first started . . . our ideas of the cheers . . . first . . . when . . . uh . . . Barbara she came to the whole fifth-grade classes and told them that we have to make our own cheers that represent us and that uh . . . then we asked Michael our music teacher if he could help us do our cheers and uh . . . we all got in groups and um . . . each group came up with a cheer . . . and we saw that . . . we got three cheers. One was Jose's group, Pierre's group and Lisa's group.

Scott: [He peers to look at other students in the classroom.] Well Jose's group consisted of Jose, Yolanda, Anjelica, Shakima and Javier. Lisa's group consisted of Lisa, Julia, Mary, Maria, Belinda and . . . uh . . . [He is trying to think of the other girls' names but couldn't name them.] . . . Pierre's group consisted of Pierre, Brian, Joshua, Claudio, Javier . . . John . . . and myself. And Yolanda's group is doing a Spanish one and first . . . uh . . . Jose would do this . . . uh . . . Spanish chant and then Yolanda and . . . uh . . . and the other people would come up this . . . uh . . . they came up with this . . . uh . . . body movement stuff . . . and then . . . and . . . Lisa's group was like this . . . shaped like a pyramid . . . and like this stand up shout out . . . something like that and Pierre's group was really funny because it was like we are the ducks in black [he places his hands under his armpits, makes a duck like motion using his arms as wings, and starts singing the cheer] . . . quack . . . quack . . . we are the ducks in black and don't forget about that . . . it was funny. And also in a way . . . we made the whole class get into it . . . we are the ducks in black . . . 208 defenders . . . that's it. [He looks over at Yolanda.]

Yolanda: And in our class we're doing cheers because . . . uh . . . I kept on writing it . . . uh . . . because I think that . . . we need to work together as a class and as a team and . . . uh . . . I think . . . we should be taking it very seriously because . . . uh . . . some of us really do want to do it. And Mrs Jones our drama teacher . . . we asked her if we could a cheer and there we did a pyramid . . . with three . . . with five children and . . . each . . . five . . . [Yolanda looks over to Scott for reassurance of the exact number of students involved in the pyramid design] . . . yes six . . . three on the bottom, two on the top, and one on the top. We took the lightest person and put them on top so that the stronger people are at the bottom . . .

Scott: And . . . we thought there could be three pyramids . . . one in the beginning . . . one in the middleish and the other one at the end . . . so that . . . uh . . . we could open it up and close it up and keep it . . . going.

Author: Who came up with the pyramid idea? [Both Yolanda and Scott look at each other before responding to my question.]

Scott: Uhh . . .

Yolanda: That was . . . uh . . .

Scott: We already started the pyramid after Roberta and . . . Youmee [first semester student teacher] . . . uh . . . uh . . . said like they . . . they said they were cheerleaders and . . . they did . . . uh . . . they would teach us and they did stuff . . . uh . . . that cheering wasn't only cheering for the team whatever but it was also showing off your acrobatic skills and then . . . cause . . . and then . . . like . . . we . . . uh . . . then we . . . then we . . . [Yolanda and Scott are distracted by the noise level in the classroom because the class is transitioning to the next classroom activity] . . . and then we . . . thought about the idea of a pyramid and . . . uh . . . we tried it successfully . . . uh . . . except that we . . . uh . . . it was funny . . . because after a while . . . I was on the bottom and after a while . . . the whole pyramid would crash down and uh . . . [he laughs] . . . it was funny . . . and . . . uh . . . we told Roberta that . . . we told Mrs Jones that we should have more time to practice that this week.

Yolanda: Mrs Jones says that we should have three pyramids . . . one for the beginning for . . . one song . . . two for the other . . . like the middle . . . and three for the last . . . and the whole thing and its . . . and that's why we should have three so that each group can have a pyramid . . . and other people can be singing or doing something. [Yolanda and Scott are called back to the class lesson in progress.]

The interview above highlights the ambiguous nature of how the cheers started in development and when and who determined the final composition of the cheer. When asked who had decided on creating the pyramid structure, for example, there were silences, gaps and uses of the sound "uh" in between their words to indicate that Yolanda and Scott were both unsure of when, who and how the pyramid idea came about. In turn, if the students were unaware of the pyramid's structural origins, then perhaps they were less sure of questioning its legitimacy in the final performance since they were unsure of which group of students and adults first suggested the choice of the Valley Girl cheer.

Conclusion: How Differences in Taste, Style and Historical Origins Affected the Cheers

The cheers constituted a complex and textured form of cultural production since they were emerging and developing over time and did not claim to be complete and finished until the very last moment of its performance. In the beginning of the production process, the students were given the freedom to take risks; therefore, the espousal of experimentation was first actualized in the students' organic labor to invent three distinct cheers that were not immediately foreseeable in the process of production. Yet, the continuously increasing reflections on the cheers increased in scope and power during many class discussions so that the content of the cheers became even more uncertain as they neared the final performance date. The evolving critical discussions that ensued surrounding what constitutes a cheer and what does not led to a dialectical discussion of aesthetics that was constantly moving and changing the form and function of the three original cheers. Even though the cheers were perceived aesthetically throughout the production process, at one point the cheers slowly became a final product defined more so by form than by function.

The relationship between the production of the cheers, which privileged the form over the function, and the performance of the cheers, which privileged the function over the form, was constantly evolving within the aesthetic discourse so that there was always a negotiation between whether either form or function should become dominant in the final absolute product. The antagonistic relationship between aesthetic form and function led to the subsequent confrontation between those subjects who produced the cheers and the critical judgments brought about to analyze the cheers from the *other subjects*, thus leading to dialectical discussions of aesthetics. Even though there needed to be a consensus between the positions of those who produced the cheers and the positions of the other students in the classroom who perceived them, the oppositions between the class cheers can be found at many levels in addition to the students' aesthetic perceptions of them. Stylistic characteristics, language choice and genre also deterred the formation of consensus amongst the cultural producers and cultural perceivers.

However, not only did the cheers differ in both form and function, they also differed in the manifestation of their essence. The cheers in many ways came to essentialize each sociocultural student group: (1) the essence of a predominantly Spanish-dominant, lower-middle-class Hispanic sociocultural group; (2) the essence of a predominantly white

English-dominant, upper-middle-class female sociocultural group; and (3) the essence of a predominantly white English-dominant, upper-middle-class male sociocultural group. The same essentialism required the students in each group to impose on the cheers what their cultural essence imposes upon them. Thus, in their cheers, the students lived up to their divided socialized selves and had differing points of view, tastes, values and dispositions as to which cheer best represented their authentic, natural and stable dual immersion classroom identity.

Specifically, taste is a sociological concept concerned with the field of cultural production; it is a product of the social conditions in which we live and it defines each individual's art of living (Bourdieu, 1987). In this chapter, the opposition between the three cheers is at the heart of the debate over taste and cultural production. Even though the cheers themselves are artistic productions that can be analyzed through the discourse of aesthetics, cheering is nonetheless a product of our American culture and thus internalizes the beliefs, values, behaviors and attitudes of different cultural groups. The relationship between the production of the three different cheers and the three different sociocultural student groups highlights how strong differences to cultural taste led the students to contest each other's cheer:

> Tastes are the practical affirmation of an inevitable difference. It is no accident that, when they have to be justified, they are asserted purely negatively, by the refusal of other tastes. In matters of taste, more than anywhere else, all determination is negation, and tastes are perhaps first and foremost distastes, disgust provoked by horror or visceral intolerance of the taste of others ... because each taste feels itself to be natural – and so it almost is, being a habitus – which amounts to rejecting others as unnatural and therefore vicious. (Bourdieu, 1987: 56)

The students in each cheer group had similar social origins that were different from the other cheer groups. According to sociologist Pierre Bourdieu (1987), social origin can be defined by multiple variables such as the mother and father's occupation, gender, race, class, ethnicity, place of residence, etc. Categories related to aesthetic appreciation such as musical culture and literary culture also distinguish people from different social origins. The kind of music one listens to and the kind of movies one watches can determine an individual's class position just as much as occupation and place of residence. Taste can unite all people who are the products of similar social conditions while distinguishing them from others who are not of the same social conditions. The Spanish cheer group, for example, was a mixed-gender group of students who lived in similar social conditions and identified themselves according to similar class, race and ethnic markers. Furthermore, their group had distinct social tastes that were different from the tastes of the other groups, which manifested themselves in their use of step movement and Spanish chants.

Oftentimes, the struggle for artistic legitimacy is based on a hierarchy of taste in which one social group is fighting to legitimize its group's social and cultural tastes. When the students made aesthetic stances against other cheers, objectively and subjectively, they were asserting their position within the hierarchy of taste and at the same time showing how its tastes are distinct from others. By making their aesthetic choices explicit, the students were also opposing the choices of other students groups. The aesthetic judgments made about each other's cheers were based on differences of taste amongst the three sociocultural student groups but also reflected how there were inherent differences between the students outside of the classroom as well. Even though a dual immersion program brings together students from different cultural, economic and linguistic backgrounds, it is inevitable that these differences will manifest themselves within the everyday life of the classroom. In turn, the tension between the three cheer groups was binding in relation to the tensions external to them and was reflective of the tensions within a pluralistic society composed of multiple races, cultures and languages.

The principles of selecting a final cheer also enabled the students to pick out and retain, from among the three cheers performed, all the stylistic traits that distinguished one cheer from another. A select sample of dual immersion student leaders, such as Yolanda and Scott, utilized their aesthetic dispositions during class discussions surrounding the cheers to perceive and vocalize specific stylistic differences amongst the three cheers and to state their preferences of taste for one over the other. Soon an informal aesthetic taxonomy developed within the classroom discourse in which some students mobilized themselves to distinguish, classify and order the three cheers by grasping each cheer's meaning, reconstructing the perceived situation of performance and pointing out the different self-positionings of the students within the cheer's production, e.g. pointing out the gender-based positionings in the Valley Girl cheer. Yet, the aesthetic arguments revolving around the cheers and the classificatory taste-based schemes for the cheers rarely rendered a universal consensus amongst the students due to the differing positions individual students occupied in the debate, the different meanings and values articulated, the opposing adjectives used to describe the artistic products, and the notably different ideals in the perception and appreciation of the three cheers.

Individual students are not exposed to the same social situations, do not hear the same music and do not see the same movies, and thus are bound to have different aesthetic value judgments that then affect the cultural productions in their classroom.

The aesthetic judgments of the three cheers also reflect what kind of cultural capital is valued within the larger school culture (Apple, 1995). The cultural transmission by schools includes *value-inculcating* and *value-imposing operations* that create certain cultural dispositions in the students who then legitimize certain cultural forms over others based on what values the school defines as dominant cultural capital (Bourdieu, 1987: 23). The cultural dispositions we acquire at home or at school subsequently lead to the cultural legitimacy and cultural norms in which we perceive, classify and memorize cultural experiences differently. The norms of aesthetic perception, for example, define the legitimate mode of perception that is used to then evaluate other artistic works and determine their competency throughout life. Within the cheers event, the dual immersion students acquired certain cultural dispositions from the experiences they gained from producing and performing the cheers. The cultural dispositions that the students gained were based on the fact that a certain kind of cultural capital was more valued in the final selection and performance of the Valley Girl cheer. Yet, by valuing the cultural capital within the Valley Girl cheer over the others, choosing the traditional cheer over the other two cheers can have hidden effects later on in the students' lives due to the positioning of some cultural dispositions over others and the valuing of certain cultural capital over other forms of cultural capital.

Moreover, when making aesthetic judgments, people apply "the perceptual schemes of their own ethos, the very ones which structure their everyday perception and everyday existence," to determine their ethical interest in an aesthetic object (Bourdieu, 1987: 59). The dissonance between an emphasis on form versus an emphasis on the affective and ethical interest can lead to ethical complicity when we give into aesthetic form over ethical interests. In this chapter, the dual immersion class placed a greater emphasis on the form of the cheers rather than on the ethics of representing themselves truthfully through their cheer, and, thus, they were liable for ethical complicity. What was essentially at stake in the oppositions structuring the aesthetic perception of the cheers was truth, and the truth of the artistic method lies in its ability to correspond directly with what is real, universal and absolute. According to Bourdieu, the ethical disposition should privilege ethical representations and subordinate the aesthetic disposition as being less valuable in judgment. Also, an ethical indifference occurs within our aesthetic dispositions when it becomes a basis for art and subsequently leads to an ethical aversion within art. *Art for art's sake* and *cheers for cheers' sake* incorporate ethical indifference and subordinate the core values of living art to the art form itself. Separated from what is right and what is duty, form for form's sake in turn diverts attention away from what is true and what is real in the art. In the cheers episode, the ethical disposition to create a cheer that best represented the true identity of the dual immersion classroom was subsumed by the desire to regenerate the historical form of cheerleading and its aesthetics of performance. Instead of demanding an ethics of representation in which a truthful cheer is valued more, most of the students instead relied on the origins of cheerleading as a foundation on which their own cheer would be constructed. Even though not all students agreed with the Valley Girl cheer, the teacher's romantic belief was that the traditional cheers are the highest and purest form.

In order to have qualitatively transformed the cheers episode so that the class could have chosen the more ethical Spanish cheer in the end, since it best represented their dual immersion identity, the artistic production of the cheers needed to have been turned against itself and its elementary concepts. In turn, there needed to be a discussion of uncertainty in which the validity of the Valley Girl cheer was questioned further (Adorno, 1998). Yet, at the same time that artistic productions turn against the status quo in terms of their form, artistic productions must also reconstitute their elementary concepts so that they are always changing and evolving their elements historically and refusing to be defined by any essential set of variables. If the dual immersion class had rejected the traditional cheer and turned against the status quo form of cheerleading, then they would have rejected the generic, common and immediately accessible cheer, which was perceived by many to be *easier* to perform than the other two cheers.

However, the other option would have been to create a totalizing cheer or pastiche that combined all three cheers by integrating them together through increasingly binding centrifugal forces, even if the three cheers were different in style and taste. Yet, by capitulating to this unity and pushing the integration of the cheers to create a new totality, would it have led to the further disintegration of the three cheers and to a lack of internal coherence amongst the three cheers? The fragmentation of the proposed classroom cheer occurred from the very beginning of the production process. An opposition to the idea of working on the cheers together initially moved the dialectical development of the cheers away from creating a heterogeneous pastiche that would have been able to synthesize different styles and tastes of performing cheers into one cheer. Yet, by turning against the status quo, and synthesizing a totality that crossed linguistic, racial and gendered borders and boundaries, would the dual immersion students have attained a form of interstitial *third space* that is able to synthesize their diverse and heterogeneous subjectivities?

The third space in this episode can be defined as a heterogeneous space that challenges the homogenizing and unifying forces of cultural production, authenticated by the originary, such as the traditional style of cheering. It constitutes the discursive conditions of enunciation that ensure that the meaning and symbols of culture offer no primordial unity or fixity; that even the same signs can be appropriated, translated, rehistoricized and read anew (Bhabha, 1994: 37). The third space is also a space of thirdness that opens up an area of *interfection* where the newness of cultural practices and historical narratives are placed in an unexpected juxtaposition that disavows earlier forms of disjunctive spaces and signs by creating a new totality (Jameson, 1991). Thus, through the splitting of the cheers into three cultural narratives and the displacement of the Ducks in Black and Spanish cheers, the disintegrative moment of aesthetic judgment could have been turned around so that a *new cheer* emerged, leading to the totality and ensemble of all three cheers as a whole. In order to attain a third space in the cultural production of the classroom cheers, the authenticity of the traditional Valley Girl cheer needed to be dehistoricized within the class discussions so that a postmodern pastiche, and thus a new totality, could have been formed from the disjunctive subjectivities of the three original cheers.

There were four particular students in the classroom, Jose, Scott, Shakima and Yolanda, who often reflected politically on the nature of the cheers during class discussions. These four students wanted to transition to a unifying cheer that escaped from atomization by grounding the aesthetic production of the cheers in a heterogeneous third space. The critical articulations of these border-crossing students during class discussions advocated that the final cheer must go beyond its objectively established borders. The class needed to strike a balance between the mimetic Valley Girl cheer, which upheld traditional cheerleading forms, and the other two constructive cheers, which pushed the rejection of traditional cheerleading forms. Even though Shakima and Scott are English-dominant students and Yolanda and Jose are Spanish-dominant students, all four students used their voices to advocate for a heterogeneous cheer that combined all three cheers and also combined both Spanish and English. The common traits amongst these four students are that they all used their student agency to voice resistance toward the homogeneous cheer and that they all seem to identify with bicultural and bilingual identities due to the fact that they were able to function academically in both the Spanish and English language throughout the school year and in both the Spanish-dominant and English-dominant social spaces of the classroom.

However, even though these border-crossing students enunciated the desire to sometimes create a third space in the cheers event, the collective agency of the class as a whole was still struggling with the complex bounds of student agency, teacher authority and ideological hegemony. The complex tensions in the cheers concerning individual student agency, teacher authority and a collective classroom agency crystallized in some students' desire to break away from the ideological bonds of traditional cheerleading but without losing the student autonomy of their collective cheers. Even though a few students protested against the traditional cheer, a few of the students also repressed their negative feelings toward the Valley Girl cheer and remained silent throughout the production process and did not voice their resistance. Some students also realized that their acquiescence and solidarity with the final class cheer was better than disavowing them entirely and in turn disavowing their class spirit.

In the end, Roberta possessed the absolute power to determine the final aesthetic composition of the cheers. The reappropriation of the cheers by Roberta nonetheless recognized the dominant aesthetic ideology of cheerleading. The deviation from student autonomy toward absolute teacher authority remained unquestioned throughout the production process by both the teacher and the students; yet, this kind of deviation can be seen as a common occurrence in the everyday classroom. As the outside researcher, I was able to notice when the development of the cheers moved away from student autonomy and toward teacher authority. Instead of relying on the students' improvisation and imagination, the teacher at one point in the dialectical trajectory substituted the aesthetic-in-itself for a formal cheerleading aesthetics. The further blurring of boundaries between aesthetics and pedagogy provided a rational teaching of what cheers should look like and sound like so that the students' direct experience of creating cheers was substituted by explicit norms and formulas. The cheers no longer sprang from the spontaneous aesthetic tastes of the students; they were now the products of an ideological hegemony rooted in the past and legitimized by the teacher.

Adorno (1998) states that essentialist thought defines what is the universal norm by negating the relativity of differing points of view and creating a pure aesthetic disposition through a return to the beginning when the definition of the artistic genre was pure and authentic. The formal character of the older aesthetic norms of cheerleading and the ignominy of its ever-same belief system clashed with the newer forms of cheerleading. The force of the old pressed against the new cheers as the qualities of the ever-same endured in favor of the timeless traditional cheer. The regression to the past occurred through both assimilation with the traditional style of cheering as well as through the powerful nature of the classroom teacher's self-posited need to return to her nostalgic cheerleading roots. The aesthetic truth content of the cheers meshed with the history of cheerleading so that a resituated truth of the past converged instead within the classroom discourse. Thus, the present temporality of performance and aesthetic composition reconstituted the past.

Oftentimes, the arguments and struggles over the value and meaning of aesthetics are situated and dated within a historical context that defines the social space in which these debates are set. The definitions of what is aesthetically beautiful or good are generated and operated in a historical structure that provides the situated context for these debates. However, sometimes the historical past and its codified and canonized achievements of mastery overwhelm the present field of artistic production (Bourdieu, 1992). The celebration of past achievements in art, music, drama and even cheerleading, connects the present artistic production to the proper traditions of the past. Anything new in the artistic field and its space of possibility is imposed upon by the history of the field. Deviations from the historical traditions of the artistic field, such as the Ducks in Black and Spanish cheers, create ruptures that are dehistoricized due to the lack of attention paid to historical properties of form and a greater focus on the social context of the artistic production. The timeless artistic objects of a purely aesthetic form constitute a corpus of canonic works, such as the traditional acrobatic cheer, whose value the field of production keeps making it indispensable, as evident in contemporary high school culture.

In the next chapter, the artistic field of drama will be highlighted to show once again how conflicts and tensions ensued over language use and linguistic borders and boundaries in this dual immersion classroom, as well as conflicts and tensions over gender, race and colonial history. We will also examine how certain border-crossing students were able to mediate the conflicts and tensions along the Spanish/English borderland through the production and performance of a bilingual Cuban play set in the historical past.

Chapter 4

Jack, Su Mama, Y El Burro: *The Performativity of Race, Gender and Language in a Bilingual Play*

Fueling the Fire for More Spanish in the Classroom: Putting on a Play

After the spring semester began in mid-January, a new student teacher, Trisha, an upper-middle-class white female who was fluent in Spanish and whose mother was also a white Spanish bilingual teacher, joined the dual immersion classroom. One of her initiatives during her student teaching practicum was to increase the amount of Spanish taught in the class curriculum. In order to increase the dual immersion students' exposure to authentic Spanish literature, Trisha decided to produce a bilingual play in March so that the dual immersion students could practice their oral and written language skills in Spanish through drama and present the play to their parents, teachers and peers in May, right before the graduation ceremonies. Trisha first asked Roberta for permission to produce a class play in Spanish and to present the play at the end of the school year. Although Roberta generally did not want to take on the great amount of responsibility that often incurs during the production of a class play, she did agree that Trisha could take on the leadership role herself and produce the play; however, Roberta helped Trisha decide which play to produce. The title of the play was *Jack, Su Mama, Y El Burro*, and it was scripted from an audiotape titled "The Cuban Storyteller." The autobiographic narrative of "The Cuban Storyteller" focuses on the narrator's cultural adaptation from rural Cuba to modern America at the turn of the 20th century. However, due to time constraints, Trisha was only able to transcribe the first section of the audiotape entitled, *Jack, Su Mama, Y El Burro*, which focuses solely on the Latino male author's childhood and adolescence in Cuba. It does not delve into the complex processes of cultural adaptation, assimilation and accommodation he experienced later through comic situations and events as an adult living in the United

States. Thus, the section that was transcribed and scripted onto paper by Trisha focuses only on Jack as a young *paesano* (peasant) living in rural Cuba with his nagging, single mother.

In terms of literary motifs, the character of Jack is written in the tradition of the *boberia* (buffoon), the total simpleton who fails to grasp symbolic and figurative language and interprets the world literally (Larson, 1991). Jack's failures to understand and communicate are humorous to the audience who laughs at his linguistic misfirings throughout the play. It is easy to see how language affects the character of Jack as a buffoon or *bobo* since words assume an important role throughout the play and create laughter by obfuscating meaning for Jack. Furthermore, the laughter in *Jack, Su Mama, Y El Burro* is produced through a series of repetitive silly behaviors from Jack that all possess a similar logic such as continually losing the money he earns at the end of the day through some mishap. This formulaic series gives rise to the stylistic and ideological idiosyncrasies of Jack's everyday speech as it is embedded in the recurring events of the play. When Jack is talking to himself in relation to his own buffoonery, he is speaking as if he is engaged in private speech with himself and is not aware that the audience is conscious of his comic thoughts and antics. The audience is shown what Jack is thinking and what he is experiencing through his periodic internal monologues. Thus, Jack as the *bobo* functions at the literal level because his words and actions attempt to realistically portray the role of a fool or buffoon in the Cuban folktale.

In *The Dialogic Imagination*, M. M. Bakhtin (1981) defines the function of the rogue, clown and fool in the context of the novel and states that the folkloric or semi-folkloric forms of novels tend to use satire and comedy by placing the rogue, clown, or fool at the center of the novel. According to Bakhtin, these figures can be traced back to classical antiquity and ancient Asian civilizations, when dramatists performed plays in public squares where common people gathered and laughed at these figures. The audience also attempts to grasp the metaphorical meaning of the fool's words and actions by becoming responsive to every joke and slapstick performance in the play. Thus, public spaces where common folk gathered took on the trappings of a public theater and externalized the figure of the clown, rogue and fool through parodic and comedic laughter. However, in this classroom, the figure of the rogue, clown and fool was evident not only in the production of the Cuban play but also in an earlier classroom episode related to the circulation of a bilingual children's book titled *Juan Bobo*, which also depicts the rogue, clown and fool but in the Puerto Rican countryside. In both the book *Juan Bobo* and the play *Jack, Su Mama, Y El Burro*, the *bobo* or buffoon's unselfish simplicity and his failure to comprehend symbolic language can be used to examine how colonial Hispanic characters from a rural peasant background are textualized as the primitive through the author's voice within Spanish children's literature and how these characters are then contextualized as the primitive in the production and performance of such texts. The relationship between the text and its situated context will run as a thematic thread throughout this chapter as we examine how bilingual classroom texts such as *Juan Bobo* and *Jack, Su Mama, Y El Burro* materialize and become understood in the context of not only race and ethnicity, but also class, gender and language differences. The inextricable link between where and how a text situates itself in the context of the everyday classroom life and how it affects the identity of the bilingual and multicultural classroom will hopefully be better understood as this chapter examines how students appropriated such texts, their characters, events, dialogue, gestures and bodily actions.

Examining the Primitive: The *Paesano* and *Jibero* in Children's Literature

To better understand the appropriation of texts such as *Juan Bobo* and *Jack, Su Mama, Y El Burro* in the context of race and ethnicity, the situated theme of primitivism will be used to examine the characterization of subjects such as Juan Bobo and Jack as the primitive. Furthermore, primitivism will be defined here from an anthropological framework which states that the primitive is an authentic being who is closer to what is natural and to Nature rather than to the artificial; who is less subject to the influences of civilized society and its advancements of technology; who performs a native resistance to a colonial hegemony; and who is a primordial being that prefers the uninhabited and irrational to the rational and controlled. The primitive discourse is also a temporalizing discourse since most of the "discourse about the alienness of the non-European Other was a discourse about development" (McGrane, 1989: 100). European civilizations came to connote the Darwinian concepts of development, progress and evolution with themselves while the Other-as-primitive, prehistorical being in Asia, Africa and the Americas became connoted with backwardness, deeply petrified beliefs and linear fossilization as opposed to linear growth. Clifford Geertz also classifies the primitive discourse as a temporal discourse but continues to state how the primitive discourse reflects more so the thought processes and thought products of the Europeans colonizers:

The primitive form of the "primitive thought" formulation – that is, that while we, the civilized, sort matters out analytically, relate them logically, and test them systematically, as can be seen by our mathematics, physics, medicine, or law, they, the savage, wander about in a hodgepodge of concrete images, mystical participations, and immediate passions, as can be seen by their myth, ritual, magic, or art – has, of course, been progressively undermined as more about how the other half thinks has become known (and more, too, about just how unvirginal reason is); though it persists in certain sorts of developmental psychology, certain styles of comparative history, and certain circles of diplomatic service. (1983: 148–149)

Within this anthropological framework of the primitive, narratives about progress and civilization produce an _imagined primitive being_ who fails to catch up to the 20th century and subsequently becomes either a marginal figure or a romanticized object (Tsing, 1993). Since the clown or fool figure is given the same characteristics of not understanding, being confused, teasing and hyperbolizing life, not being taken literally, acting as if life was a comedy, and parodying others, the clown or fool character takes on the characteristics of the primitive when set against a backdrop of colonial imperialism and rural landscapes. The primitive thoughts of characters such as Juan Bobo and Jack become material for laughter and parody; however, what ramifications does the performativity of the primitive buffoon, situated in the rural Hispanic colonial countryside, have for the context of a bilingual classroom?

The following sections of this chapter first examine the text of the children's Spanish book, _Juan Bobo_, how this text circulated and traveled throughout the space of the dual immersion classroom starting from its situated place on the Spanish library shelf, and finally how the primitive character of Juan Bobo in the book came to personify a Hispanic male student in the classroom. Jose became known throughout the school year as Juan Bobo, the name given to him by his English-dominant peers due to his physical traits, thus highlighting how such texts can be used to examine the context of race and ethnicity in the bilingual and multicultural classroom. Next, the chapter will examine how another primitive subject, Jack, in the production of the play, _Jack, Su Mama, Y El Burro_, was not kept in place as the primitive subject by the very same Hispanic male student identified earlier as Juan Bobo. Now Jose was able to reinterpret his scripted role of the primitive subject by changing the words spoken by his character Jack, the buffoon, and thus subvert the primitive discourse by rewriting his spoken text. In the end, the dynamic within the production and performance of the play, *Jack, Su Mama, Y El Burro* was one of student transformation, in which the concepts of race and ethnicity, as well as language and gender, as depicted by primitive characters such as Juan Bobo and Jack, are ultimately brought to bear on larger questions of identity, legitimacy and authenticity in the dual immersion classroom.

Yet, the depiction of primitive characters such as Juan Bobo and Jack also call into question larger complex issues related to how race and ethnicity are performed as the Other by young students in the fantasy space of a bilingual and bicultural play and also in the real space of their own dual immersion classroom. The dynamic of Otherness came into play as these sociocultural identifications of primitive subjects became traveling signs signifying the unresolved tensions between the two languages, cultures and the two sociocultural student groups in this class. The dynamic of Otherness also came into play in the context of gender and language when male subjects played female characters, female subjects played male characters, and English-dominant students played Spanish-dominant characters in the production and performance of the Other within this Cuban play. Furthermore, within the colonial countryside of multiracial, Spanish-speaking nations such as Cuba and Puerto Rico, where race relations can be traced to their slave past, issues related to the theoretical concept of national identity as constructed difference will be also addressed in this chapter when we examine how a sense of Cubanness and Puerto Ricanness was constructed spatially and visually in the signifying texts. The representation of the indigenous, folkloric colonial past was evident in the visual depiction of the spatial landscapes in which both Juan Bobo and Jack were situated, either through the rural Cuban scenery painted for *Jack, Su Mama, Y El Burro* or the illustrations in *Juan Bobo*.

Juan Bobo: A Traveling Sign of Social Relations in the Classroom

On the Spanish bookshelf, *Juan Bobo* was a popular children's book that most of the dual immersion students read for their Spanish book reports. Since every two months they had to read a book in Spanish and write a report in Spanish summarizing and analyzing the books they have read, the students often chose a Spanish book from the classroom library and asked each other informally which one to read first, depending on the book's level of Spanish sophistication. The story of *Juan Bobo* was a popular text that subsequently was the topic of many Spanish book reports due to the fact that it was an early elementary-level Spanish book, targeted for Grades 2–4, and the fifth-grade students in this classroom found it to be less challenging than the other Spanish books on the shelf. Since the book *Juan Bobo* was a highly read book, one can posit that *Juan Bobo* was a text that traveled through the hands of many dual immersion students in this classroom, and this section in turn locates the *Juan Bobo* text and situates it in specific yet shifting classroom contexts. By tracing the residues that the text leaves behind in its travels throughout the classroom space, the researcher is able to stop its itinerary and draw implications as to how its deployment affected the larger classroom life. Once appropriated by classroom subjects, texts such as *Juan Bobo* acquire a new identity as they slowly become naturalized within the traversed space of the classroom. It is the researcher's role to locate those situated moments of textual appropriation and examine the production and performance of such appropriation by marking and analyzing the spaces in which the meaning of the text is enacted.

Furthermore, the textual voyage that *Juan Bobo* took will be recounted in this section by narrating how its itinerary became a topic of classroom discourse – starting from its use as a normative text for the Spanish book report assignment and then to the personification of Juan Bobo, a young Afro-Hispanic character growing up rural Puerto Rico, in the everyday life of the classroom. More specifically, the textual journey of *Juan Bobo* throughout the dual immersion classroom will be interpreted through a semiotics framework in which one utilizes the ability to read a map of *Juan Bobo*'s travels in relation to its points of reference and contact within the classroom discourse. In turn, I will examine when and where *Juan Bobo* the text is talked about and in what contexts. Only in this sense can we speak of a topography positing the travel of a text such as *Juan Bobo* throughout the classroom and its endless chain of reference and signification, even if it bears an unwelcome witness to the wanderings, deviations and departures from the figural meanings in *Juan Bobo* the written text (Abbeele, 1992). Thus, we will travel along the various routes that the text *Juan Bobo* took, starting from the bookshelf to the classroom discourse and then to its appropriation by human subjects.

We can begin by applying topological theories of language here in which a Spanish book report becomes a question of choosing the right *route* for getting an above average grade in Spanish literacy. Most of the students chose the easy route by reading elementary children's books such as *Juan Bobo* in Spanish for their two-page book report assignments. However, at the same time, an overwhelming concern in the dual immersion program was that the selection of reading books in Spanish at each grade level was indeed limited and the students often relied on Spanish *baby books* such as *Juan Bobo*. Studies have examined the paucity of children's literature written in Spanish by Hispanic-American authors and its effect on the quality of bilingual education programs. Gonzalez-Jensen (1997) found that (1) many of the available books come from Spanish-speaking countries or are translations of English works into Spanish; (2) a high degree of imbalance exits among the genres; (3) few books are published for students in late exit or maintenance bilingual programs; (4) evidence of a lack of "author balance" exists with several prominent authors writing many more books than others and few male authors represented; and (5) relatively few of the children's books were written by Mexican-American authors. Her conclusions mirrored the same issues that PS 2000 faced as well in terms of providing high-quality, award-winning bilingual children's literature.

On the back cover of *Juan Bobo: Four Folktales from Puerto Rico* (Bernier-Grand, 1994), the description of the book is as follows:

> Juan Bobo, do this! Juan Bobo, do that! Mama puts Juan Bobo to work whenever he is having a good time. But he always finds a way to make work fun – like using baskets instead of buckets to carry water, or sprinkling the pig with Mama's favorite perfume.

The book is divided into four Puerto Rican folktales that are written in English in the first half of the book and then written in Spanish in the second half of the book. In the first chapter, "The Best Way to Carry Water", Juan Bobo's mother asks him to bring water from the stream but Juan, who is a young adolescent, is wearing his *diablo* (devil) mask and is busy chasing chickens. After yelling at him to get the two buckets of water, Juan eventually brings the water to his mother but in two straw baskets, and the water drips out before Juan Bobo reaches the front door. In the second chapter, "A Pig in Sunday Clothes," Juan's mother states that Juan must either go to church with her or take care of their farm pig. Juan decides to take care of the pig but then he takes the pig to church, and in the process, he dresses up the pig in his mother's best clothes, shoes, jewelry and perfume. By the time his mother shows up to the house, she is fuming at Juan Bobo because the pig is wearing her best Sunday clothes and rolling in the mud. Next, in "Do Not Squeeze, Do Not Scratch . . . Do Not Eat," Juan Bobo and his mother visit Señora Sota's house for dinner; however, due to the fact that his mother thinks that Juan does not have any manners while he eats, he goes home with an empty stomach. In the last chapter, "A Dime a Jug," Juan's mother scolds him for tasting the sugarcane syrup from the jugs because she wants him to sell the jugs of syrup for a dime each. However, Juan goes through a series of silly mishaps in which he loses the syrup before he even gets to sell it. When his mother states that the syrup is for "widows with black hats" at the church, he mistakes the black hornets swarming in front of the church as the widows his mother is referring to and subsequently lets them drink the syrup. But Juan Bobo finds four dimes on the way home and gives his mother the money. She believes that Juan actually sold the jugs of syrup instead of giving it to the black hornets. At the end of the book, Juan's mother walks into his bedroom and says, "Tonight you can eat as much as you want!" Juan replies, "No thank you, Mama. Tonight I am very full!" He goes off to bed with a smile on his face but without eating any food.

In the book's colorful illustrations, the artist places dramatized and exotic emphasis on Juan Bobo's blackness, which is characterized through his physical features: copious, black, naturally kinky hair; dark black skin; wide nose; drawn in forehead; prominent jaw and full mouth. On the one hand, these features serve as archetypes that typify the character's physical being, on the other hand, they make an aesthetic impact on the reader. Yet, blackness is often folklorized and celebrated institutionally as part of the nation in Puerto Rico; however, this inclusion and celebration complements ideologies of *blanquemiento* (whitening) and race-mixing that distance blackness to the margins of national identity and romanticize blackness as primitive remnants of a past era (Godreau, 1999). Furthermore, similar to the delineation of black characters as the primitive being in early 20th-century American children's books, Juan Bobo's character was also depicted as being "moved by instinct rather than logic, as prone to imitate rather than initiate action, as excitable and immoderate, as self-deprecating and clownish" (MacCann, 1998: 83). The portrait of Juan Bobo can be summed up as variations of black plantation tales and adventure tales in American children's literature and in which Juan Bobo is characterized as a cross between a Hispanic minstrel clown and the ultimate buffoon in the Puerto Rican sugar plantation. Thus, the folklorization of blackness and an elemental and stereotyped black psychology are essential to the creation of Afro-Hispanic characters such as Juan Bobo who are situated in a discourse of premodern primitivism.

In *Juan Bobo*, Bernier-Grand (1994) depicts the primitive life of Juan Bobo in rural Puerto Rico as exemplified by a return to Nature, and thus, the book becomes a *novela de la selva y la tierra* – a novel of the jungle and earth. The wilderness of the jungle foregrounds the author's own nostalgia for her childhood in Puerto Rico as noted in the preface, but it also posits Nature as an alternative to development in *jíbero* (rural peasant) Puerto Rico. The semiotic ties between Juan Bobo and the green environment around him contrast strongly with modern society and its exchange of commercial commodities. In *Juan Bobo*, Nature and the primitive protagonist become identified with one another in the tropical landscape, which is seen as the only consolation. However, this contrast between the premodern and the modern promotes cultural myths in children's literature such as the idea of primitive cultures preserving wilderness much more so than industrialized cultures. In many ways, the environment in which Juan Bobo lives becomes portrayed as an archaic utopia and a perhaps postmodern cultural resistance to modernity. Yet, at the same time, the book does not highlight humanity's alienation from Nature, global poverty and inequality; instead, the book ironically illustrates the utopian celebration of primitive wisdom that rarely translates into empowerment for Juan Bobo, who seems happy to the reader even though he is a poor and impoverished character who goes to bed without eating food at the end of the book.

In addition to the emphasis on Juan Bobo's blackness and his surrounding physical environment, the author delineates the primitive mind of Juan Bobo as indifferent to logic and one that prefers mystical explanations based on invisible connections among the objects that surround him, such as the straw baskets with water and the jugs of syrup with the hornets. The four stories within *Juan Bobo* are all told through the protagonist Juan Bobo's point of view and how he is unable to see beyond the illogical paradigm afforded to him by the author. However, even though the protagonist Juan Bobo arrives at illogical conclusions, he is still using a distinct process of reasoning to arrive at those conclusions, such as the reasoning that black hornets do resemble widows wearing black hats. The use of experiment and deductive reasoning by Juan Bobo does exercise a certain logic within his reasoning. Thus, the question then becomes whether primitive subjects such as Juan Bobo are located in a pre-rational stage of development or whether they employ a non-Western logic that uses a different kind of reasoning process to describe phenomenon such as black hornets (Levi-Strauss, 1966).

The pre-rational stage theory automatically constructs a teleology in which a primitive pre-rational stage is necessarily followed in time by a civilized and developed rational stage. On the other hand, the non-Western logic best serves the purpose of establishing a positive view of primitivism that can be associated with "a non-linear notion of time, closeness to the natural world, to generate myths, and in sum, a greater artistic capacity in contrast to the 'scientific' tendency of the modern mind" (Camayd-Freixas & Gonzalez, 2000: 100). However, by denying multiple types of reasoning, notions of causality and temporal dimensions associated with the West to non-Western nations such as Cuba and Puerto Rico, are authors such as Bernier-Grand in turn perpetuating images of social and economic underdevelopment in non-Western nations to its young readers? Are bilingual children's books such as *Juan Bobo* subordinating a primitive discourse of Puerto Rico to the modern discourse of the United States?

From one point of view, the non-Western literary styles of *transculturadores* (transculturals) such as Bernier-Grand do present a Hispanic response in children's literature that finds local equivalents and does not copy the Western literary style found in American children's literature. As the author, she has to create a psychology for Juan Bobo that seems more a result of her own authorial intuition and observation rather than a product of American archetypes. Bernier-Grand (1994) uses this paradigm logically to create a web of primitive belief systems that she feels characterize Puerto Rican folktales. In the beginning of the book, the author makes note that

> for decades Juan Bobo, the invention of rural story tellers of Puerto Rico, has been the most popular fictional character on the island. Although some of Juan Bobo's "noodlehead" behaviors also occur in the folklore of other countries, the oldest and best-known Juan Bobo stories authentically illustrate what life was like for poor rural areas of Puerto Rico at the beginning of the twentieth century. In retelling a few of these old tales, I have used my own voice and have tried to preserve some of rural Puerto Rican flavor. (Bernier-Grand, 1994: 1–2)

Thus, *transculturadores* like Bernier-Grand attempt to recover a primitive view of Hispanic culture that may seem completely foreign to the contemporary American reader. Even though the supposed anonymity of protagonists such as Juan Bobo and the atemporality of this Puerto Rican folktale do not necessarily reflect the individual personality of its author, the textual representation of Juan Bobo tries to supposedly represent the cultural values of the ethnic community from which the author comes from.

Yet, even though the author's main purpose may have been to preserve her cultural traditions, she is still employing a form of writing that turns her primitive subject, Juan Bobo, into primitive discourse. The ideological contradictions between the use of archaic writing techniques by the author and the author's nativist discourse opens up the possibility for an author who is a native of Puerto Rico to harbor the same prejudices commonly associated with Western inscriptions of the primitive discourse. Yet, at the same time, the positive views of primitivism support the stability of collective folk traditions that challenge the chaotic, sterile traditions of Western modernity (Fass Emery, 1996). In turn, depending on the ideology of the transcultural author who is employing the primitive discourse, the primitive protagonist can be either degraded or exalted for thinking differently or can be represented as either inferior to Western culture or superior to Western culture. Thus, a paradox is produced in books such as *Juan Bobo* because they are a way of giving the Other a voice through a romantic view of primitivism, but they are also a way of silencing that authentic native voice through a form of primitivism that is essentially racist.

Bernier-Grand's characterization of Juan Bobo seems to fall nonetheless within the category of elementary or schoolish images of black characters given by romantic novelists where there is no authentic black being, just a primitive subject with innocence, illogical reasoning, natural rhythms and ties to the earth. The picturesque and superficial world of Juan Bobo inevitably gets fixed within the *naturalistic-nativist-typicalist-vernacular* method writing that never arrives at the depth of things or the really transcendental (Barreda, 1979: 137). In order to achieve this depth, the novelist must move beyond natural space and black animism and replace it with the notion of becoming in time as opposed to remaining situated permanently in a primitive space. In turn, the black protagonist must be seen in different time periods besides colonial Hispañola and must move beyond static spatial dimensions and move toward changing temporality: "The Cuban protagonist is placed in space, in nature, whereas in the novel of Haiti, without losing his relation to the earthly context, the principal character is an integral part of time, of history" (Barreda, 1979: 154). Not only is the story of Juan Bobo a primitive artifact of the communal culture in rural Puerto Rico, but also its anonymous features represent a Puerto Rican tradition that does not seem to have changed much since colonial times even though the book was published in 1994. The absence of historical change in *Juan Bobo* frees the Puerto Rican culture from an obsession with time and presents its truths as if they were eternal, universal truths that are not subject to mutation and instability. But is this depiction of Juan Bobo what the dual immersion students saw as eternal truths of Puerto Rico as well? Did they see Puerto Rico as a primitive nation that is inhabited by subjects such as Juan Bobo who resist modern social formations and rational ideas?

The psychological effects of reading children's literature such as *Juan Bobo*, that are attributed to primitive production, to ideas about the

communal, and to atemporal stories that recreate the way of life in primitive societies, did manifest themselves in some way or another within
the larger context of this dual immersion classroom discourse. The
perception of cultural differences between Puerto Rico and the United
States and of social and political relations between the primitive and the
modern become clearer in the classroom discourse when seen through
the contextualized symbolism of the Afro-Hispanic human body. Specifically, the body of one particular Hispanic student in the dual immersion
classroom, Jose, a Spanish-dominant, lower-middle-class male student
whose parents are from the Dominican Republic and Puerto Rico, became
contextualized as the Afro-Hispanic archetype. By naming Jose as "Juan
Bobo," the dual immersion students collectively illuminated the nature
of the link between signifier and signified in which the circulating Spanish
children's book, *Juan Bobo*, began to take on a different sort of signification; soon a subtle substructure developed in the classroom based on
language, on naming and on manipulation. The sign of *Juan Bobo*, the
book, established a one-to-one correspondence between itself as a sign
and the referent, Jose. Initially, it was Brian, an English-dominant white
male student from an upper-middle-class background, who first identified and named Jose as Juan Bobo because of the clownish way Jose acted
in class and the iconic properties of Jose's body: his strangely shaped
skull; copious, black, naturally kinky hair; dark mocha skin; wide nose;
drawn in forehead; prominent jaw; and full mouth. Thus, Jose became
an emblematic figure of Otherness in the dual immersion class due to
the physical traits perceived by his peers as having the same traits as the
primitive protagonist Juan Bobo.

Throughout the academic year, Jose's bodily contours became an object
of humor and ridicule. Furthermore, since many of the students read the
story of *Juan Bobo*, they soon began associating Jose's physicality with
Juan Bobo and soon Juan Bobo became the metonym for Jose. The other
students, both Spanish-dominant and English-dominant, conferred with
each other and from their conferring power they named and identified
Jose as Juan Bobo throughout the school year and in both formal and
informal spaces. Brian's citing of Jose as Juan Bobo initially began this
process of naming in Spanish, but for Brian, an English-dominant student,
this naming process was a way of playing with the Spanish language as
well. Throughout the school year, he often used Spanish in class to create
silly names and phrases that became a site of a unique pidginization of
the two languages. During one Spanish spelling lesson, Roberta, the
teacher, called on Brian to read his Spanish sentence aloud for the Spanish
word *probable* (probably). Brian replied, "*Probable*, it's *probable yo* will be

un doctor." When the class laughed at Brian's pidgen Spanish, he responded, "I understand Spanglish!" Thus, by Brian first signifying the primitive protagonist Juan Bobo with his friend and peer Jose, the name became the effect and token of playing with Spanish for him and for creating a hybrid understanding of the Spanish language. Yet, the dynamic of Otherness came into play as these sociocultural identifications of primitive subjects become signs of larger unresolved tensions between the different sociocultural student groups in this dual immersion class.

In turn, the book *Juan Bobo* was not a dead object sitting on a bookshelf; instead, it was speaking and signifying. The students in the class were reading it, perceiving it and localizing it by having this text occupy a specific function in the classroom culture. Juan Bobo was not a dead character; he was passing through a series of mediating links and came up against a real human body when the students inscribed Jose as the person inside the book *Juan Bobo*. Even though Jose and Juan Bobo are located in differing time-spaces, separated by a century and the spatial distance of nation-states, for his peers, the real world in which Jose was situated did not have a sharp categorical border against the represented world in the text. The dual immersion students were the readers of the text and were subsequently renewing its meaning by making no distinction between Jose, who was a fellow student in their everyday world, and Juan Bobo, the Puerto Rican protagonist who was represented in the world of the text. The real and the represented worlds were tied up with each other, and Jose found himself in the mutual interaction between these two worlds. Jose became a part of the creation since most students in class now began referring to him not by his real name but mostly by the name "Juan Bobo." Even though he lived outside of the text as a human being living his own biographical life, the dual immersion students became creators of Jose's fictive Afro-Hispanic self. Thus, the signification of the name "Juan Bobo" and the book *Juan Bobo* reflect the interrelations between the primitive protagonist known as Juan Bobo and the object *Juan Bobo* and how they both provided an index to Jose, the student, and a mask for the dual immersion classroom's troubling alter ego that still needed to address its brewing racial tensions.

In *Lost Subjects, Contested Objects* (1998), Deborah Britzman talks about the recurring repressive discourses in the life of schools, such as the racist, primitive discourse surrounding Juan Bobo, and how these discourses remain repressed within the unconscious of the classroom until they are brought to the surface through critical inquiry and dialectical discussions. Britzman further states that the normalization of race often occurs through the body so that obvious, natural features of the body, such as those exhibited by Jose, become mechanisms of power in which all bodies are then categorized as either proper or improper bodies. English-dominant students such as Brian and Shakima were constantly engaged in repeated indexical gestures to signify Jose as Juan Bobo, isolating Jose through name-calling, through gazing with their peers and through other modes of *pointing out* Jose's improper physical characteristics as Juan Bobo's, thus enabling a text/subtext distinction central to the dual immersion students' interrelations.

Brian, who often manipulated the Spanish language to coin silly phrases and make fun of other students in Spanglish, first baptized Jose as Juan Bobo during their literature circle discussions in which the character in his story was named "Juan Bobo" but the literary characterizations in his story reflected Jose's actual presence in the classroom. Even though the teacher and the student teacher did not suspect anything when Brian was reading his story aloud, most of the other students were giggling and whispering Jose's name underneath their breath because they knew that Brian was really writing about Jose disguised as Juan Bobo. In turn, Juan Bobo was used on the literal level of a proper name to identify Jose with iconic signs such as his unusually shaped skull, Puerto Rican socio-cultural background and Spanish-speaking ability, and also as a kind of metaphoric label of identifying Jose with certain indexical signs such as the class simpleton or buffoon (Peirce, 1986). The verbal legitimization of Jose as Juan Bobo was never contested by Jose during the literature circle discussion and was never contested at other times in other classroom spaces, since he often shied away from any overt confrontation with his peers and instead fell silent. Even though he was embarrassed, Jose could not stop the other students from calling him Juan Bobo, and often he had to defend the unusual shape of his skull, even with his own friends. Furthermore, the misnaming of Jose as Juan Bobo was never questioned enough by his close peers to deconstruct its inherent assumptions, especially since the qualities expressed in the characterization of Juan Bobo did not necessarily match up with the qualities within Jose as an individual. Both the classroom teacher and the student teacher were also unaware of this name-calling since it often occurred in informal spaces such as the playground, the hallways, and the cafeteria, places where children often escaped the panoptic gaze of the adult authority figure.

The everyday classroom practices around name-calling are oftentimes organized around a principle of displacement in which a student's status or place in the social hierarchy can be displaced when a name such as Juan Bobo becomes contingent with that person and cannot be avoided. Substitute names such as Juan Bobo are not simply negations of the real name but often point toward something else as well (Keane, 1997). Strategies of displaced naming, such as Juan Bobo, point to the existence of something that is suppressed in the classroom culture as well. The ritual of name-calling can be seen as a displacement of student agency in which targeted students such as Jose are challenged and their self-possession and esteem are threatened in the eyes of classroom Others. By baptizing Jose in public as Juan Bobo, the act and process of name-calling moves out of intimate circles and becomes a part of general social relations in the classroom. All this displacement and name-calling points back to what is not being spoken in the classroom discourse about interpersonal student relations between the two sociocultural student groups so that name-calling continually constructs the very center of social relations that is apparently being presupposed. However, there were a few students, such as Spanish-dominant students like Javier from Puerto Rico, who challenged the originary act of name-calling enacted by a few English-dominant students such as Brian and Shakima. In fact, he led a small movement to create social boundaries between those students who still identified Jose as Juan Bobo and those who did not due to its demeaning nature.

Ironically, the notoriety that Jose gained as Juan Bobo throughout the school year by some of his English-dominant and Spanish-dominant peers led to Jose's subsequent role-playing of Jack, another Afro-Hispanic buffoon, in the class production of a Cuban bilingual play, *Jack, Su Mama, Y El Burro*. Jose's role as the central *bobo*/buffoon character added primacy to his original label as Juan Bobo. However, Jose's own attempts at self-definition seemed to contradict his fictional role as a *bobo* in the play, given his strong academic performance in class and subsequent entrance to a renowned magnet middle school. Even though Jose sometimes used his student agency to challenge the name he had been identified with by his peers, Jose was also a complex student with other conflicting, multiple roles within the social context of the classroom: he faced the problem of not asserting and losing control of his identity through name-calling while at the same time gaining the recognition of his peers and his teachers for his academic performance; he became associated negatively with the name Juan Bobo but subsequently took on the role of another buffoon in the class play; in the cheers episode he lead the Spanish cheer; and in music class he advocated the singing of Spanish songs. Jose was also a border-crossing leader in the classroom and often voiced issues and concerns over the marginalization of the Spanish language but strangely did not challenge the name-calling. Nevertheless, in the next section, we will see Jose as that border-crossing student who challenges the linguistic inequities in the bilingual play.

Jack, Su Mama, Y El Burro: Examining the Primitive Discourse in a Cuban Play

Semiotics relates to signifying systems in which the perceptual object, such as the *Juan Bobo* text, is examined within the codified boundaries of the sign and what it signifies as it conjoins itself to a specific referent. Jose's body became lost in a chain of reference between the signifier and signified, so that Jose's body, the signified, was read and embodied as Juan Bobo, the signifier. However, in order for Jose's body to be *lived* as Juan Bobo, both the signifier and the signified must be involved in a mutual relationship within a field of observation conducive to seeing such positional categories. And such a field of observation was eventually constructed when the class decided to put on a performance of *Jack, Su Mama, Y El Burro*, a Cuban comedy play based on a fictional character who is also an Afro-Cuban buffoon like Juan Bobo.

The play begins with Jack's mother coming on stage and saying, "*Jack! Jack! No tenemos comida en la casa, tienes que trabajar!* Jack! Jack! We don't have any food to eat and you have to get a job!" Similar to Juan Bobo, Jack goes out to look for a job and ends up working on a farm milking cows, cleaning the barn and picking mangoes off the orchard trees. At the end of the day, the farmer approaches Jack and says, "*Jack, hiciste muy bien!* You did a good job! For that I am going to give you, *los mangoes que comiste*, the very mangoes that you ate, and your very own silver coin." However, as Jack walks home, he drops the silver coin foolishly in the pond when he stands on a bridge watching the fish below. In the end, Juan returns to the house without food and confronts his mother:

Mama: *Aye . . . que bueno! Esta noche vamos a comer.* (Mama starts singing). *Arroz, arroz, arroz, nos gusta comer arroz!* Rice, rice, rice, we are going to eat lots of rice. Give me the money Jack! (Mama holds out her hand).

Jack: (Jacks acts out what happened when his coin dropped into the river). Estaba mirando los pescaditos, se cayo y KERPLUNK!

English translation:
[I was looking at the fish and then the coin dropped and KERPLUNK!]

Mama: *Pero, que lo tuyo, muchacho?* What is the matter with you? Don't you know that when you get something like that, you should take it, put it in your pocket, and walk home.

Jack: (Jack acts out putting it in his pocket.) *Ponga en el bosillo?*

English translation:
[Put it in the pocket?]

Mama: That's right! Put it in your pocket.
Jack: (Jack nods his head). Oh! Ah!

The next day when the farmer gives him a jug of apple cider as a reward for the same chores, Jack pours the apple cider in his pockets just as his mother advised him the previous day. However, by the time he gets home, the apple cider has dripped out of his pockets, and his mother scolds him again for his illogical thinking. The play goes through a series of mishaps in which Jack takes his mother's advice literally and somehow does not end up coming home with any food to eat. Finally, in the sixth act, the farmer gives Jack a *burro* (donkey) as his reward, and Jack carries the *burro* home on his back just as his mother had advised him to do so with the slab of meat that he lost the other day when he dragged it on the ground and the street dogs ate it. Meanwhile, as the *burro* is slung over Jack's back and is slobbering down his face, Jack passes in front of a rich factory owner's mansion, *la casa del dueno de la fabrica*, who has a young daughter that has been crying for two years straight for no reason. But when she sees Jack and the slobbering *burro* on his back, she starts laughing hysterically, and the factory owner subsequently gives Jack four bags of gold as a reward for making her finally laugh. Jack's mother is elated when Jack comes home with the gold and sings, "*Arroz, arroz, arroz, nos gusta comer arroz!*"

At the end of the play, the character of Jack transforms himself from a simpleton or *bobo* to a *discreto* or wise man. Jack's newfound sensibility at the end of the play surfaces as well in the type of language he employs; it becomes more sophisticated and stylized as Jack displays an awareness of his new state of being. Jack's half-witted speech patterns disappear as he celebrates with his mother that they will finally have *arroz* (rice) to eat that night. Yet, throughout most of the play, Jack is truly a comic character; his speech and actions create humor, and the audience reacts to the comic effects of his silly behaviors. Jack's movements on stage were also stylized and codified according to the buffoon character type. Most importantly, the basis for all of Jack's comic characterization is his mishandling of language and the communicative act; he is a character whose linguistic misfirings form the essence of his characterizations. Furthermore, Jack's comic manipulation of language combines well with his physical humor and adds texture to the comedy through such actions as falling down on the stage, changing the intonation of his voice to sound dumb and dumber, and scratching his skull often to show his slow thought process, which he presents as an internal monologue.

However, when the clown or fool is the main protagonist, as in *Juan Bobo* and *Jack, Su Mama, Y El Burro*, the clown or fool also goes through a stage of transformation that has enormous significance because it leads to a *folk consciousness* in which the meek becomes powerful and power is displaced from the feudal lord to the folk (Bakhtin, 1981). In particular, the clown or fool uses the device of *not understanding* and being simple-minded and naive in order to expose feudal unreasonableness. By winning the admiration of the factory owner and acquiring a large sum of money for doing so and making his mother happy, Jack the protagonist gains a form of equivalence that contrasts with his lower-class status. The play's fairytale conclusion gratifies the wishes and beliefs of wealth that make bearable the difficult life of an illiterate peasant such as Jack (Tillis, 1998). Yet by destroying the ordinary ties between the common folk and the ruling class, the unexpected connections and organic union between Jack, the daughter and the factory owner may also produce a *false consciousness* that distorts the authentic nature of the relationships between the working and the ruling class that were often established and reinforced through cultural traditions and sanctioned by political ideology.

Even though the play begins with the collective life of Jack and his mother, the progression of events in the play isolates Jack from his mother as he transitions to the time of labor when Jack's mother sends him off to find work and when he returns home with food to consume. Jack's everyday life of consumption with his mother is separated from the labor and production process of Jack working on the farm and receiving commodities in exchange for his labor. Time in the play is measured in phases via Jack's agricultural labor in the six sequenced acts in the play. Furthermore, time is profoundly spatial and concrete as Jack moves between where he dwells and where he labors. Thus, the narrative movement in the text helps build a *folkloric time* in which Jack goes through temporal cycles: he leaves the home to go to labor on the farm; earns a reward at the end of the day for his labor; loses the reward along the way home; gets yelled at by his mother for not having any rice to eat that night; and then returns to work the very next day in order to bring food to his mother (Bakhtin, 1981). The mark of a constant cyclical repetition deters the possibility of time moving forward and treading beyond the premodern stage of development in 1900 in colonial Cuba.

Furthermore, both the book *Juan Bobo* and the play, *Jack, Su Mama, Y El Burro*, try to create a real and imagined place where the authors attempt to recapture the simple life of old Cuba and Puerto Rico. This primitive ideal of the past was also sought in the present when the dual immersion classroom recreated the life of the primitive protagonist, Jack, in their play production. When the dual immersion class began producing and performing the play, *Jack, Su Mama, Y El Burro*, they were building on an *aesthetic typology of primitivism* in which the signs of primitivism are seen most clearly in the arts such as drama and literature (Camayd-Freixas & Gonzalez, 2000). Both the children's book *Juan Bobo* and the play *Jack, Su Mama, Y El Burro* show a different combination and predominance of categories of primitivism that highlight the conflict between the modern, characterized by the application of intellectual reason and intelligent production, and the Afro-Hispanic protagonists' rejection of rationalist thought.

Even though the students only performed the first part of *Jack, Su Mama, Y El Burro*, the rest of the Cuban folktales depict the narrator's transition from his bucolic past with his mother to his modern life in New York City, where the bilingual script transitions into more English and less Spanish. As the narrator moves from his past in Cuba to his present situation in New York City, there is a sense that the narrator is taking on a paternalistic, patronizing role toward his inferior Cuban past. The devaluation of his Cuban history also reflects the turn-of-the-century socialist thought in the early 1900s that was grounded in the binary between civilization and barbarism as Western European nations began colonizing Africa, Asia and Latin America. The prevalent sentiment at that time in Cuba was also the preoccupation with the unassimilation of primordial non-white racial groups from Africa into modern Latin American society. As early as 1501, African slaves were first brought to Cuba by the Spanish *conquistadores* but directly from Spain and not directly from Africa. It is estimated that over one and a half billion African slaves were brought over to Cuba between the years 1517 and 1880. The largest percentage belonged to the West African Yoruba group known in Cuba as *Lucumis* (Amor, 1969). The Portuguese first mentioned the power of the Yoruba kingdom in their voyages along the West Coast of Africa during the early 1500s. The influence of the West African slaves' Yoruban culture into Cuban society during the colonial period led to the hybridization of Hispanic and African cultures that we see today in both the written folk text of *Juan Bobo* and the performative text of *Jack, Su Mama, Y El Burro*.

Both *Juan Bobo* and *Jack, Su Mama, Y El Burro* also illuminate how a Hispanic writer who employs archaic writing techniques is not able to fully support the political relevance of the text and thus reproduces the marked borders between rational modernity and irrational premodernity. The

author's use of archaic writing techniques for aesthetic purposes subsequently places into question the value of the written work and
jeopardizes political progressivism (Benjamin, 1986). In order to produce
socially and politically relevant works, the use of archaic writing techniques and premodern cultural elements does not necessarily guarantee
political value but may only guarantee aesthetic value. The folk element
in *Jack, Su Mama, Y El Burro* never became politically problematic since the
play is a scripted performance that incorporates the mimetic retelling of
fixed lines and predetermined role distribution among two or more actors.
Thus, it adheres to the traditional aesthetic and communicative models of
the performing Cuban community (Tillis, 1998). However, in modern
Cuban literature, the work of Alejio Carpentier, for example, deals more
specifically not only with the aesthetic traditions, myths and legends of
Africans as they are still preserved in Cuba, but also with the political initiation of young Afro-Cuban protagonists into mainstream Cuban society.

In the mid-1900s, the figure of the Afro-Cuban protagonist became a
subject of polemic literature since "he" became a symbolic representation
of the oppressed sector of Cuban society, especially in Alejio Carpentier's
novel *Ecue-Yamba-O*. For many modern Cuban writers, the Afro-Cuban
character was a proletariat representative of the poorer classes who
needed attention and aid by Cuban writers much as the slave had in the
19th century; however, their interest was more sociological than literary.
To other Cuban writers, however, the Afro-Cuban protagonist was representative of a race and culture and thus "his" ancient myths, legends
and traditions brought from Africa were to be researched, studied and
collected in a scientific manner. In turn, the Afro-Cuban folktale needed
to be kept alive from generation to generation through oral and written
transmission by Cuban authors, even if the folktale archetype was archaic
and reproduced the sociocultural norms and stereotypes endorsed by
Spanish colonialism.

Folklore studies in general can be defined as the science that collects
and studies the beliefs and practices, customs, social and political institutions and the popular literature of the people, which is what the class
production of the play attempted to do through its oral narration of a
Cuban folktale, *Jack, Su Mama, Y El Burro*:

> *El folklore es la ciencia que estudia el saber del pueblo, lo que el pueblo humilde*
> *va aprendiendo y practicando durante su vida, de generacion en generacion,*
> *y que aceptando y practicado por la gente llega a formar la base de su vida,*
> *de su modo de pensar y obrar, de su religion; en fin de la base filosofica de su*
> *vida material y espiritual.* (Amor, 1969: 78)

English translation:
Folklore is the science that studies the knowledge of the village, what the humble village will be learning and practicing during its life, from generation to generation, and which accepted and practiced by the people comes to form the base of its life, of its mode of thought and work, of its religion; in short the philosophic base of its material and spiritual life. (Amor, 1969: 78)

Furthermore, according to Amor, the folktales or *cuentos* of Afro-Cuban culture can be categorized into three categories: (1) the stories of African gods and their counterparts in the Catholic religion; (2) the stories of the animals used by the Afro-Cubans to teach the maxims of their philosophy of life; and (3) the stories of the people of their society told in colorful and realistic detail, such as *Jack, Su Mama, Y El Burro*. In turn, the Afro-Cuban folktale is often a literary reflection of the characteristics, philosophy and customs of the folk. Specifically, one characteristic attributed to the Afro-Cuban protagonist in the folktale is *lightheartedness* in which the protagonist is filled with constant merriment. In *Jack, Su Mama, Y El Burro*, the protagonist is also depicted as a lighthearted young man who finds himself in several predicaments due to his buffoonery. Laziness is also another characteristic attributed to the Afro-Cuban protagonist in the folktale and is portrayed in an admonitory form of practice that is not to be imitated. The constant nagging from Jack's mama to find a job and to find something to eat for the family is another plea to save the family from ruin and from the Afro-Cuban male's laziness. Even though archaic folktales such as this one lack political progressivism, most Afro-Cuban folktales are didactic in form since they purport to teach either a moral or religious lesson through short cultural narratives. In *Jack, Su Mama, Y El Burro*, the didactic narration is contained in the actions and predicaments of Jack, as well as in the mother's repetitive dialogue, and in turn the moral principles are hidden in his primitivism.

Challenging Gender Roles in the Production of the Play

Role-playing is not just a literary technique; it is also a psychological phenomenon. The students in this dual immersion classroom did not accept every convention of traditional role-playing in their student production of *Jack, Su Mama, Y El Burro*; instead, they held auditions in which students were selected for the part they tried out for democratically by their peers and their teachers. In many ways, the play provided a fantasy space within the formal curriculum because it presented an imaginable space that did not materialize into strict limits and prohibitions of role-playing: a boy can play the part of a woman; a girl can play the part of a man; a Spanish-dominant student can play an English-speaking character; and an English-dominant student can play a Spanish-speaking character. By challenging the symbolic order of role-playing through the democratic process of student auditions, the dual immersion play transcended rationality and orthodoxy through gender-role inversion and cultural-role inversion and allowed boys to play girls, girls to play boys, and English-dominant students to play Spanish-dominant parts in the fictional play.

On the day of their auditions for *Jack, Su Mama, Y El Burro* in early February, under the guidance of the student teacher, Trisha, the class observed each student who went up to the front of the blackboard and auditioned for the part that s/he wanted to play. Yet, the character the dual immersion students chose to play in *Jack, Su Mama, Y El Burro* and chose to present to other people in the audience also depended on their individual nature. In some ways, the students adapted themselves by means of a personality from the play that either they themselves or their peers felt best expressed their individual natures, such as the push by peers for Jose to play Jack because of his semiotic link to *Juan Bobo*. Psychologist Carl Jung (1923) labels this way of relating to the external world through a fictional production as the *persona*. By taking on either the persona of Jack, his mother, the daughter, the farmer, the factory owner, the dogs, the cow and the *burro*, the students were not trying to deceive the audience; instead, they were accommodating themselves in accordance to the persona/character they wanted to portray on stage. As a result, the students confronted their own individual problems of identity by playing a role that did not necessarily match their external worlds and thus they assumed a masked persona while on stage in the fantasy space of a bilingual play.

After all the auditions, the class voted on who would play which part. They decided that Scott should play Jack's Cuban mother. Both Jose and Alice should share the part of Jack, a young Cuban male. Julio should play the Cuban farmer. Javier should play the Cuban factory owner. Mary should play his Cuban daughter. Emil should play the *burro*. Brian should play the cow, and Sunny and Maria should play the dogs. In turn, a few English-dominant white students, such as Scott, Alice and Mary, were involved in cross-cultural representations in which they were playing Spanish-dominant characters and were subsequently more methodologically self-conscious and more receptive to the multiple perspectives and practices involved in representing cultural Others. Their task was now to act out a dramatized Spanish-dominant, Hispanic Other and give a plausible account of the Other through their own construction and representation of the Cuban characters. Engendered in the process of representing a character from a different culture, Alice, Mary and Scott had to cross over to the Spanish language and to Cuban culture. However, as Alice, Mary and Scott were rehearsing their Cuban characters, they were also attempting to claim an access to some truthful portrayal of the Other and defining their characters in relation to the mimetic realism of what it means to be a Spanish-speaking, Cuban character from the colonial 1900s. Moreover, Alice, Mary and Scott were not only characters in the Cuban play, but they were also somehow both *subject* and *object* of the transformation required to represent a fictional character from a different culture, speaking both as a Spanish-dominant, Hispanic character and as a white actor playing a Spanish-dominant, Hispanic character. As their voices oscillated between being themselves and being their Spanish Other character, an uncanny effect was produced. The tone, pitch and volume of their voices changed as they morphed into their Spanish-speaking, Cuban characters, sometimes of a different gender, and subsequently their voices wavered between the performance and production of the real and imaginary.

Another deictic shift occurred in relation to gender due to the fact that Alice portrayed a Hispanic male while Scott portrayed a Hispanic female. Alice and Scott's hermeneutic challenge was not only to figure out what was happening in the Spanish parts of the play but also how to narrate their parts of the play in Spanish and from the perspective of someone from the opposite sex, sometimes with a great degree of hesitancy in their voices. Alice and Scott focused on the mechanisms of identification, projection, transference and idealization of the Spanish Other as they operated in the discourse of the narration. Their narrative constitution of the Spanish Other in the Cuban play subsequently raises the possibility of a different, non-ethnocentric way of relating to Otherness. When I interviewed Alice at the end of the performance as to why she wanted to play a male role and as to why an English-dominant student wanted to perform a Spanish-speaking part, her response was as follows:

Author: What about your role as Jack in the school play? What did you think about that? Why did you try out for that? What about your Spanish there?
Alice: I think that was more . . . rehearsed words and I'm kinda of . . . I like acting and I'm kinda of good at remembering lines even if it

is . . . no matter what language it is in cause I am in the Metropolitan Opera and we sing in German and Italian and I have no idea what I am saying. But . . . I guess I have an okay accent and I like saying words. I just don't know what they mean. So I kind of . . . I got the basic idea . . . then I knew what each word in my lines meant because they were very short. So . . . then I could as Jack . . . like . . . sort of like if I left something out I can add a tiny thing to make up for it.

Author: In what language?

Alice: Well . . . see it was sometimes . . . in Spanish and sometimes in English. So in Spanish like . . . I could add . . . I could change . . . a word or something. Like I did that once by mistake. And it was okay as long as I made the meaning clear . . . cause as long as I knew what was happening . . . I could sort of make the meaning clear with my body movements even if I couldn't say the words. So that's why I really liked it. Also, I thought it was a really funny play and I like to make people laugh. So . . .

Author: Did you understand your lines by the end of the play?

Alice: Yeah . . . I didn't really know them exactly word for word. I got the basic idea like *hombros* is shoulders. So I got the basic idea that I am putting it on my shoulders. I knew the story in English so . . . it kind of worked out that way.

Author: How did you feel about playing the role of Jack, a male character? How did you feel about playing Jack next to Jose?

Alice: Well I thought that he was a bit better. He was better at the Spanish but he didn't use many body movements. I used like a few more body movements. But in third grade I played a . . . the boy of the "Three Year Nap." It's always been a girl playing it. No one knows why. But the girls always seem to be the ones that end up playing it. Not the boys. Even though it's a boy's role. I guess at this age it doesn't really matter cause none of us are . . . or like . . . like none of the boys' voices have changed and stuff. So you can't really tell . . . the difference . . . once you're on stage. And . . . I guess it doesn't matter who plays it . . . as long as they are qualified . . . whether it's a boy or a girl or a cat . . . as long as they can do it. So . . . I got kind of used to playing boys cause in the opera . . . I play little orphan boys and stuff . . . because the costumes fit me. And . . . you know . . .

Author: I noticed that you played a boy and Scott played a woman. How did you feel about that?

Alice: I thought it was really funny . . . [laughs] . . . but I thought he was . . . I thought that I would not have made as good a mother . . . and I don't think he would have made a good as Jack. I think it was just right. Also . . . I added at the end . . . it was really funny when he took off his wig and I took off my hat. It was sorta off like . . . we could have been switched. But we weren't because we were right for our roles.

Alice's responses to the above questions reveal underlying issues related to the corporeal and linguistic problematics of producing a bilingual play in a fantasy space. The dual immersion classroom's production of the play dealt with corporeal problematics due to its cross-gender role-playing, in which the body became an ambiguous site of gendered subjectivity. In addition, their production also dealt with linguistic/textual problematics when English-dominant students played Spanish parts, which will be examined later.

First, in terms of corporeal problematics, the body became a site of corporeal and subjective elements that resisted reduction to the mere textual representation of gender. The portrayal of Mama by Scott and the portrayal of Jack by Alice posited a gender consciousness in the classroom that was caught up in the ambiguity of corporeality and subjectivity. Yet, the possibility of Alice being a lesbian and Scott being gay was never discussed in the fifth-grade students' conversations during the production of the play. Issues related to homosexuality in general were discussed more often outside of the classroom during gym class and drama class when and where the students were also required to perform their sexuality as males and females through either dramatic stage acting or physical play in sport teams. In fact, one particular incident had occurred earlier in a drama class when the drama teacher reprimanded Alice for calling a male student a *fag*. Even though the class had dealt with homosexual name-calling in other classroom spaces, the issue of homosexuality did not come up during the production of the play itself. Furthermore, because of certain physical and psychological similarities present in both sexes at this stage of human development in the fifth grade, it was physically possible for students to play the role of the opposite sex with the aid of a clever disguise and lots of stage make-up.

However, the manner in which Alice portrayed a male character and the manner in which Scott portrayed a female character were culturally coded and inscribed so that they both were abstracting what it feels like being a man or woman in our structurally gendered society where there is a dominant heterosexual border placed between maleness and femaleness. The role of the mother and the princess were conventional female roles but the stereotypical representation of these two female characters in the text was never questioned or critiqued in their performance. Even though Scott reembodied the female body on stage and Alice reembodied the male body on stage, they both did not try to subvert the traditional imaging of gender. Instead, they consigned themselves to a sexually demarcated physicality in which they were unable to transcend their gendered embodiedness of femaleness and maleness. Scott made sure he presented a clearly defined female version of Mama while Alice made sure she presented a clearly defined male version of Jack. In turn, Alice and Scott's modalities of bodily comportment, motility and spatiality were characterized more by physiological origins of maleness and femaleness as opposed to social origins of gendered identity. In this way, the character of Jack and the mother were subordinated to corporeal parameters in which language, gesture and self-extension were subsumed in gendered codes and theatrical realism. Scott made sure he acted like a real woman, and Alice made sure she acted like a real man while playing their parts on stage. In turn, the performance of gender became solid and fixed so that the actor's body on stage was externally reified and objectified.

Even though Alice and Scott used their sense of agency to challenge gender norms by playing a character of a different gender, their portrayal of the character was not a critical reworking of constitutive gender norms. By staying within a highly gendered regulatory schema, both students' construction of the opposite gender was always in relation to the normative cultural construction of gender. Furthermore, their performance of the opposite gender on stage was also linked to the materiality of the body in which their costumes, movements and gestures were reflective of normative cultural constructs. There was never a critical discussion of the process by which a bodily norm is identified, assumed, appropriated and taken on by the choosing subject, such as Alice and Scott, who voluntarily constructed gender through their instrumental actions on stage. According to Judith Butler in *Bodies That Matter* (1993), gendering is a dual process in which speaking subjects such as Alice and Scott are both subjected to gender norms as well as subjectivating gender through their own sense of agency. Yet at the same time, it is necessary to keep in mind that the conditions of their gendered portrayal of the opposite sex emerged and operated in the context of a scripted play in which they were required to take on a gendered persona for a primarily theatrical performance. The moment Scott and Alice purport to represent the feminine and masculine their characterizations naturally displace the feminine/masculine and what remains is a specular figure of Mama and Jack.

Furthermore, since Jack was portrayed by both Jose and Alice, the presence of Jack's character was also caught up in ambiguity on stage due to the impossibility of corporeal self-possession and unity with one actor's body. Though both Alice and Jose managed the technical aspect of this character by wearing the same type of denim overalls with a white T-shirt underneath, baseball cap and sneakers, the body portrayed by Alice never coincided with the body played by Jose. This circular physicality of Alice as Jack and Jose as Jack never resulted in a rooted identity for the character of Jack. As Alice exited off stage after one act, there was a temporal gap before Jose entered on stage for the next act. The vanishing point when Alice exited and Jose entered became a moment of absence since the spectator perceived that Jack's lived body had disappeared. Nonetheless, the bifurcated mode-of-presence between Alice and Jose created a form of symmetry in which both actors had an equal number of acts in their portrayal of Jack's character and balanced each other in their separate pursuits.

In the earlier interview, Alice talked about making the body come to life, to give her body its full weight, dimension and its physical presence on stage as Jack. In order to construct a physical and sensory space filled with the presence of her body on stage, Alice constructed a fantasy space invested solely by the body as opposed to a theatrical space invested with language. Even though the body's living presence asserts a physiological irreducibility that challenges the stability of a female student representing a male character, Alice talked about bringing physiology under control and disciplining her body with the physical and emotional staging of a male character within the stage's exacting field. Moreover, throughout the school year, Alice was a student who often challenged gender norms through her words and actions, such as choosing to join the boys in the building of a human pyramid in the cheers episode. In the following field notes, Alice responded to a challenge posed by Jose and Julio about her gender identity:

Jose: Alice you act like a boy!
Julio: [You're like a boy!]
Alice: [She waits a few seconds before responding.] If you don't like me because I act like a boy, then that means you don't like yourself because you're a boy!

Furthermore, during the creative writing circle on Wednesday mornings, Alice often shared her stories relating to gender, which sometimes parodied the hyper-feminine female students in the dual immersion class such as Lisa who she named as the Valley Girls:

Alice: You know ... Valley Girls are people who use words like "like" and ... "whatever" ... "whatever" ... they go ... they walk around the mall [she puts her fingers in the air to motion she is putting the word "mall" in quotes] . . . and talk like Valley Girls . . . like some people in this class.

At one point in the study, Alice came up to me while I was taking field notes and said that she wanted to share her Barbie doll collection with me. When she returned with the plastic case of Barbie dolls, they all had their hair shaved, and Alice decided to exchange and combine body parts, as well as sew her own punk-rock clothes for the Barbie dolls.

Nevertheless, the cross-gender role-playing by Alice and Scott provided a stronger foundation for humor in *Jack, Su Mama, Y El Burro*. Even though the humor did not come from the cross-dressing itself, it did create a comic effect at the end of the play when Alice and Scott decided to reveal their *true* gendered identity. Humor and dramatic irony converged at the last moment of the play when the actors and actresses were taking their bows, and Alice removed her baseball hat to reveal her short curly blond hair and Scott removed his wig to reveal his short buzzed sandy hair. In the school's large auditorium, the audience, composed of all the dual immersion parents in the front rows and other PS 2000 monolingual classrooms in the back rows, laughed when it became aware of the fact that Alice was portraying a male and Scott was portraying a female. Their duplicitous intentions also brought about the observation that Scott and Alice were able to finesse their histrionic abilities and change from playing the role of one sex on stage to playing that of another at the moment when the play was completed. This moment of gender reconstruction can be also be seen as a gap and fissure that opened up instabilities in Alice and Scott's normative gender constructions during the earlier performance on stage. The final bow at the end of the play produced a moment of reconstituting possibility that had the power to undo the very effects by which the male and female sex was produced by Alice and Scott during the performance so that gender came undone through this final moment of gender reconstitution. The audience's reaction to this moment of revelation produced a gasp at first and then laughter, thus drawing a line between what was and was not constructed along gender lines in real space and in fantasy space (Butler, 1993).

After the completion of the play's final performances in May, photographs were posted on a classroom bulletin board from the play. There were two pictures of Scott in his drag costume: one showed him in the process of becoming a woman in which Yolanda was applying make-up to his face, and the other showed him fully disguised as a woman after his make-up and wig were fixed onto him. One day when the second grade dual immersion students came to Roberta's classroom to read Spanish books with their Reading Buddies, Scott began crying hysterically in the back of the room near where the photographs from the play were displayed. Roberta ran over to him when she heard him wailing from the other end of the classroom. Scott explained to her that the second-grade students were laughing at the pictures of him in drag. So as a result, Roberta went over to the bulletin board and removed both photographs. However, Scott walked toward her as she was in the process of removing the photos and stated that it was okay to keep the photo of him in full drag posted on the bulletin board. In turn, Scott was making a distinction between him becoming-a-woman versus being-a-woman on stage. His decision to remove the photo in which he was becoming-a-woman while Yolanda applied make-up to his face removed his fear of ridicule and cushioned the shocking impact of an apparent change in gender identity. Yet, he was psychologically prepared to accept the idea of him playing a woman on stage. Scott was comfortable being fully attired in female clothing but was not comfortable with the process of becoming a woman. At the same time, by weeping and displaying his hurt feelings in front of everybody in class, Scott was challenging gender norms for fifth-grade boys by becoming-less-masculine in front of all his peers, as well as the pervasive dichotomy between what is maleness and femaleness, and thus creating a vulnerable sense of oneness – he is biologically a boy, yet feels comfortable playing a fetishized older, nagging rural peasant Cuban woman on stage, but is unrepressed about weeping over the image of him becoming-a-woman.

Challenging Linguistic Borders and Boundaries

During the production of the play, English-dominant students, such as Alice, Scott and Mary, were learning how language and linguistic control function in the Spanish language. The dramatic performance in the play required Alice, Scott and Mary to come to terms with the Spanish language gradually by means of trial and error during rehearsals. Their occasional mistakes in Spanish production during the rehearsals illustrated the evolutionary nature of their transformation from not having spoken much Spanish in the beginning of the school year to being comfortable playing a Spanish-speaking character in the second semester. Yet, Scott's intonation and delivery in Spanish had a broken quality at times, which was questioned by his peers as well as by Roberta; his Spanish words were joined together but lacked the flow and cadence of a native Spanish-speaker and his/her unifying trajectories of normal speech. When Brian offered a suggestion regarding a correction in Scott's Spanish lines, Scott was offended and answered angrily, "Yes! I've heard it eight times!" At another point in the rehearsal process, Claudio noted that he could not understand whether Scott was saying either *"perro"* (dog) or *"pelo"* (hair). The physical effort Scott put into squeezing the Spanish words out was evident in his face during this linguistic struggle. However, by rejecting the phonocentric privileging of speech, Roberta allowed Scott to subvert language by overemphasizing his corporeal presence on stage as Jack's mother. In turn, Roberta gave equal status to dramaturgy, in which the actor's presence on stage (gestures, movements, mobility) is given equal status to the linguistic text. For example, instead of emphasizing whether Scott knows how to correctly pronounce *barrer* (to broom), she stated that it was much more important for Scott to grab the broom and act out a sweeping motion so the English-dominant audience understood what *barrer* means in Spanish through this action. Yet, the repetitive and reductive structure of Scott's dialogue gave him sufficient rehearsal time to overcome the obstacles of delivery in Spanish before the final performance date for an audience of parents, peers and administrators. Scott retained a link between the phonic qualities of Spanish and the embodied utterance so what he said in Spanish was given physiological reinforcement through his bodily actions.

Thus, one of the outstanding features of this bilingual play was the heightened degree of student participation from English-dominant students such as Scott, Alice and Mary. For the most part, there were key sections of Spanish dialogue in the play that the actors repeated frequently throughout the script. This repetition of dialogue in Afro-Cuban folktales was often deleted in Cuba in order to make concessions to the European reader. However, *Jack, Su Mama, Y El Burro* is a distinctly Cuban folktale that has been written for a bilingual audience, and it grabs the audience through its comedic play on repeated words. Yet, one of the concerns brought up by a few Spanish-dominant students was that the play did not have enough emphasis on real Spanish and that there needed to be an increased number of Spanish words in the play. The student teacher originally created the dramatic text by transcribing one section of an audiotape given to her by Roberta entitled *The Cuban Storyteller*. However, after the students read her transcript of *Jack, Su Mama, Y El Burro* from *The Cuban Storyteller*, Trisha began the production process with a brainstorming session in which the students offered suggestions as to how to produce the play and the different student groups that would need to be formed such as the costume, scenery and music groups. Some of the suggestions included adding more characters, bringing in a real dog, building a cardboard house for Jack and his mother, changing the ending of the play, adding in the part of the narrator, making Jack wear overalls and a baseball cap, and creating more real sound effects. However, in the middle of the brainstorming session, Claudio suggested that they add more Spanish into the original script after they had just listed the different student groups needed for the play:

Trisha: Eso es un folklorico ... eso es un folklorico Cubano ... y vamos a ... hacerlo en español y en inglés también. This is going to be a bilingual ... Cuban folktale ... so that our audience can appreciate en español pero también en inglés también. [Trisha is cupping her right hand and left hand together to show how the two languages are in sync with one another. Then she calls on Claudio who has his hand raised.]

Claudio: [He raises his hand.] But there are not many words in Spanish. I think we need to add more Spanish words.

Trisha: Que hay solamente algunas palabras o frases en español. Quisas Claudio ... podemos escribir más frases en español? Que piensas?

English translation:
[That there are only a few words and sentences and Spanish. Claudio thinks ... can we write more sentences in Spanish? What do you think?]

Claudio: [He nods his head up and down in agreement with Trisha.]

Trisha: [Trisha moves to the other side of the room and addresses the students there but in English.] Claudio is mentioning that maybe there are not enough lines in Spanish. *Es possible que podemos ... nuestra clas e ...* [Trisha moves her hand across as if she is writing in the air] *podemos añadir más lineas en español?* [Trisha moves her hand in a wave motion to show future time.] *Claro que sí ... claro que sí ...* [Other students raise their hands.] *Claro que sí Claudio. Buen idea.* [Trisha writes down his idea on the chart but can't figure out under what category she would place his idea.] *Voy a poner aqu í ... "Añadir más español."* [Trisha creates a new category on the chart paper and titles it *"Añadir más español"*. Then she turns around and solicits more student responses.] *Que más?*

English translation:
[Trisha moves to the other side of the room and addresses the students there but in English.] Claudio is mentioning that maybe there are not enough lines in Spanish. Is it possible ... that our class ... [Trisha moves her hand across as if she is writing in the air] can we add more

lines in Spanish? [Trisha moves her hand in a wave motion to show future time.] Of course yes . . . of course yes. [Other students raise their hands.] Of course Claudio. Good idea. [Trisha writes down his idea on the chart but can't figure out under what category she would place his idea.] Let's put over here . . . "Add more Spanish." [Trisha creates a new category on the chart paper and titles it "Add more Spanish". Then she turns around and solicits more student responses.] What else?

Julio: Trisha . . . Trisha . . . we need a farm . . . *una granja.*

After Claudio made his suggestion, Trisha stated that it was a wonderful idea and wrote it down on the brainstorming chart of suggestions, which was later hung up on the classroom wall. Even though Claudio did not have an acting part in the play, he had read the script carefully enough to realize that only few repetitive Spanish lines were dispersed throughout the script. Yet, when the class began the production of the play, Claudio's suggestion was never discussed further by either the students or the student teacher. The rehearsal process did not begin with a new script that included more Spanish dialogue; they resorted to the use of the original English-dominant script. However, during one of the dress rehearsals, Jose began to spontaneously add more Spanish lines into the play in order to further develop his character, Jack, and to lend a more realistic credence to the Cuban play. For example, instead of just saying *"los pesquitos"* (the little fish), he changed the line to *"los pesquitos bonitos"* (the pretty little fish) and subsequently added more inflection to his facial gestures when saying this new Spanish line. Also, during the scenes in which Jack receives compensation from the farmer for his labors, both Jose and Julio decided to add more Spanish into their dialogue. After they finished saying their newly improvised Spanish lines, Trisha replied angrily, "But it's all in Spanish! I think we need to add a little more English." The student teacher was the play's producer, and thus, she was adamant against Jose adding in more Spanish dialogue due to the fact that she wanted to stay true to the text and did not want to alienate the English-dominant audience of parents, peers and administrators.

For Trisha, the written script was a blueprint for the performance and was also a text that contained a specific discipline of the body, stage and eye. In its directions for the setting, speech and action, the dramatic text coordinates the elements of performance and puts them into play; when reading through this text, according to her, the student actors needed to seize these elements in specific relationships. By increasing the quantity of Spanish in the play, Trisha feared that Jose and Julio would overlook the quality of the Spanish that they were adding into the dialogue; the relation between what they were adding in Spanish to the existent English and Spanish dialogue; and the manner in which they were expressing their Spanish use (Grice, 1975). Furthermore, since the play was transferred over to the written form from the original audiotape by a white, upper-middle-class, female student teacher, who was fluent in Spanish, there was much more attention given to the rhythmic aspects of the bilingual dialogue as opposed to what the students wanted to signify from the dialogue and the possibility for making new meanings and expanding the characters.

Here the student actors' interpretations of the text intervened with the student teacher's authorial production of the play. The student teacher's analysis of the English-dominant dialogue and linguistic interaction in the play required her to recognize the primacy of the script in its original written form. For her, the script was both the text and the pre-text for the play's production and performance. Working from the realist tradition, Trisha approached the performance field through a formal scripting and with specific, a priori bodily configurations and perceptual orientations grounded in a traditional understanding of the dramatic text. However, when Jose and Julio enabled a more experientially intricate understanding of the text, they were seeking to disclose the richness of phenomenal variables such as the Spanish dialogue by reembodying the text and drawing out their Hispanic characters even further by adding more Spanish words.

By moving beyond the teleological point of realization in the play's script when the student teacher originally transcribed the audiotape onto paper, the two Spanish-dominant, Hispanic male students created an intrinsic component to the original dramatic text by seeing it differently and through their insights as native Spanish speakers, perhaps questioning Trisha's over-Anglicized scripted characterization of Hispanic protagonists.

However, since Roberta was the *real* classroom teacher in the eyes of both the students and Trisha, the student teacher, Roberta challenged Trisha's reservations against increased Spanish dialogue and gave Jose and Julio power to create more authentic Cuban protagonists through their own indigenous use of Spanish and their portrayal of Hispanic characterizations. By mediating the discursive borders between Spanish and English in the production process, Roberta was able to ignore the gaze of the English-dominant audience and instead reinforced a more realistic depiction of the Cuban characters by allowing Jose and Julio to creatively play with form and technique, gain expressive and emotional force through distortion and stylization, and in turn, use their sense of performative freedom to change the law of proportion between Spanish and

English. There were two intertwined processes developing in the early stages of the play's production: Trisha sought to follow the script's original dialogue but Roberta wanted to develop the script much more loosely by allowing students to interpret it for themselves. Furthermore, in addition to adding in more Spanish into the original script, Roberta was also adamant about making sure the narrator introduced the play in both Spanish and English: "*Para nuestra obra ponen todo en dos idiomas . . . no solamente en inglés . . . es un folklorico Cubano*" ("For our play put everything in the two languages . . . not just in English . . . it is a Cuban folklore"). Even though these two processes of production were at odds with one another, Trisha eventually revised the script and the tension between these processes soon receded since Roberta possessed greater teacher authority.

As the student actors read and reread the script during the rehearsal process, they were searching for a better way to approach the bilingual text's reading and its performance. Soon, the students found new ways of reading the script, ways that moved away from the use of Spanish in the past and toward the use of Spanish in the present. By allowing students the possibility of revising the ways they present the text, Roberta allowed the play to move away from a synchronic, systematic frame of language and closer to a diachronic, daily trajectory of language (Saussure, 1965). For example, when Jose added more lines in Spanish and increased the amount of Spanish dialogue between his character and Julio's character, he felt that it was absolutely necessary to eliminate the archaic elements of Spanish in the original text. He wanted to achieve a modernization by adding in new ways of speaking Spanish. Thus, Jose was appropriating the production of Spanish in the play and rewriting his character so he appeared as a modern figure and not a primitive figure.

The kind of space produced on the rug area during rehearsal time also allowed actors such as Jose and Julio to play with language in the script and to play with their characters because there was a heightened degree of fluidness and freedom during rehearsals. During rehearsal time, there was a cacophony of student voices as the actors rehearsed their parts, as the scenery crew hammered and painted, as the costume group played with make-up and wigs, and as the teachers were busy walking around and making sure each group was on task in the different spaces of the classroom and hallway. The following field notes highlight how the rehearsals gave the students both space and time to change and shape the form of the play as they discussed the nature of its production:

Trisha is going through a dress rehearsal with the actors. Jose and Julio are improvising their lines in Spanish. At 10:30 am, the classroom is abuzz with a cacophony of noises. The different student groups are all walking around the classroom and working on their part of the play. "I made up the line," says Julio when he adds the word "hot" in Spanish to the word "cider." Then Jose goes off track and starts joking around with the animal actors instead of focusing on his dialogue with Julio. "I looked at his udders!" screams Jose as he plays jokingly with Brian who "moos" back to him. Julio now gets tired of waiting for Jose and doesn't put as much enthusiasm in his dialogue. "You've got to have presence," says Roberta to Julio when she walks by the actor area on the rug space. At 11:00 the whole class came together at the rug area to discuss last-minute concerns with the play. Joshua says his group has finished the drawings. Shakima and Yolanda say their group has figured out the music for the initial scenes. Shakima says she will use the drums for sound effects when Jack drops the coin in the water. Then Alicia asks if they should have music for the mother's "*arroz*" (rice) lines. Roberta says that the refrain, "*arroz, arroz, nos gustamos comer arroz*," is a famous refrain from a children's song. "For anybody who is Latino, who was brought up in that culture, that melody hits home," says Roberta. I was afraid that the predominantly non-Latino audience would not know this refrain.

Furthermore, Roberta's decision to allow for more Spanish dialogue was a characteristic turn in the scripting of the play and she continued to play an important role in the later stages of the play's development. The archaic mode of Spanish dialogue within the original script was soon eliminated due to the students' desires for more modern colloquial Spanish in the play. In attempting to give his character a more positive role within the play, Jose reworked his Spanish dialogue into modern ways of speaking Spanish. Yet, even though more colloquial Spanish was integrated into the script, the core of the illogical primitive subject was still kept in place. Nobody ever questioned why Jack was characterized as a buffoon and why his use of archaic Spanish words and intonations helped characterize him as an unintelligent Afro-Cuban peasant.

When Jose and Julio pointed out the need to change the Spanish in the play to a modern-day vernacular Spanish, they were also pointing out the gap between the *uttering self* as a character on stage and the actor's *I of utterance* by separating themselves as the speaking subject from the character in the play (Garner, 1992: 130). Their radical changing of the script alluded to the fact that the character's delivery of Spanish seemed unnatural to them and did not mark the speaking subject well because the Spanish dialogue seemed to float free of deictic connection to themselves as the speaking Hispanic male subject. Therefore, it was not geared toward a pragmatic spatio-temporal use of Spanish. Yet, by adding in new Spanish dialogue situated in the temporal dimension of the present, Jose and Julio created a temporal ambiguity in the play because the narrative slipped from Spanish that was used in the past to Spanish that was used in the present. For example, Jose changed the line *"Agarra con una cosita"* ("Grab it with something") to *"Agarra con un cordon"* to ("Grab it with a piece of rope"). However, in his next line, he kept the original Spanish words, thus moving sporadically from a more colloquial use of Spanish to an antiquated use of Spanish. This effect was compounded by the fact that it was only Jose and Julio who were shifting into the Spanish present while all the other actors remained rooted in the original text. On the other hand, the English-dominant students were not comfortable transforming the scripted dialogue in the play and did not reinvent the scripted dialogue nor use the Spanish language to create new dialogue. Thus, it was only Jose and Julio who foregrounded the linguistic attributes of the bilingual Cuban characters and took ownership of the Spanish dialogue, meanwhile, Alice and Scott foregrounded the actor's corporeality through their gendered subjectivity. Yet, even though Alice and Scott disguised their gender through an affected style, it was much more difficult for them to disguise their English-dominant linguistic identities. Subsequently, when Jose and Julio added in more Spanish, they often alienated the other English-dominant actors such as Alice and Scott who did not attempt to add in more Spanish lines, even though their characters were subsequently affected by Jose and Julio's Spanish improvisations:

Jose: "Ese es peligroso" [Jose added in this new line.]
Scott: What does that mean? [Scott looks puzzled.]
Jose: It means that it's dangerous.
Scott: Okay.

Rehearsing on the Rug: A Possible Third Space

Many of the linguistic changes that Jose and Julio brought about to the play's performance were proposed and discussed at length during the rehearsal process, which took place predominantly on the rug area or *alfombra*. The rehearsal process, unlike the final performance, was a trial-and-error process in which the actors were seeking to find the best way to perform. This process can also be defined as a quasi-personal performance because the audience is lacking, and the actors themselves become the imagined audience. The labors of an actor come through in the rehearsal process and come to comprise the production process itself. The rehearsal process also allows actors to scrutinize themselves and their co-presence by providing the alternative time needed to apply an aesthetic frame to the production process. During the rehearsals, the actors become much more aware of what they were saying and how they were saying it so that their reflexivity included awareness that the aesthetics of their performance will count significantly as well. The playing space of rehearsal time, in turn, established an aesthetic frame in which the structural properties of the production process, such as the dialogue in the script, opened themselves up for questioning as the student actors played and experimented with their words and actions, trying to create something new and different.

While working within the rehearsal space every Tuesday and Thursday morning, the rug area became a dwelling in which the student actors were able to affirm their differences, speak from the diverse locations of their own histories, and strive to engage their desires through creative expressions (de Certeau, 1984). An improvisational, uninhibited process, based on human instincts and the ability to act out ideas and play with ideas, characterized the rehearsal space in which the student actors improvised their actions and dialogues. During the last two months before the final performance, the student actors explored, developed, expressed and communicated ideas about their characters through dramatic enactment. In turn, the students made the rehearsal space their own in which they were able to play with dialogue, sound, symbol and movement. The rehearsal space also offered the students the possibility of transgressing over sociolinguistic borders using their voices to challenge how the Spanish language was structured in the play and how gender was to be performed on stage. In some ways, the rehearsal space can be seen as a third space that opened up multiple possibilities for the hybridization of language, gender and race. The rehearsal space created an opening for transformation that allowed the students to move beyond the technical aspects of the play's production and toward an awareness of the deeper dimensions of linguistic equality and equity. Real and fictional arenas came together in the rehearsal space so that students were able to voice the inequalities and conflicts between Spanish and English, for example, through their metalinguistic discussions of the play's fixed English-dominant script.

The fluid and unstructured rehearsal space also allowed for the possibility of metalinguistic conflicts to occur. The rehearsal process that took place on the *alfombra* allowed the dual immersion students to resignify the confining limits placed on the investment of the Spanish language. Within the framing of the rehearsal space, the students were mobilized enough to offer a counter discourse that dialectically restored the marginalized Spanish language within this dual immersion classroom. In turn, the rehearsal space became a *third space* for the dual immersion students because the third space is where subjects call into question the hegemonic force of that very regulatory schema (Bhabha, 1994). The disidentification of the play's script as a text that promoted equality between the two languages was needed to question the regulatory norms of language in this dual immersion classroom and equally crucial to the rearticulation of democratic contestation within the open, fluid rug area.

While the fixity of structuralism divides and bounds Spanish and English by virtue of their dyadic differentiation within the dual immersion matrix, the third space opens up discursive possibilities through the constitutive *outside* of hegemonic positions. Both Jose and Julio's positions, for example, were voiced outside of the logic behind an English-dominant framework underlining this dual immersion classroom. The constrained appropriation of the Spanish language within the play's production process opened up linguistic possibilities through student agency. Instead of identifying with the normative demands for English, the students decided to craft a different signification of what the play's production process constituted for them as Spanish-dominant students who were subjected to the pressures of an English-dominant ideology in the original script. Yet, the pressure to conform to an English-dominant ideology did not foreclose the possibility of agency, furthermore, the students used their voiced agency, even if it meant that they would be situated in opposition to the power and authority of the student teacher, Trisha.

When the vector of power endemic to English overshadows the Spanish language, then it is inevitable that this English dominance will become vulnerable to criticism, by both English-dominant and Spanish-dominant students, when it ignores or devalues the Spanish language, since its own structured construction depends on the Spanish language for its binary framework. The hegemony of the English language in dual immersion classrooms often initiates a set of criticisms from multiple perspectives that can also call into question the premises underlining dual immersion programs. The interarticulations of power between the two languages and the destabilization of the structural stasis of the English-dominant norm deflect and expose the unequal production of the Spanish language. Nonetheless, by including more Spanish in the play, the dual immersion classroom acted differently during the performance of the play in comparison to their performance of the cheers in the previous chapter.

For example, in the performance of the play it seemed as if the dual immersion students were reversing the gaze of the English-dominant audience, consisting of parents, peers and administrators, by not being controlled by the necessity to perform predominantly in English. By subverting this linguistic objectification, it was as if the dual immersion classroom raised its head and fixed the English-dominant audience in a stare and asserted a linguistic subjectivity that reversed the assertion of a spectatorial power as found in the production of the cheers.

On the day of the actual performance, even though the English-dominant audience of parents, peers and administrators did not entirely comprehend the Spanish dialogue, they did not render themselves invisible either and were able to pick up on the physical cues of the actor's corporeality and laughed in all the right places. The audience's response was overwhelmingly positive, and they cheered and clapped at the end of the performance, even though they might not have understood it in its entirety. Once again, in comparison to the production of the cheers, the gaze of the audience was reciprocal. However, the power shifted from the spectatorial gaze of the English-dominant audience to the Spanish-dominant production of the play, thus the dual immersion classroom was able to reclaim itself from the earlier cheer spectacle. Alice and Scott also confronted the audience's gaze through their gendered bodies, just as Julio and Jose confronted the audience's gaze through their use of greater amounts of Spanish: "The reverse gaze catches me in the act of looking, challenging the *ecstasis* by which I 'surpass' my corporeal boundaries through the outer-directness of vision" (Garner, 1992: 50).

Nevertheless, when Jose and Julio took linguistic flight by changing lines and using the Spanish vernacular, they were still paradoxically rooted in the same place, rural Cuba *circa* 1900, and could not escape from it. Even though Roberta was willing to allow students to create new dialogue in Spanish, the spatio-temporal structures of language in the play still reflected the structures of an antiquated perceptual space of Cuba as defined by the scenery on stage. The realism of rural Cuba *circa* 1900 resisted the autonomy of the students' spoken word and their demands of verbal verisimilitude by still orienting the characters and the scenery to the physical surroundings of the past, thus compressing the space on stage into the space of the narrative. Changing the Spanish dialogue from the past to the present, from there to here, the students were challenging the fixed tableau of an antiquated Cuba, which nonetheless never moved and never changed. *Here* existed as a discursive manifestation that the students felt was subject to correction and semantic reinvestment, but this *here* also reflected conflicting modes of scenic presence on stage. But in the field of performance, at the moment of living the text, the stage became an inhabited space, articulated by the actors' bodies and their relationships to each other and to the objects on stage. Thus, even though the play's setting was moored in an antiquated spatio-temporal world, the discursive space of words and actions attempted to reconfigure the autonomous *mis-en-scène*. Jose and Julio were engaged in reconfiguring the play through an improvised vernacular speech that eclipsed the material past setting of the play, and thus, reasserted the presence of the Spanish language throughout the production of the bilingual Cuban play, regardless that the primitive landscape did not change.

Cuba: An Imagined Space of Spanish Colonialism

Spatiality in the performance of a play can be defined as the enacting relationship between the actual field of vision created on stage and the field of vision perceived by the human audience. Under the spectator's gaze, the actor's presence actualizes the dramatic text into a space of performance. The spectator, actor and character together seek to situate themselves in relation to the non-Cartesian theatrical space, both real and make-believe, which surrounds them. On the one hand, the stage creates a scenic space that is objectified by the spectator's perceiving eye as a field of vision. At the same time, this same field of vision is subjectified by the physical actors who inhabit the scenic space but in a situated place on stage. Furthermore, the theatrical space in the production of *Jack, Su Mama, Y El Burro* also became an *orientated space* when its stage was situated in terms of objective variables such as frontality, angle, depth, point of actual perception and the laws of visual dynamics so that a border was placed between the illusionary world on stage and the real space of the spectator (Garner, 1992). However, the objective dimensions of the theatrical space are also constituted by possible subjective variables in the play's production such as the setting, costumes, the actor's body, props, sounds and lighting. The objective and the subjective thus intertwine themselves on stage.

Furthermore, in the production of *Jack, Su Mama, Y El Burro*, the dual immersion students in the scenery, costume and music production groups were able to reproduce an objectified backdrop of native tropicalism through a fusion of animal, human and plant forms that visualized the everyday scenery in the play from the naive peasant subjectivity of Jack, the Cuban buffoon. Most of the female students were in charge of the costumes, and they used everyday materials such as cotton balls and string, along with papier-mâché material, to design the animal costumes for the *burro* and the dogs as well as the costumes for the main charac-ters. Many of the minority students, such as Yolanda, Shakima, Javier and Alicia, worked with their music teacher, Michael, to create the orchestra music for the play. Since they also performed in the afterschool percus-sion music program, the mostly Spanish-speaking Puerto Rican and Dominican students used several different kinds of percussion drums to recreate the Afro-Cuban tribal music of Cuba as well as the sound effects of Jack's mishaps. The scenery production group of dual immersion students, consisting of all English-dominant students, established a sense of *Cubanness* by objectively coding the scenery in the play as distinctly Cuban through several thematic and formal procedures: emblematic plants such as mango trees; oblique perspectives on the painted scenery screens that offered impressive images of the green land; the thatched huts on the horizon; and the endless blue sky.

The scenery was a significant element in coding the premodern past in a much subtler way than the play's language. Similar to Rousseau's idealized state of nature and his noble savage Emile (1979), a remote exotic landscape was recreated in *Jack, Su Mama, Y El Burro* as the dual immersion students constructed the actual physical setting of the play. They fashioned orange balloons to green papier-mâché trees to depict the mango groves of Cuba. They painted bucolic, butcher paper screens to depict the rural backdrop of the folk play. And they displayed cultural artifacts, such as woven straw baskets and a wooden plank bridge, on the actual stage to recreate and revive an authentic primitivism that was more spontaneous and intuitive in its creation than the student teacher and teacher had ever imagined.

The final setting for the play was framed in a pastoral tableau in which the stage was conceived with pictorial precision by the select group of English-dominant scenery students and their art teacher. This scenery group decided to paint three screens to spatially conceptualize the back-drop for three different locales in the Cuban play: one panel depicted Jack's cottage in the rural countryside; another depicted the farmer's land covered in tree groves; and the third panel depicted the daughter's window set inside the factory owner's mansion. These three scenic panels created a framing device to heighten the appearance of a pastoral tableau through its material icons; however, the framing device also marked the stage with indexical references that oscillated between the rural poverty of Cuban *paesanos* (peasants) and the bourgeoisie reign of factory and land owners. The three square screens were also mobile since the students placed wheels underneath each painted screen, which was framed by a wooden panel. This mobile setting, which evoked rural Cuba *circa* 1900, also integrated a sceno-graphic setting in which real objects placed in front of the painted screen, such as a wooden basket full of mangoes, established a contrast between its own reality and the objects that are drawn from it. By establishing this stylistic juxtaposition, the students were working toward particularizing the play through a physical materiality that closely justified its historical/geographical details. These movable props privileged certain nodal points in the scenic field, such as the authentic life-size wooden bridge dividing Jacks' rural poverty from the landowner and the factory owner's wealth. At the same time, they asserted a powerful opaque materiality common to folk drama in which the setting becomes naturalized as the primitive. Scenic naturalism and verisimilitude were championed in folk drama in order to make the stage not simply stand in for reality but become it, yet at the same time, there is also the potential for its own subversion.

For example, in the play, there was a passage from the mother's house to the farmer's house where Jack went to work, however, in order to get to the farm, Jack had to cross a bridge every day. The wooden bridge functioned as a border between the poverty-stricken boundary where Jack lived with his mother and the farm where the landowner oversaw the production of food commodities. Notions of identity were developed here between the people and the land and between power and property. Jack dwelled on the threshold between two bounded spaces of unequal wealth and thus functioned as a mediator between the peasant and the landowner; he was able to cross borders and transgress over class-based boundaries as he moved back and forth between the two scenes. The frontier space between Jack's dwelling and the landowner's farm created an openness and situated itself in a paradoxical place where the peasant and the landowner interacted, even though they were aware of their Otherness due to differences in class and social status. However, as Jack traversed from one place to another, living a kind of *border existence*, he was caught up in comedic situations that caused him to somehow loose the commodity that he had earned from that day's labor (Huerta, 1999). Thus, as he was traversing from one bounded space to another, he nonetheless returned to the space of rural poverty in the end without the rewards of his labor that he earned on the other side of the border, where he negotiated his worth with the land and factory owners.

Furthermore, *Jack, Su Mama, Y El Burro* created a picturesque setting of Jack's borderline existence that was framed through the constant movement of Jack's in-between scenarios and through the means of a road that wound through the local town starting from Jack's own rural home to the landowner's farm. The *chronotope of the road* returned again toward the end of the play when Jack had a random encounter on the road with the factory owner's daughter who turned from her window to look at Jack and then intersected with Jack's life by chance at that particular spatial and temporal point (Bakhtin, 1981). The factory owner's daughter and Jack would have normally been kept apart by class-based differences and spatial distance but here they met *on the road* by accident. Their lives and destinies collided with each other and within a particular moment that collapsed the social distance between them. For Jack, the road was a point of departure from his rural dwelling, and it was also a place for events to unravel. Time flowed along the road that Jack took from his home to his work. It was only in the denouement that events governed by chance replaced the cyclical time of the folkloric everyday and the familiar territory of Jack's rural dwelling was replaced by the fantasy space of rich factory owners and mango groves. In the end, the play had a capacity for transformation because it was Jack who went back to his rural, poverty-stricken dwelling with a large sum of money from the factory owner. The gradations of social hierarchy were evident in this chance encounter on the road and were made concrete when the factory owner offered Jack a large sum of money for making his daughter laugh, which may have seemed petty for such a large financial amount. Yet, the four bags of gold also represented a fetish desire for capital consumption since even Jack fell into the trap of fetishizing the gold money that he received for his comic buffoonery.

Conclusion: From Fantasy Space to Real Space and the In-Between

Theatrical space allows for the possibility of illusion so things in reality are not what they seem to be. The elements of performance create a make-believe world that supplants the present real world of the classroom and thus allows students to travel and imagine a world outside of their everyday classroom reality. Furthermore, the entire field of performance is subject to a mimetic play in which everything is always other than what it is and each object and subject is caught up in a play of Otherness in which they become something or someone other than themselves. In turn, the theatrical space of performance infuses a space of alterity that seeks to displace the actuality of everyday life in the classroom reality by producing a fantasy space distinctly different from real space.

Yet, at the same time, the border between the fantasy space and the real space is by nature produced by binary operations that exclude what constitutes the imaginary from what constitutes the real so the fantasy world never crosses over into the real world and the real world never crosses into the fantasy world. For example, the students questioned the lack of Spanish in the play's production but never stepped outside of the fantasy space of the play's production to question the real modes of bilingualism in the actuality of everyday life within their own classroom. Even though the imaginary form of the play and its script allowed the students to talk about the displacement of the Spanish language in the dramatic text, the students never made a connection between the unequal proportions of Spanish in their staged simulation of bilingualism within the fantasy space of the play and the unequal proportions of Spanish within the real space of their actual classroom. Thus, there was no in-between space produced that allowed metalinguistic discussions related to the marginalization of Spanish text in the play's script to transgress beyond metaphysical frontiers and subsequently move toward a grander metalinguistic discussion of the marginalization of Spanish within the everyday life of their own larger classroom context.

However, two student actors, Jose and Julio, did employ the Spanish language to create new possibilities in the play. By consciously adding in distinct vocabulary words that contrasted with the written discourse but were in sync with the play's motifs, both Jose and Julio were exposing the dilemmas concerning who has the control, power and authority in the production of a class play. The link between linguistic convention and social hierarchies between students and teachers came into play when Jose and Julio foregrounded language through metalinguistic discussions in which they became conscious of their own characterization in the play. They commented on specific dialogue in the play and proposed the possibility of transforming their characters through a self-conscious manner. The production of the play reached a moment of threshold, defined by Bakhtin (1981) as a metaphorical breaking point caused by a crisis or break in sequence, when Jose and Julio made a decision to change the lines in the play so they were no longer anachronistic. They became creators in the production process and moved freely in their own time; they also violated the objective course of the play by creating a sharp distinction between representing language in their present time and represented time in the original lines. Thus, the power of language to constitute the imaginary space was the focus of attention as the student teacher, students, and Roberta struggled over how the scripted text should be actualized, produced and performed on stage. Nonetheless, the theatrical mode of fictional presence remained separated from the experiential actuality of the classroom because students never transgressed over the boundary between *what if we added more Spanish to the dramatic text* and *what if we added more Spanish in the classroom's everyday language text.* Even though it was a given that the play's production was fueled by the presence of a difference between the Spanish and English languages and the absence of equal numbers of Spanish dialogue, this linguistic inequality never manifested itself and disclosed itself even further in the students' mode of address during the everyday classroom discourse.

Nevertheless, since the hierarchy produced between the two languages in the play's production was challenged and contested, especially in relation to what was excluded along the borderlands, the events examined in this drama chapter did eventually produce a *third space* in the linguistic borderland between Spanish and English. If the third space is defined here as a site constituted by metalanguage's appearance and the revelation of the dual immersion classroom's contradictions and where it needs to improve – then Julio and Jose's use of metalanguage can be read as a manifestation of the third space. In these sites of metalanguage, the "I" abandons the self to the Spanish Other in the mirror, saying we are here as a dual immersion class, let us look at each other in terms of language and culture, let us get to know each other, and let us resolve our faults and meet our needs and desires. Claudio originally pointed out the lack of Spanish in the script during the brainstorming session and first opened up a desiring space for the Spanish Other. During the daily dress rehearsals, Julio and Jose also used metalanguage to show resistance and struggle toward linguistic borders and boundaries; however, they also knew that it was necessary to keep on moving with the rehearsals in order for the metalinguistic discussions to not fall into pieces. In this sense, the metaphor of the third space can be located when and where the dual immersion students addressed the troubling lack of Spanish in the production of the bilingual play. However, their contestations, disruptions and radical rearticulations did not necessarily lead to the restructuring of borders in their everyday classroom reality.

By nature, binary operations are formulated through the exclusion of disruptive possibilities that can be opened up by a third space. The erasure and exclusion of the Spanish language from that binary gave back a false, contradictory and specular reflection of the dual immersion program. The exclusion of Spanish thus haunted the boundary between the two languages as an internal ghost of sorts, and for some subjects such as Claudio, this loss became a source of unsatisfied desire. The displacement of Spanish can be traced through its sense of loss and the students' subsequent mobilizations to recover the Spanish language within the third space. The desire to return to that originary moment of Spanish equilibrium was also a desire to reconstitute the dual immersion mode of signifying equality between Spanish and English. Acts of differentiation and separation of the two languages motivated the students to refuse the loss of one language over the other and subsequently to return to an idealized sociolinguistic hybridity – the third space.

Yet, even though the teacher allowed the possibility of students being reflective and critical about the marginalization of the Spanish language, their inquiries never went beyond the content of the play in order to examine the underlining characterizations and depictions of social class, cultural background and cultural biases in the play. Even though the students were encouraged to be analytical, not enough time was allotted to be truly reflective and to grasp the contradictions in the characteriza-tion of the play's main protagonists, especially in terms of race and ethnicity, and to grasp the wider social and political undercurrents at work in the play. The subtle and hidden oppression within Spanish folk dramas such as *Jack, Su Mama, Y El Burro* often go undetected and remain repressed unless time and space are provided for students to critically analyze the historical and cultural context of the script and realize what was hidden in the cultural codes that they were reproducing and performing on stage.

In turn, it is worth noting that the dual immersion classroom never explored the various aspects of folk primitivism in either the book *Juan Bobo* or the play, *Jack, Su Mama, Y El Burro*, especially from a critical post-colonial perspective and through critical inquiry. A critical postcolonial perspective can be defined as the voicing of a subversive discourse within the dominant colonial culture; furthermore, Spivak (1990: 69) advocates the catachrestic strategy of *reversing, displacing and seizing the apparatus of value-coding* found in colonial discourse in order to bring about a post-colonial critique. A critical discussion during a class meeting regarding how the character of Jack was portrayed in the play or how Jose was named Juan Bobo could have triggered a critical consciousness of how such texts are situated in the context of race and ethnicity and how these texts code values regarding race and ethnicity. However, both *Juan Bobo* and *Jack, Su Mama, Y El Burro* were organized dominantly by aesthetics and thus the representation of ethnic identity in the two protagonists was never questioned through a catachrestic strategy of reversing the values codes associated with these two primitive protagonists. In turn, the performance of *Jack, Su Mama, Y El Burro* can be posited as the *returning gaze of the colonized* since it reappropriates the colonial identity by laying claim to the cultural origins of primitivism and upholding images of the native as both primitive savage and rustic idealist (Camayd-Freixas & Gonzalez, 2000). Overall, the cultural production of *Jack, Su Mama,*

Y El Burro in this dual immersion classroom did not make any political statements and changes against the colonial depiction of its Afro-Cuban protagonists. Instead, its main objective was to reproduce the folk aesthetic in its public performance rather than present a radical post-colonial performance.

Since the play utilizes a folk aesthetic, it is important to note that the performance of folk dramas, such as *Jack, Su Mama, Y El Burro*, follows strict rituals and formal behavior encoded in the liturgical order: (1) folk drama is often performed in an open space such as a public square or street; (2) folk drama involves a direct address done in a declamatory style in which the actor talks with the audience; (3) folk drama does not allow for intimacy between characters; (4) the folk characters are without exception stereotypical; and (5) the language and movement on stage is often ideographic so that it becomes heightened (Tillis, 1998). *Jack, Su Mama, Y El Burro* aligns itself most clearly with the ritualized aesthetics of Afro-Cuban folk theatre and makes no proclamations about postcolonial political projects. While the characters on the whole are stereotypical in *Jack, Su Mama, Y El Burro*, these stereotypes are very much rooted in the daily life of the local peasant culture, and thus, would seem conventional to a Cuban audience.

By its very nature, folk plays do not consciously show a conflict between individuals or social groups such as the landowners and the landless. In folk plays, the actors are not active, motive powers of their fate. Thus, the content of folk plays takes plots from everyday life and imitates the satirical, peculiar and funny characterizations of the folk peasantry and its topical humor. They are performed within the frame-work of folk customs and are in stark disagreement with social dramas that challenge stereotypes and position characters in conflict-ridden scenarios. The folk play's reliance on the idea of tradition is problematic when seen through a political lens; tradition becomes a criteria for constraining and modifying aesthetic formulas in the production and performance of folk plays. In turn, ritual plays like *Jack, Su Mama, Y El Burro* can never serve as a premise for the analysis of Otherness and as a subject of the analysis of Otherness. A redefinition of the folk would entail changing the long-standing ritual equations of what the folk equals to in ritual performance. The content of the folk would have to move away from what is already foreknown to the audience to perhaps what is untraditional in the folk, such as the notion of a postcolonial subject who reverses the colonial order.

Folk plays thus speak in terms of prescriptive and fixed behaviors as opposed to invariance and improvisation, which on the other hand, explicitly recognize the spontaneity of the actors and characters on stage to change any scripted stereotypes. Ritual-like performances in folk plays also entail a lack of critical awareness by the actors of what one is doing and saying on stage. Furthermore, in this type of performance, the ritual of peasant life is enacted within a frame of make-believe and fantasy. There is no expectation on the part of the performers or the audience that any action or creative expression from an individual or group agency will result in changes of outside reality. Yet, can the criteria of tradition become unmoored from the production of a folk play and still remain distinctly a folk play? What essentially constitutes a sense of the folk in its performance? Do the student actors have to accept whatever is encoded in the canons of the liturgical order that they are performing on stage for a specific school audience?

The critical examination of *Jack, Su Mama, Y El Burro* is an artistic presentation needed to get behind the piece itself. However, as John Dewey stated in *Art as Experience* (1934), artistic productions are often isolated from the human conditions that produce them and thus often work against critical pedagogy because they do not always allow for the critical investigation of the sensitivities, tastes and aesthetics that produced them originally. Style also can subsume any deviation from the status quo so that the aesthetic production of a class play overlooks the political message hidden within its text and context. It is rare for students to probe the layered meanings within an artistic production, such as the production of the class cheers and the production of the bilingual play, due to faithfulness to aesthetics. However, critical pedagogy advocates examining the historical and subjective origins of a work of art and asks whether there is the possibility of imagining and creating other aesthetic productions (McLaren, 1997).

Thus, the aesthetic production of class plays and other spectacles such as class cheers needs to be examined in relation to its underlying ideologies. This relationship between aesthetics and ideology must be seen as a dialectical relationship in order for us to probe what lies beneath the production, performance, consumption and representation of aesthetics. The beliefs and values embedded within aesthetic productions need to be critiqued further in order to realize how they are governed by dominant ideologies such as the racist ideology governing the speech and behavior of primitive protagonists such as Juan Bobo and Jack. The values, beliefs and relationships depicted in *Jack, Su Mama, Y El Burro* need to be specifically questioned by bilingual educators, especially in observing how cultures such as the Afro-Hispanic culture are being affirmed or ridiculed in the production and performance of a bilingual play or book.

For example, at the end of *Jack, Su Mama, Y El Burro*, the contradictions related to race, class and gender are never addressed or resolved because of the spurious harmony produced in the ending when the main protagonist does not protest the poverty and injustice he experiences. Instead, he takes the bags of gold offered to him by the rich factory owner.

Furthermore, the dominant ideologies of race, class and gender that go into producing the fictional reality of a class play need to be interrogated in order to determine how these dominant ideologies affect the students' everyday life inside and outside the classroom. Drama must go beyond the traditional space of predictable performance and must point to the possibility of questioning the status quo outside of the fantasy space (Pinar, 1976). A critical aesthetic pedagogy thus allows one to examine the concepts of cultural production and reproduction within aesthetics and education and in relation to dominant ideologies (Greene, 1978). Moreover, critical pedagogy enables students to empower themselves and transform their social reality through processes such as a play production so students realize that scripts are not neutral and value-free.

In order to assert their sense of agency, students must play a large part in the pedagogical process of determining what form and function the play will eventually take on during its performance. By positioning students as critical agents rather than as actors or performers, students will more likely be engaged in critical acts of cultural production such as reversing the binary between the Spanish and English languages and rewriting the scripted text to address issues related to how race, class and gender are portrayed. Furthermore, in order to create a culture of self-reflection in the classroom, it is important to develop a pedagogy of drama that reveals what interests the roles serve in *Jack, Su Mama, Y El Burro*, how they become institutionalized, how they are historically constructed, and how they can be resisted, undone and rethought outside of the binaries that define them within the structures of inequality and oppression, such as modern America and premodern Cuba and rational Americans and irrational Afro-Hispanics.

In conclusion, the class production of *Jack, Su Mama, Y El Burro* enacted scenes in which the relationship between race identity, history and power was never problematized, unlike language and gender. The aesthetic principles guiding the production of the play did not open up the possibility of a critical, political and emancipatory aesthetic that offers an opportunity for students to employ the categories of voice, difference and community in order to interrogate their scripted roles. The wider configurations and discussions of ideology and power need to be integrated within a critical pedagogy of drama, the aesthetics of cultural production and the politics of performance so that the hidden ideologies within the text and context of the performance are revealed. In doing so, an ethnical discourse can develop to inform how a bilingual play is being produced and performed by the classroom subjects, how identity is constructed in relation to both real and fictional subjects, such as how Jack, Mama, the landowner and the factory owner are being performed in relation to cultural domination, power and agency. In the next chapter, we will examine a weekly Spanish music program that was integrated into the dual immersion classroom. We will see how once again hidden ideologies manifest themselves in the cultural production of Spanish folk music and how when the students performed the Spanish folk music they were in turn reproducing these hidden ideologies of race, class and gender, even though they were learning the Spanish language through music and coming more closer to their Spanish Self than ever before.

Chapter 5

The Flow and Movement of Music: Appropriating the Third Space

A Brief History of Music Education: A Struggle between Structure and the Sublime

In the classical and medieval periods of European history, music education was instituted as a branch of science and mathematics. The ancient Greek scholars strongly felt that the work of musicians was the work of mathematicians due to the fact that both disciplines are grounded in the conceptual themes of multitude and extension, quantity and size, as well as both disciplines possessing powers of ethical character development derived from their abilities to purify the soul. Thus, music was taught after geometry and arithmetic so students could apply their mathematical understandings to both vocal and instrumental musical practice (Hatch & Bernstein, 1993). Ratios, integers, proportions, fractions and the linear progression of sounds within the tonal range were all curricular topics that bridged music and mathematics together in ancient Greek education. The structural theory of music in ancient Greece also emphasized the symmetry of mathematical tonal patterns and how the stability of those tonal patterns was sustained throughout time. The ancient Greek scholars greatly valued the structural properties of *musical harmonia* and stated that the highest value in music lies in its ability to imitate the natural order of things in the mathematical and scientific world.

Yet, the pleasure music afforded was considered both irrelevant and dangerous when choosing music for educational purposes. In fact, music's affective potency was considered at times a threat to the purification of the human soul due to the risks of the soul becoming unguarded, uncontrolled; rather, music was seen solely as a subject that should be used to teach reason and morality. Even though the Platonic philosophy in ancient Greece greatly stressed the need for authentic music and playing instruments, the music was nevertheless not to be too stylistically

217

different from the main corpus of orderly, harmonious and controlled music that was considered important for social and moral development by the Greek scholars. Toward the end of the Platonic educational system and the beginning of the Aristotelian era, music and song were being replaced by philosophy and rhetoric, as well as the disintegration of its claims of ethical character development. Aristotle steered away from the strict Platonic philosophy of music and differentiated between musical goodness and the goodness of what music initiates. Unlike Plato, Aristotle accepted music's ability to seduce the soul and give it pleasure; yet, Aristotle believed that the pleasure we gain from music is purely cognitive and contemplative rather than social-affective (Bowman, 1998).

For Plato, music served ornamental purposes while for Aristotle music had the potential of being first beautiful, and as the happiness from musical pleasure increases, music then moves from the beautiful to the sublime. The sublime can be defined as the moment when the listener experiences the vastness and incomprehensibility found in music. Beauty and ornament also blend into music whenever there is a flowing melody; however, music that is rich and strange at the same time produces the sublime: "Music is considered to be sublime if it inspires veneration, beautiful if it pleases, and ornamental if it amuses" (Zon, 1999: 25). The inherent qualities of sublime music, its vastness and incomprehensibility, were abhorred by Plato because of their power to allow individuals to lose themselves in the music. Mystics and theologians often used sublime music to entrance individuals into believing the message hidden within the music and its forms. Religious music often mimics the sublime musical experience because the listener's self-consciousness is supposedly obliterated by the controlling powers of the sublime. The individual forgets her/himself in the music and barriers between the musical object and the perceiving subject are removed. The sublime is thus associated with self-absence as music becomes the powerful agent in the listening experience. Ritual music is also often associated with the sublime because it also builds up a revelatory perception through the musical text. Unlike modern music, the ritual song and its notions of populism renders ritual music more popular and in spirit with the masses. Ritual music causes the masses to induce themselves into a moment of revelatory abandonment (Zon, 1999).

Later on in Western history, in the medieval system of liberal arts schooling, music was seen more as a science alongside astronomy due to the similarities in their conceptual abstractions of time, motion and revolution, of what is limited and what is boundless, and similarities in numbers and in reason (Lippman, 1999). However, due to shifts in paradigms brought on by modernity in Western civilization, music was designated later as a corollary to the study of grammar and language due to once again structural similarities in musical and linguistic composition and the part-to-whole interrelationships of words and musical notes. A generative grammar of music began to develop in the 20th century based on the fundamentals of harmonics and rhythm that matched closely with the generative grammar theories from linguistics and cognitive science (Chomsky, 1988). Similarly, the more recent generative grammar theory of music also emphasizes that a universality is inherent in music from different cultures and that there are certain parameters that distinguish each particular culture's music from the universality of all music. During the 20th century, letters, syllables and words were being compared with the generative grammar of music, which included tone, pitch, temporal duration of notes and other musical elements – since both sets of elements and units could be manipulated to develop different levels of discourse as well as different types of music. The structural composition of both linguistic elements and musical elements is what gives meaning to both linguistic and musical texts. In turn, the epistemological classification and categorization of music in Western education has evolved throughout the past thousand years due to its ability to find structural parallels with multiple disciplines, such as mathematics, science and linguistics. Furthermore, music has always come to serve multiple purposes in society: there is an aesthetic to music; theology has used music to inculcate the masses; music is used metaphorically to represent political power; and in education, music has been used in public schools for a variety of reasons, such as the assimilation of the immigrant masses through patriotic school songs.

In the American educational system, the early forms of music education were first employed in the public schools at the turn of the 20th century when the Pestalozzian theory of music education was being implemented. Song material chosen by the teacher had to reflect the cultural standards of Western European society, especially German classical music, and the songs were sung in rote with emphasis on good vocal tone before any sight-reading of the music (Volk, 1998). Once again, the music curriculum was seen as an object that had the spiritual power to cleanse the thoughts, feelings and souls of the public schools' immigrant students, who were largely from poor, rural Eastern and Southern European nations, and lift them up morally and spiritually from their newfound poverty in urban slums. Since early music education was grounded in the Germanic tradition with its Germanic folk songs and advocacy of character development, there were conscious attempts at the national level to exclude the presence of African-American spirituals and slave hymns from music textbooks due to their so-called primitive nature at the lower end of the musical evolution, as defined further by the rhetoric of Social Darwinism that spread throughout the field of American education in the early 20th century. Furthermore, spirituals and slave hymns were also condemned for their power to induce a moment of the sublime when the human soul is carried away from its bodily presence. Yet, as American involvement in World War II increased, the Germanic tradition of classical music education was slowly eliminated from the public school curriculum and was replaced instead by the didactic teaching of patriotic songs that celebrated the nationhood of solely the United States. The National Education Association was holding several meetings at that time to stress the need for the standardization of national American folk songs with patriotic themes that were *genuine, authentic and cultural* (Volk, 1998: 43). Subsequently, incoming immigrant groups were inculcated in the public schools with this music-based process of assimilation and Americanization through the singing of national patriotic songs such as Yankee Doodle Dandy and the production of pageants and other musical performances to celebrate our nationhood. However, there were a few leaders in the field of education, such as John Dewey and Jane Addams, who advocated instead for the teaching of bilingual songs and folk dancing from the students' own immigrant cultures in order to create mutual respect for different cultures within the public schools through the music curriculum:

> Music, having sound as its medium, thus necessarily expresses in a concentrated way the shocks and instabilities, the conflicts and resolutions, that are the dramatic changes enacted upon the more enduring background of nature and human life. The tension and the struggle has its gatherings of energy, its discharges, its attacks and defenses, its mighty warrings and its peaceful meetings, its resistances and resolutions, and out of these things music weaves its web. (Dewey, 1934: 236)

Today, in the contemporary American educational system, music has been practically eliminated from the public school curriculum due to the fact that it has been classified in the past fifty years as one of the fine arts. Subsequently due to budget cuts and the return to a basics curriculum that focuses strongly on mathematics and science, many struggling public school systems decided to dismantle their fine arts curriculum, including music education. Yet, during the last few years, there has been a growing resurgence in music education due to its celebrated cognitive benefits.

Musicology today has also been influenced by a number of other disciplines such as linguistics, computer science, philosophy, semiotics and anthropology, and thus the study of music is returning to its original interdisciplinary roots. However, the most profound contributions to recent music education have been made perhaps due to the result of the rapid progress in cognitive psychology in education. Cognitive musicology, in particular, is an area of musicology that studies musical *habits of mind* and how music can produce defined conceptual schemas within the mind that have a logic of their own and are beneficial for cognition. For example, Howard Gardner's Theory of Multiple Intelligences (1999) states that musical intelligence is one of the seven main intelligences that need to be encouraged and developed in the public school curriculum for its cognitive benefits. Musical intelligence, for example, encompasses the capability to recognize and compose musical pitches, tones and rhythms, and thus, a strong musical intelligence allows students to understand the rhythm and variations of the music. Yet, students must be given the opportunity to create, communicate and understand meanings made out of musical sound. In relation to the behaviorists, the cognitive musicologists do not presume that there is a simple causal relationship between a musical stimulus and a student response. Cognitive musicologists instead feel that the phenomenal experiences produced by musical stimuli help develop a sophisticated, complex mental function that moves as a process within the mind and helps further develop cognitive complexity (Serafine, 1988).

The Role of Music in Bilingual Education

Some educators, however, currently feel that music should fall under the multicultural education category so that music education can not only increase the students' cognitive capacities but also teach them about different cultures and their respective musical repertoires (Volk, 1998). Due to the increasing ethnic diversity of students at the national level and the increasing degree of globalization on an international level, multicultural music education states that students will be able to better understand their world and the people living in their world if they study global music cultures. Listening, performing and composing music from a different culture are ways to create plural aesthetic experiences in which students begin to acknowledge music as a universal language since it can be found in every existent cultural group and is able to cross and transgress over boundaries and thresholds. Furthermore, instead of creating a dichotomy between Western music and non-Western music, multicultural music education advocates teaching a fuller range of musical pieces so students can begin to see similarities and differences in the conceptual and structural understandings of music from one culture to another. However, one of the difficulties of teaching multicultural music education is the difference in musical scales between Western music and non-Western music and finding music educators who understand the different variables between multiple musical scales and then are able to teach these variable scales to students.

Furthermore, the field of bilingual education has also recognized the power of music to teach a second language such as Spanish and English through the use of vocal texts. Music in bilingual and ESL (English as a Second Language) classrooms is fundamental to teaching pronunciation, grammar and vocabulary, as well as for teaching cultural songs and teaching the geographical contexts of those cultural songs. There are also cognitive functions common in processing both language and music that are necessary for second language acquisition. Steven Krashen (1983) states that language learning is different from language acquisition because music allows for the subconscious internalization of language learning while the learning of language rules and grammar allows for the conscious internalization of language. Krashen defines the *din in the head* phenomenon as the use of music, especially vocal songs, to induce the involuntary, subconscious acquisition of language in students. According to many bilingual teachers, music also has social and emotional benefits because the students are gaining confidence in using the second language through music and thus do not face the same kinds of performance pressures found in formal language learning. Studies that have implemented the use of music in bilingual and ESL classrooms have found that sounds, words, phrases and sentences of the second language may suddenly pop out in the subconscious – even without the presence of any musical stimulus – and ring insistently in the student's head, or may be deliberately retrieved, repeated, analyzed and associated with certain situations and experiences within the memory (Schunk, 1999). The function of this mental rehearsal of spoken language through music is analogous to that of *audiation* – hearing music in one's mind, not only for the cognitive rehearsal of musical text, but also for the *ontogenetic development of the second language* (Murphey, 1992). When a song is running through the head, the language student will involuntary rehearse the speech within that song, even if exposure to the song has been short-lived. Thus, the inclusion of music and songs in bilingual and ESL classrooms is a progressive step toward achieving a multisensory approach to second language development.

The development of a positive self-image and increased self-esteem are two more important benefits of music education cited by multicultural educators who target largely urban and minority public school students (Banks, 1997). Multicultural theorists contend that if minority students are exposed to the music from their respective cultures then their identities will be shaped and validated by their ancestral origins; music thus becomes a way to achieve a secure sense of self through the strong identification with one's cultural origins. A feeling of being psychologically secure develops through the continued exposure to musical experiences grounded solely in one's culture. Yet, others fear that the teaching of specific cultural songs and music leads to a static depiction of that particular culture in the musical texts, as opposed to the portrayal of a dynamic music culture that is multiethnic and always changing. Smith (1994) argues that multicultural music education can also be defined predominantly as *folkish Romanticism gone bad* because multiculturalists often view music education as fundamentally folk in character, the roots of which can be found in the countercultural movements of the 1960s.

The use of folk music for political gains, its use to develop a communal identity among listeners, and the overall emphasis on the mimetic performance of insular ethnic music as opposed to the discursive study of formal Western music are the three main reasons why opponents to the multicultural movement in American education feel that the overemphasis on a global village, folk music curriculum is changing our American musical culture for the worse. Folk music for them is strongly related to a tradition of performance, as a ritual, as communal in nature, and sometimes even as tribal because the instruments and music tend to replicate premodern sociocultural activities. Thus, critics of multicultural education advocate a music curriculum that will provide students with a classical orientation to music and its structural elements (timbre, tempo, phrasing) by developing their interpretive and appreciative capacities for music through aesthetic experiences. By focusing on music as an aesthetic object and not as a performance, critics want students to learn how to talk about music and its form, content and contexts. Smith (1994) outlines five components of a music curriculum that focuses on aesthetic learning, as opposed to focusing on multicultural learning, by moving students through five consecutive phases of discursive knowledge related to music: (1) an exposure and familiarization to the music; (2) a perceptual training of music in which the teacher is guiding the students through the listening; (3) an historical awareness of the music; (4) the exemplar appreciation of music; and (5) a critical analysis and aesthetic judgment of music. Thus, instead of immersing oneself in multicultural music through performance and sheer listening, critics of multicultural education are advocating for the building of discursive knowledge about music through more information, not experience.

The following sections of this chapter will examine the implementation of a Spanish folk music program at PS 2000. It was initiated by the dual immersion parents so the students in all the dual immersion classrooms could increase their levels of Spanish language proficiency and their discursive knowledge of music through the singing of Spanish folk songs. Through the production of vocal sounds in the Spanish language, the dual immersion parents, predominantly the white, upper-middle-class parents who were spearheading this music program, were hoping that their children would learn to communicate more fluently in Spanish by discovering the varieties of sound possible with their own Spanish voices; by understanding the small inflexions, timings and dynamic changes in the Spanish folk songs; and by initiating vocal play in Spanish by playing voice games, improvising songs and singing known songs over and over with the guidance from a native, Spanish-dominant folk musician (Young & Glover, 1998). Yet, the implementation of this music program at PS 2000 was faced with issues and concerns at the local level that have been faced historically and universally in music education.

The struggle between creating a music program that focuses on controlling the senses through the formal study of its elements versus allowing for the power of music to induce moments of the sublime will be examined closely in this chapter, as well as the use of music to teach language skills, to teach about other cultures and to increase cognitive complexity. The ethnographic context of this chapter will carefully document and reflect upon the meaning of the musical texts consumed in this fifth-grade dual immersion classroom, the musical practices and performances themselves, the effects of music on the social actors, including both the listeners and the performers, and the analysis of these effects in relation to musical agency. How music education works in the social and academic life of a dual immersion classroom and how its significance changes based on the social context at particular moments and under particular circumstances will provide an analytical lens on music consumption, especially in relation to the inculcation of a second language such as Spanish. Student and teacher responses to the enacted musical practices and performances, both visceral and conceptual, will tell us how the Spanish folk music was experienced differently by different recipients and how those differences allude to larger sociocultural differences amongst the students in terms of race, class and gender. The musical perceptions, interpretations, valuations, comportments and feelings of all the social actors – students, parents and teachers – will together help frame the musical experiences described in this classroom episode.

In *Sound, Speech, and Music* (1990), David Burrows creates a topology for analyzing musical experiences in which he designates three fields of study: (1) Field I is the examination of the mobile, changing body in a physical space during the entire musical experience; (2) Field II is the invisible and intangible space where thoughts take place, the Cartesian *res cogitans* where the mind functions and where mental schemas are developed from the musical experience through concepts and images that subsequently enter the memory; and (3) Field III is the field of the spirit where listeners can transcend the limits of bodily existence and enter into a state of the sublime where they loose all sense of reason. The body, the mind and spirit are three areas where music is spatialized and localized, thus, in the following sections of this chapter, the three fields that Burrows outlines will also be used to frame the musical experiences in this dual immersion classroom. The physical space where the musical experiences occurred will be examined carefully in relation to its architectonics and how the subjects' bodies were arranged, configured and projected within this sonic space. Furthermore, categories of Field I include what is inside and outside the bodily space; the withinness and withoutness of certain bodies within that space; the separation and connection between the bodies, between bodies and objects; and the protective space inter-polated between certain individuals and sociocultural groups. The mental space of Field II will be analyzed through the social consensus of the entire class community and their agreement of what effects the musical experi-ence produces in their collective mental space, based on the connecting concepts and images from subject to subject during the musical experi-ence. In turn, Field II takes off from the use of the senses in Field I and begins to develop mental schemata, conjectures and expectations for the lived musical experience. Field III includes the spiritual sense of self and heightened degrees of self-awareness that occur during a sublime musical experience in which our sense of self is centered everywhere and its periphery nowhere – an *oceanic feeling* that suffuses the listener during the musical experience. There is also an increased communal awareness during the moment of the sublime that projects a Hegelian universal self in which the divide between Self and Other is attenuated. Field III is thus a way to transcend the bodily existence and limits found in Field I through this intense commitment to sounds found in the sublime musical experi-ence. Burrows (1990) also states that listeners can operate simultaneously in all three fields of perception and can move and forth from one field to another and interweave their musical experiences from all of them. This chapter in turn will examine how the social actors moved back and forth from one field to another to weave together a unique musical experience.

Ya Me Voy: Lourdes and Her Transnational Music

One of the main concerns that always resurfaced during the dual immersion meetings and discussions amongst the parents, administrators and teachers was the need to hire more specialty teachers who were fluent in Spanish so the dual immersion students could learn art, music and even physical education in the Spanish language. At the beginning of the year, during an October dual immersion meeting, the parent association established a budget from their own monetary funds that allowed the school to hire a musician from outside the school faculty who could come in part-time and teach the students Spanish songs. Subsequently, the dual immersion parents first went in search of *native* talent using the resources that were available to them in order to advertise the music position. Then the dual immersion parents channeled the selected applicants toward the dual immersion teachers who acted as experts in the Spanish language and acted as functionaries who knew who was a successful music teacher. The teachers later interviewed the potential applicants and gave their feedback to the parents. Thus, the dual immersion teachers were seen as ethnic *insiders* who ostensibly possessed superior knowledge of their students' cultural needs than the predominantly upper-middle-class, white parents who were spearheading the music program. Musicians who interviewed for the part-time position tried to make peace with this uneven relationship between the dual immersion parents and dual immersion teachers in the selection process as they were shuffled from the main office to each individual classroom so that everyone approved the final applicant. In the end, Lourdes was selected as the native musician who would come in every Tuesday and Thursday and teach folk songs in all K-5 dual immersion classrooms.

In her selection, a distinction was made by the teachers between naive folk musicians who play traditional music versus cultural activists who consciously strive to pass on certain musical forms and revive others to the students (Glasser, 1995). For them, Lourdes' music pedagogy involved the cultural preservation of music rather than just transmitting music unconsciously. Her energy and intelligence allowed her to plan Spanish music lessons that were designed to represent the best music of each Hispanic ethnic group. Also, Lourdes seemed to the teachers and parents as if she was an *authentic* folk musician since she was a newly arrived immigrant who lived in *El Barrio*, where many of the Puerto Rican students also lived, and thus was seen as a cultural insider by all the adults. Since she lived in the neighborhood, Lourdes' son was also enrolled at a well-known dual immersion program in a nearby elementary school, and she traveled back and forth between the two schools to teach music. Everywhere she went, she carried her *guitara* (guitar) and once she even brought her son to the classroom so he could accompany her on the drums. Lourdes' livelihood was based on her musical skills and thus she soon became a cultural figure in the immediate dual immersion community.

Yet, in order to fully understand the effects of Lourdes' Spanish music production, it is vital to understand the role that Lourdes played at the school, the settings in which she worked, the musical repertoires she played for the dual immersion students, and the symbolic meanings of such music both for Lourdes and for other members of the dual immersion community. In her very first lesson, Lourdes had all the fifth-grade students seated in a circle on the rug. She then joined the circle on the rug with her *guitara* in one arm and her musical sheets in front of her on the rug floor. The very first question she asked the students was what kind of Spanish music they listen to regularly. The students started listing many popular Hispanic singers who happen to have recorded a few songs in Spanish but sang predominantly songs in English with a few Spanish lyrics, even though they catered their music to the mainstream American market. Artists like Jennifer Lopez, Mark Anthony, Christina Aguilerra, Santana, Shakira and Ricky Martin were listed as the Hispanic singers the students listened to on a normal basis, thus establishing a fine distinction between the popular and the folkloric. At this point, Lourdes reiterated to the students that they will learn to sing authentic, quintessential Spanish music using indigenous instruments and genuine lyrics. Lourdes privileged traditional folk music and did not leave room for exploring the popular Hispanic American singers whose new combinations of music were drawing in an English-dominant mainstream audience in the United States. Emphasis was placed instead on the difference between home music listening and school music listening and the different functions that they each served. Lourdes reported that home listening was linked with enjoyment, emotional mood and social relationships, whereas school music was associated with motivation for learning Spanish and being active in the Spanish language (Boal-Palheiros & Hargreaves, 2001).

Lourdes defined her music as a rich repository of song, dance and folktales with which nearly all the students soon identified themselves. Subsequently, the music produced during Lourdes' lessons reinforced the dual immersion identity of this classroom. Some of the music highlighted the rural-to-urban paradigm that many immigrant Spanish-dominant students could relate to personally, as well as music that highlighted the variety of regional, linguistic and class backgrounds of ethnic Hispanic groups and their various national identities. The following quote highlights Lourdes' multicultural framework for the music curriculum:

Lourdes: *Es muy importante que ustedes cantan música de diferente paises latinamericano porque no todo la música latinamericana tiene el mismo sabor.*
English translation:
[It is very important that you sing music from different Latin American countries because not all Latin American music has the same flavor.]

Furthermore, the spatial interplay of Lourdes sitting in an enclosed circle with her instruments at her side, the students huddled on both sides of her, and Roberta watching and listening from afar, since she was technically on her preparation period, led to the production of a social space that reflected the openness and fluidity found during other moments on the rug area. The use of folk music is often identified with a sense of community and collective power that Lourdes also wanted to reproduce by performing particular folk songs. Subsequently, these songs allowed Lourdes to share her cultural past with the students, such as the cultural traditions she grew up with in Puerto Rico:

Lourdes: *Mira . . . chicos . . . yo tengo música nueva para hoy . . . hoy comenzamos en diciembre . . . y en el fin del diciembre es la Navidad. Y en la nuestra cultura latina . . . la música de la navidad es muy especial . . . del día veinte-cuatro . . . pero lo que hacen en la Navidad latino no es necesario dar regalos . . . porque en los otros paises . . . este . . . el intercambio de regalos no se usa . . . no existe . . . es simplemente mucha música . . . mucha fiesta . . . mucha allegría. La Navidad era el único tiempo que mi mama nos dejamos a tomar un poquito de vino . . . golpean un poquito en el intero . . . pero sola- mente un poco vino . . .* [Students start laughing.] *También acaloramos un lechón. Saben que es un lechón? Un cerdo . . . okay . . . en la casa . . . temprano por la mañana mis padres mataron el cerdo en el patio . . . desacaban las cosas en el dentro . . . mi papa no hizo nada después . . . porque ponemos un parro del medio . . . del cerdo* [Lourdes pretends she is stabbing the pig with a sharp stick.] *Y salía por la boca . . . después lo ponieron encima de dos . . . cómo se dice en español . . . estacas . . . encima de dos estacas . . . que son dos cosas que suspendieron el cerdo . . . y el abajo es un fuego.* [Lourdes pretends she is spinning the pig around the stick and over the fire.] *Y todo el día*

. . . mi papa . . . le damos vueltas a esta cerdo . . . y cuando era a las cuatro de la tarde . . . a las cuatro . . . ya acaba . . . y metieron el cerdo en la boca . . . es delicioso . . . y esa era romantica. Y mi mama cocina mucha arroz . . . mucha ensalada . . . y era comida especial . . . después y comen muchas frutas . . . la Navidad viene de las raices de Puerto Rico. Entonces hoy . . . yo voy a formar la oportunidad para este clase hermosa . . . para cantar un poco de esa música de la Navidad.

English translation:
[Listen . . . children . . . I have new music for today . . . today we are beginning with December . . . and at the end of December is Christmas. And in our Latin American culture . . . Christmas music is very special . . . on the twenty-fourth day . . . but on Christmas we do not necessarily exchange gifts . . . because in other countries . . . this . . . this exchange of gifts is not used . . . it does not exist . . . it's simply a lot of music . . . a lot of parties . . . a lot of fun. Christmas was the only time my mother would give us a little wine . . . it would hit us inside . . . but only a little wine. [Students start laughing.] We also roast a *lechón* . . . do you know what is a *lechón*? It's a pig . . . okay . . . in the house . . . early in the morning my parents would kill the pig on the patio . . . we would fill it with things inside . . . then my father did nothing . . . because we put a stick in the middle . . . of the pig. [Lourdes pretends she is stabbing the pig with a sharp stick.] And it came out of the mouth . . . then we would put it on top of . . . how do you say this in Spanish . . . *estacas* . . . we would put it on two stakes . . . they are two things that suspend the pig . . . and underneath is the fire. [Lourdes pretends she is spinning the pig around the stick and over the fire.] All day . . . my father . . . would give us turns to spin the pig . . . and when it was four o'clock in the afternoon . . . at four o'clock . . . it was finished . . . and we would put the pig inside our mouths . . . it was delicious . . . and it was romantic. My mother also cooks a lot of rice . . . a lot of salad . . . it was a special food . . . then we would eat lots of fruits . . . this Christmas tradition came from Puerto Rico . . . that's why today . . . I'm going to create the opportunity for this lovely class to sing a little of the Christmas music.]

Lourdes also wanted to create equality between her voice and the students' voices by sitting in an enclosed circle on the rug. She did not want to be the chief participant in the singing and instead advocated a dynamic interplay between her voice and the students' voices in order to create a polyphony of voices within this sonic space. The music-making functioned primarily as a communal activity, and like other communal performances, it too strengthened the degree of solidarity within the collective classroom community. The greater sense of community and social solidarity during and after the musical performances led many Spanish-dominant students such as Yolanda and Javier to share their native knowledge of the Spanish songs with the English-dominant students and assist them to better learn the words, their meanings and the melody.

Furthermore, the ethnic boundaries between the Puerto Rican and Dominican students were not maintained stringently during Lourdes' musical performances. On the contrary, the sociocultural boundaries between the students became more ambiguous in comparison to other times on the rug space during class meetings and the creative writing circle when the boundaries were marked by a structured seating order. The students did not try to separate themselves into different social groups and mark off distinct ethnic boundaries during the music lessons; instead, they found a common cause in Lourdes' music along with the other student groups who also enjoyed the diverse musical genres and nationalities found in Lourdes' songs:

Lourdes: *Seguimos con algo nuevo que lo trajé . . . otra canción . . . una canción nueva . . . y este canción no es de suramerica . . . este canción no es de chile . . . este canción es de caribe . . . okay . . . es dominicana . . .*

English translation:
[We will continue with something new that I brought . . . another song . . . a new song . . . and this song is not from South America . . . this song is not from Chile . . . this song is Caribbean . . . okay . . . it is Dominican.]

Students: Yeah! [They start clapping.]

There was a fluid collective identity produced during Lourdes' musical performances that did not embody the divisive reality found in other moments and places within their classroom life. Rather, the students crossed ethnic, national, class and geographical boundaries and thus maintained their collective identity as a dual immersion classroom. When they sat together on the rug, the videotape data captured a different kind of social setting where there were less distinct borders and boundaries between the different sociocultural student groups. Most of the students were reclined on the rug floor, sprawled over each other, and their bodies were positioned randomly in a much more relaxed state of being with their hands and heads moving freely in syncopation with the music. It can be argued that when music is performed in a social context it can sustain a sense of community and become social cement for creating cohesion and continuity. Lourdes' music lessons did not produce the sociocultural borders and boundaries that separate cultural insiders from cultural outsiders, e.g. Puerto Ricans versus Dominicans and English-dominant versus Spanish-dominant. Instead, there was a physical sense of a whole group unity amongst the dual immersion students in which the criteria for ethnic membership and in-group acceptance was based on the music that bound the students and teachers together:

Lourdes: *Este canción viene de chile . . . este mujer que hacer este canción . . . una composidora . . . una mujer que murió al final de los años secenta . . . casi secenta . . . y ella es muy conocida en todo latinamerica . . . pero ella es solamente una composidora . . . ella también cantaba . . . ella es una cantadora también pero es mas famosa para una composidora . . . porque ella escribía . . . su nombre es . . . o era . . . Violetta Parra . . . okay . . . esta canción es muy especial . . . porque habla de uno a darle gracias a la vida . . . es muy importante . . . porque estamos aquí . . . y de que respiramos . . . de que tenemos el sol . . . ella le da a gracias a la vida . . . para el sonido de los canarios . . . le da gracias para los sonidos de las palabras . . . pienso que es muy importante que hay cosas tan linda en la vida . . .*

English translation:
[This song comes from Chile . . . the woman who did this song . . . the composer . . . a woman who died in the 70s . . . almost the 70s . . . and she is very famous in all of Latin America . . . but she is not only a composer . . . she also sings . . . she is a singer also but is more famous for being a composer . . . because she was writing . . . her name is . . . or was . . . Violetta Parra . . . okay . . . this song is very special . . . because it talks about giving thanks to life . . . it is very important . . . because we are here . . . and that we are breathing . . . that we have the sun . . . she is giving thanks to life . . . for the sounds of the canaries . . . she is giving thanks for the sounds of words. I think that it is very important that there are many beautiful things in life . . .]

Jose: *Yo tengo gracias a mi vida.*
English translation:
[I give thanks to my life.]

Lourdes: *Vamos a cantar esta canción . . . yo voy a cantar . . . ahha! . . . su maestra se la sabe . . . ella puede cantar conmigo . . .*

"Gracias a la vida que me ha dado tanto
Me dio dos luceros que cuando los abro
Perfecto distingo lo negro del blanco
Y en el alto cielo su fondo estrellado
Y en las multitudes al hombre que yo amo."
[Roberta has joined the circle and is sitting next to the students.]
Okay . . . vamos a . . . toda la música es casi la misma . . . es casi misma . . .
vamos a hacer junto la primera estrofa . . . pueden hacer la primera conmigo?
Tratar. Se sienten que la canción es un poquito difícil . . . nada mas tratatla
. . . el año pasado . . . el cuarto de tercer grado . . . un tercer grado a que iba
mi hijo . . . cantaron esta canción y le penetraron bastante bien . . . vamos a
hacer la primera estrafa . . .
[Students join her and sing the first verse together.]
English translation:
[Let's sing this song . . . I will sing . . . ahha! . . . your teacher knows it
. . . she can sing with me . . .]
"I thank life that has given me so much
It gave me two stars and when I open them
I can tell perfectly the black from the white
And make out in the high sky its many lights
And amidst the crowds, the man that I love."
[Roberta has joined the circle and is sitting next to the students.]
[Okay . . . we will . . . all the music is almost the same . . . almost the
same . . . we will do the first stanza together . . . can you do the first
with me? Try. Some may feel that this song is a bit difficult . . . just try
it . . . last year . . . a third grade classroom . . . a third grade that my
son went to . . . sang this song and performed it well . . . let's do the
first stanza . . .]
[Students join her and sing the first verse together.]

However, even though there was heightened camaraderie amongst
the students, there were nonetheless different levels of student awareness displayed during Lourdes' weekly music lessons: (1) some students
displayed attentive awareness; (2) others displayed inattentive awareness;
and (3) a few displayed non-attentive awareness (Addis, 1999). Even
though the degree of awareness might change from individual to individual and from situation to situation, learning Spanish through music
allowed for cultural sharing, in-group acceptance and the possibilities
of beneficial exchanges between the English-dominant and Spanish-
dominant students. Yet, there were many moments during Lourdes'

lessons that four white, English-dominant male students in particular (John, Pierre, Joshua and Brian) would often seem distracted. So Lourdes would occasionally stop during her lesson to call their attention and sometimes asked the Spanish-dominant students to help these English-dominant students and bring them into the musical fold:

Lourdes: *Ponen atención aquí . . . no tengo mucho tiempo . . . la mirando . . . Brian . . . John . . . vengan chicos . . . todos van a leer . . . vamos . . . estan cansados?*

English translation:
[Pay attention here . . . I do not have much time . . . look at it . . . Brian . . . John . . . come on boys . . . we are going to read . . . let's go . . . are you tired?]

Yolanda: Wake up everyone!
[Yolanda addresses the group of four boys sitting nearby: John, Pierre, Joshua and Brian.]

Lourdes: *Porque miren . . . a esos niños . . . es más difícil pero para ustedes . . . es más fácil . . . entonces ayudan a ellos . . . traen ellos . . .*

English translation:
[Because look . . . for those boys . . . it is more difficult but for you guys . . . it is much easier . . . so help them . . . bring them along.]

Yet, there were other times when the English-dominant students marked their presence overtly during Lourdes' musical lessons. In the following transcript, an English-dominant student's absence, Brian, was felt by the Spanish-dominant students when it was time for the next song, *Los Locos* (The Crazy People), which many of the white male English-dominant students such as Brian, John, Pierre and Joshua enjoyed:

Lourdes: *Vamos a hacer "Los Locos" . . .*
English translation:
[Let's do *"Los Locos"* . . .]

Claudio: Brian isn't here though . . .

Lourdes: *Qué?*
English translation:
[What?]

Students: Brian isn't here today . . .

Lourdes: *No entiendo . . .*

English translation:
[I don't understand . . .]

Claudio: Brian isn't here and we can't . . .
Roberta: *Con permiso* . . . May I ask what Brian has to do with this song?
Claudio: I'm saying that because . . . because he likes that song . . .
Roberta: Why? . . . I missed your explanation. What's your explanation?
Yolanda: He said Brian likes that song but he is not here.

Lourdes: *Oh Brian! Sí! El amigo mío! Ah . . . sí . . .*

English translation:
[Oh Brian! Yes! My friend! Ah . . . yes . . .]

Music and Pedagogy: Western versus Non-Western Ways of Teaching Music

In terms of Lourdes' pedagogical style, the most common technique for teaching music is when the teacher plays the music and then the students imitate the music until they can fully master it. At first, the music is learned roughly and then the teacher places more attention on the finer details in order to produce a concentric circle of learning in which the musical repertoire is repeated for mimetic purposes with a focus on the holistic quality of the performance (van den Bos, 1993). Lourdes' teaching methods were based predominantly on a non-Western, concentric circle, holistic pedagogical style that closely matched her non-Western musical repertoire in which the Spanish music was taught in its full context and expression. The analytical approach, on the other hand, is used to describe the pedagogical style of Western music in which a linear methodology is used to teach music. The focus on playing instruments and the transmission of music through notation is prevalent in the analytical approach. The breaking up of the music curriculum into separate abilities such as rhythmic control, reading written music and musical theory is also reflective of the analytical approach. However, in the holistic approach, the importance of playing and experiencing the music takes precedence over any form of musical analysis since the emphasis is placed on the natural context of music learning.

Yet, the teacher's role is much more active in the analytical approach because s/he has to assess the progress of each student, then create and select an appropriate musical repertoire for her/his musical diagnosis. In turn, the music teacher needs a range of methodologies and techniques to use with the varying student abilities as opposed to the holistic approach to music education in which greater importance for the music teacher is placed on being a good musician. Furthermore, the emphasis on analyzing music through its rhythmic patterns, melody, expression and technical ability can deter the students from concentrating on the musical meaning within the vocal texts. The overemphasis on techniques and methods of playing music can also decrease student motivation through a series of repetitive exercises in which the students do not have as much auditory control of the musical experience. When propagating a natural context for language learning through music, educators prefer to play popular songs and simple folk songs rather than the study of classical music that trains students to read notes in exercise books and analyze music through separate entities such as melody and rhythm. In turn, when Lourdes visited the dual immersion classroom every Thursday afternoon, the students were inculcated in a holistic approach toward music, which they felt reproduced a festive ethos during every musical experience with Lourdes. The students remembered those experiences not only as entertainment but also for their practical function of learning Spanish. On the other hand, when they attended their regular music class, the students were exposed to an analytical approach to music in which they learned to play instruments and read musical notes.

Unfortunately, since Lourdes worked on a part-time basis at the two dual immersion schools within the district, she eventually left PS 2000 near the end of the school year because she received a full-time position to teach Spanish music at another public school in a different district. Her new position also included a higher salary and benefits so Lourdes left PS 2000 by April of that school year. Within this atmosphere of turnover and turmoil over losing Lourdes, the dual immersion parents at PS 2000 began searching for a replacement and found a young male musician from Ecuador whose style of teaching was different from Lourdes' style of teaching. Whereas she used a holistic pedagogical style, Alfredo used an analytical pedagogical style in which the students sat at their desks while he lectured to them on the history of musical instruments and the analysis of musical elements. Now the students rarely were given the opportunity to sing a series of Spanish songs one after the other as they did previously with Lourdes. Instead, they sat motionless at their desks, turning around restlessly, and soon lost their attention during Alfredo's lectures. Needless to say, Alfredo did not return the following school year and was only able to teach a few lessons in the end. The following transcript is of the very first lesson he presented:

Alfredo: *Ecuador es* . . . [Alfredo draws a map of Central and South America and shows the borders of Ecuador in relief form] *el país donde solamente hablan español. Entonces . . . yo soy de Ecuador . . . hace muchos años . . . algunas personas se usan muchas cosas . . . cosas de la naturaleza . . . como cañas . . . para construir instrumentos. Saben que son cañas?* [Alfredo begins to draw a sugar cane stalk along with its leaves.] *Entonces . . . la gente de las montañas andes cortan las cañas . . . y hacen instrumentos como esos . . .* [Alfredo goes to his bag and takes out a wooden flute.] *Yo trae solamente uno pero hay miles, miles instrumentos . . . me gustaría que ustedes conozcan esos . . . porque muchas veces . . . tocan la música en la casa, en la televisión, en el carro, en el teatro . . . pero muchas personas no sabemos como se llaman esos instrumentos. Esos instrumentos tienen historias . . . tienen un sistema de clasificación . . . que un señor puso . . . este instrumento* [Alfredo points to the wooden flute in his hand] *es un instrumento del aire. Y los instrumentos del aire . . . del veinto . . . se llama "aerofonos."* [Alfredo writes this word down on the blackboard.] *Entonces . . . este instrumento . . . este instrumento es de las montañas . . . se uso en todos los andes . . . en las montañas.* [Alfredo points to the map on the blackboard.] *En las montañas hay mucho veinto fuerte . . . y se usa el sonido del aire . . .* [Alfedo blows into the wooden flute.] *El sonido natu-raleza. Entonces . . . cortan las cañas, se acaban un tubo de esta caña, y ponen en la boca . . . pero con seis orificios en el tubo . . . este es un instrumento aerofono que se llama "quena."* [Alfedo writes down quena on the black-board.] *Y se usa la quena para cantos de amor y pena . . . este instrumento es algunos veces allegre y algunos veces triste.* [Alfredo finishes the lesson with the classification and naming of instruments in accordance to the different groups.]

English translation:

Ecuador is . . . [Alfredo draws a map of Central and South America and shows the borders of Ecuador in relief form] a country where they speak only Spanish . . . thus . . . I am from Ecuador . . . and many years ago . . . some people used a lot of things . . . things from nature . . . like sugar cane to make instruments. Do you know what *"cañas"* are? [Alfredo begins to draw a sugar cane stalk along with its leaves.] Thus . . . the people from the Andes mountains . . . cut the sugar cane . . . and made instruments like this . . . [Alfredo goes to his bag and takes out a wooden flute.] I only brought one but there are many, many different instruments . . . I would like you to know those instruments . . . because a lot of times . . . when we play music in the house, on tele-vision, in the car, in the theatre . . . there are a lot of people who don't know what those instruments are called. These instruments have a history . . . they have a system of classification . . . that a man put into place . . . this instrument [Alfredo points to the wooden flute in his hand] is a wind instrument. These instruments of the air . . . of the wind . . . are called "*aerofonos.*" [Alfredo writes this word down on the blackboard.] Thus . . . this instrument . . . this instrument from the mountains . . . that they use in all of the Andes . . . in the mountains . . . [Alfredo points to the map on the blackboard.] In the mountains, there is a strong wind . . . and they use the sound of the air . . . [Alfredo blows into the wooden flute.] A natural sound. Thus . . . they cut the cane, make a tube out of it, and put in the mouth . . . but with six holes in it . . . this wind instrument is called "*quena.*" [Alfredo writes down *quena* on the blackboard.] And you use the "*quena*" for love songs and songs of pain . . . this instrument is sometimes used for happiness and sometimes for sadness. [Alfredo finishes the lesson with the classification and naming of instruments in relation to the different classification groups.]

Since Lourdes used mostly vocal texts that were presented in a holistic pedagogical style, the students concentrated on the Spanish words and did not concentrate on the melody much and did not pay excessive attention to Lourdes playing the instruments. Lourdes instead maintained a fine balance between playing music authentically as promised to the students and also getting the maximum reuse of the songs she had already presented to them so that they would perfect their Spanish through recycled songs and their imitation of these recycled songs. The experience of singing the Spanish songs rhythmically and with a great degree of loudness had a great deal to do with the heightened qualities of student motivation found in Lourdes' lessons. The songs that increased in speed also were the ones that increased the dynamic swell of loudness in the classroom, a loudness that was tolerated by Roberta only during Lourdes' lessons. Overall, there were an ebb and flow of pitch, crescendos and speed that developed from the fluctuating and impulsive surges and calming resolutions from song to song.

By moving quickly from one song to another, Lourdes produced a forward moving propulsion in her music lessons that followed a logic of continuity and consecution, which eventually enveloped the students in spirit from start to finish. Subsequently, there was a steady rhythmic pulse to Lourdes' lessons as she moved toward a resolution that always ended with the same song just as she always began her lesson with the same song. Timing the songs and sequencing the songs in a certain pattern

allowed Lourdes to keep building momentum throughout each successive phase of her music lessons because the sequencing produced a
serialism that opened the students' eyes to repetition and symmetry within
the musical experience (Lippman, 1999). The following transcript shows
how quickly Lourdes transitioned from one song to the other and moved
students along a series of three songs within minutes; however, the
following transcript also provides evidence of the gender-based structural
borders and boundaries that are often produced in musical productions
when girls are asked to sing one part of a song while boys are asked to
sing another part of the song based on differences in text and melody.
In fact, many of Lourdes' music lessons reproduced bounded gender
positions that remained unquestioned; thus, there was no crossing of
gender borders and boundaries within the music lessons as evident in the
drama chapter:

Lourdes: *Chicos . . . perdóname . . . la palabra "Guantanamera" viene
de la palabra "Guantanamo" y es una provincia de cuba . . . digan
"Guantanamera" . . . repitan . . .*
English translation:
[Boys . . . excuse me . . . the word "Guantanamera" comes from the
word "Guantanamo" and is a province in Cuba . . . say
"Guantanamera" . . . repeat . . .]

Students: *"Guantanamera"*

Lourdes: *No . . . digan "Guan . . . tan . . . a . . . mera"*
English translation:
[No . . . say "Guan . . . tan . . . a . . . mera"]

Lourdes and students: *"Guantanamera, guajira, guantanamera . . .
Guantanamera, guajira guantanamera."*

Lourdes: *Ahora solamente las chicas . . .*
English translation:
[Now only the girls . . .]

The girls:
  *"Yo soy una mujer sincera
  De donde crece la palma
  Yo soy una mujer sincera
  De donde crece la palma
  Y antes de morirme quiero
  Echar mis versos del alma."*

English translation:
"I am a very modest woman
From where the palm grows
I am a very modest woman
From where the palm grows
And before I die I want
To cast my verse from my soul."

Lourdes: *Y ahora los caballeros . . .*

English translation:
[And now the boys . . .]

The boys:
"Yo soy un hombre sincero
De donde crece la palma
Yo soy un hombre sincero
De donde crece la palma
Y antes de morirme quiero
Echar mis versos del alma."

English translation:
"I am a very modest man
From where the palm grows
I am a very modest man
From where the palm grows
And before I die I want
To cast my verse from my soul."

Yolanda: Lisa, are you a boy?
Maria: Javier, you're a boy . . . sing.

Lourdes: *Bien . . . muy bien . . . para terminar . . . vamos a hacer "En Mi Viejo San Juan" y después "Gracias a La Vida." Donde estan las copias de la semana pasada? De "Mi Viejo San Juan" y "Gracias a La Vida." Donde estan?*

English translation:
[Good . . . very good . . . to finish . . . we will do "In My Old San Juan" and then "I Thank Life." Where are the copies from last week? Of "In My Old San Juan" and then "I Thank Life"? Where are they?]

Claudio: *Lo perdió.*

English translation:
[I lost it.]

Lourdes: *Perdió? Chicos . . . seguimos . . . ustedes necesitan los papeles en sus manos . . . ya preparados? Es muy importante que lean las palabras . . .*

nos fuimos con "En Mi Viejo San Juan." [Lourdes now stands up with her guitar and walks around the circle and begins singing together with the students.]

English translation:
[Lost it? Boys . . . let's go . . . you guys need the papers in your hands . . . are you ready? It's very important that you read the words . . . we will go with "In My Old San Juan." [Lourdes now stands up with her guitar and walks around the circle and begins singing together with the students.]

Lourdes and students:
  "En mi viejo San Juan
  Cuantos sueños forjé
  En mis años de infancia
  Mi primera ilusión
  Y mis cuitas de amor
  Son recuerdos del alma

  Una tarde me fui
  A esa extraña nación
  Pues lo quiso el destino
  Pero mi corazón
  Se quedó junto al mar
  En mi viejo San Juan

  Adiós, adiós, adiós
  Boriquen querida
  Tierra de mi amor
  Adiós, adiós, adiós
  Mi diosa del mar
  Reina del palmar"

English translation:
  "In my old San Juan
  I had many dreams
  During my childhood
  My first illusion
  And my love woes
  Are memories of the soul

  One evening I left
  For that strange nation
  My fate willed it
  But my heart

Stayed by the sea
In my old San Juan

Goodbye, Goodbye, Goodbye
Dear Puerto Rico
Land of my love
Goodbye, Goodbye, Goodbye
My goddess of the sea
Queen of the palms."

Lourdes: *Bueno . . . ahora vamos a hacer "Gracias a La Vida" otra vez . . .*
Estamos preparados? Quiero que todos leanlo . . . porque es muy bueno para
ustedes a leer . . . y mejorar su lectura . . . y mejorar su dicción . . . su pro-
nunicion en español . . . esta canción es más trabajo pero yo quiero que ust-
edes lo hagan . . . por favor leen conmigo . . . yo voy a parar en el medio si yo
veo algien no leyendo . . . hay mucha gente con copias . . . [Lourdes motions
students who don't have a paper copy of the song to move next to
someone who has a copy of the song.] *Digále "Por favor puedo leer con-*
tigo?" No . . . no . . . papi . . . mira . . . [Lourdes motions Brian to sit next
to Yolanda who has a copy of the song.] *Puede compartir sus canciones.*
Yolanda la tiene . . . y sientate alreador de Yolanda . . . caballeros . . . nos
fuimos . . . "Gracias a La Vida."

English translation:
[Good . . . now we will do "I Thank Life" once again . . . Are you ready?
I want everyone to read it . . . because it is very important for you to
read . . . to improve your reading . . . and improve diction . . . your
pronunciation in Spanish . . . this song requires more work but I want
you to do it . . . please read with me . . . I will stop in the middle if I
see someone who is not reading . . . there are a lot of people with copies
. . . [Lourdes motions students who don't have a paper copy of the song
to move next to someone who has a copy of the song.] Tell them "Please
can I read with you?" No . . . no . . . young man . . . look . . . [Lourdes
motions Brian to sit next to Yolanda who has a copy of the song.] You
can share your songs. Yolanda has one . . . so sit near Yolanda . . . boys
. . . let's go . . . "I Thank Life."

Lourdes and students:
"Gracias a la vida que me ha dado tanto
Me dio dos luceros que cuando los abro
Perfecto distingo lo negro del blanco

Y en el alto cielo su fondo estrellado
Y en las multitudes al hombre que yo amo

Gracias a la vida que me ha dado tanto
Me ha dado el oido que en todo su ancho
Graba noche y día grillos y canarios
Martillos, turbina, ladridos, chubascos
Y la voz tan tierna de mi bien amado."

English translation:
"I thank life that has given me so much
It gave me two stars and when I open them
I can tell perfectly the black from the white
And make out in the high sky its many lights
And amidst the crowds, the man that I love.

I thank life, that has given me so much,
It has given me the sound, that in its expanse
Records night and day, crickets and canaries
Hammers, turbines, barkings, showers,
And the tender voice of my beloved."

Lourdes: *Fue muy bien . . . la última canción . . . acabar con "Allegre."*
[The students do not need their music sheets because they have memorized this song. Everyone gets up and starts clapping and dancing to this song before they transition to their desks.]

English translation:
[That was good . . . the last song . . . we'll finish with "Happiness."]
[The students do not need their music sheets because they have memorized this song. Everyone gets up and starts clapping and dancing to this song before they transition to their desks.]

The serialism of songs highlighted above produced an experience of music in which the connectedness of songs created a motion and movement, a flow of consciousness and a moment-to-moment progression that contrasted with music that was performed in discrete, isolated, unconnected acts during the music lessons with Alfredo. Furthermore, the repetition of certain harmonic and rhythmic progressions produces a kind of chain effect in which a song such as *Buenos Días Sol, Buenas Noches Luna*, which Lourdes played at the beginning of each music session, acts as a kind of introduction that sets up each musical experience with a sense of wholeness:

Buenos Días Sol, Buenas Noches Luna
(de Puerto Rico)

Buenos días sol,
buenas noches luna.
Hoy quiero cantar
y decirle al mundo
que no vale la pena
discutir . . .
Simplemente es mejor sonreir
Por eso es que . . .

Coro:
Sonar es vivir,
sonar es vivir.
Unamos las manos
Para, para, pa', para, para ser feliz.

Puedes darme ilusión,
puedes darme tú vida
para embelesar
con colores y luz
el jardín de mi vida.
Conamor . . .
lograremos un mundo mejor.
Por eso es que . . .

Coro:
Buenos días sol,
buenas noches luna.
Hoy mi corazón
esta lleno de luz,
esperanzas y risas.
No es el fin . . .
Hoy comienza un mundo feliz.
Por eso es que . . .

English translation:

Good Morning Sun, Good Night Moon
(from Puerto Rico)

Good morning, sun. Good night moon,
Today I want to sing and tell the world

That it is better
Not to fight . . .
It is better, simply, to smile
And that is why . . .

Chorus:
To dream is to live
To dream is to live
Let's join our hands
To, to, to, to be happy.

You can give me the illusion,
You can give me your life
To embellish with
Colors and light
My life's garden
With love . . .
Let's achieve a better world.
That is why . . .

Chorus:
Good morning sun,
Good night moon.
Today my heart
Is full of light,
Hopes and laughter.
This is not the end . . .
Today is the start of a happy world.
That is why . . .

The repetition of songs such as *Buenos Días Sol, Buenas Noches Luna* throughout Lourdes' lessons allowed the dual immersion students to memorize the text of the Spanish songs in syncopation with their musical structures, thus connecting musical intelligence with linguistic intelligence through the interrelationship of words and melody, text and tone. Sometimes even phrases within the songs were repeated several times, a ubiquitous characteristic of vocal music that is not found in everyday speech in Spanish or even in prose and poetry. The familar phrases from the songs made sense to the students each time Lourdes performed them while newly sounding phrases from unfamilar songs were much more difficult to comprehend readily in meaning and took several repetitions before the text became meaningful. Furthermore, music is often seen as the interplay of new musical sounds and text against retained older musical sounds and text in which we are always developing interrelationships between the old and the new sounds so that we may develop a schema for music (Lippman, 1999). The repetition of this rhythmic pattern of musical sounds and Spanish text also produced a certain sense of satisfaction amongst the students because of the expectations that Lourdes satisfied each time she visited the classroom, thus creating a feeling of necessity. Her use of serialism regularly produced a crescendo in which the songs increased in speed, pitch and the level of loudness in the classroom built up until the pace decreased and the students' spontaneity and expressiveness moved toward resolution as the class period ended. Moreover, there was never a feeling of incoherence or a breakdown in the propulsive forces of continuity produced in Lourdes' flowing music lessons because she never tired in her rapid compositional skills and quick techniques of presenting the music within that hour-long time period.

The Power of Music: Moving Closer Toward the Spanish Other

According to Lippman (1999), the forward motion of a musical experience can also produce a flow of consciousness similar to a stream of consciousness that goes beyond a simple stimulus/response reaction and involves a cognitive appreciation of music's complex nature. The perception of sadness in a moving piece of music, for example, can lead us to being in a mind of sadness, then being in a state of sadness itself:

Consciousness and sound have a profound ontological affinity with respect to time and because human nature is what it is, music is a quasi-natural representation of possible states of consciousness to human beings such that, at some level of awareness that is not ordinarily that of what one is attending to, we are presented with those possible states of consciousness by music; that is, music brings them to mind, *if not always to the conscious mind*. (Addis, 1999: 72)

In terms of the content of the songs, since Lourdes was Puerto Rican herself, as well as Roberta the classroom teacher, much of the Spanish music content produced in the classroom was Puerto Rican folk music. Furthermore, many of these songs portrayed ordinary people in everyday situations. The Puerto Rican students who lived nearby in *El Barrio* found Lourdes' songs to be traditional Puerto Rican music that they were accustomed to listening to at home in their urban enclaves. The patriotic words and familiar phrases in many of the songs strongly identified them as Puerto Rican. Even though the life experiences of many of the Puerto Rican students were reflected in Lourdes' songs, it was never essential for the English-dominant students to have knowledge of those life experiences in order to comprehend the music as well as to appreciate it. In fact, most of the dual immersion students took these songs to their hearts and made them into enduring memories, which says a great deal about their own needs and longings, about their personal relationship with Lourdes, and their output in Spanish. When the dual immersion students listened to Lourdes' Spanish songs every Thursday afternoon, they authentically imitated the musical sounds that they had produced the previous week with Lourdes, by mimicking the words down structurally and associatively, and by duplicating the intersensory consciousness that they had experienced in the past through such mimesis. In the hallways, on the playground and in other spaces and places outside of the classroom, I often encountered the dual immersion students singing Lourdes' songs aloud to themselves. In fact, I also found myself singing the more popular songs that Lourdes presented during her weekly lessons.

The mimetic faculty was exhibited mostly by the English-dominant students who copied and imitated the Spanish songs and thus yielded into becoming the Spanish-dominant Other during Lourdes' musical performances: "The capacity to mime is the capacity to Other" (Taussig, 1993: 19). For the English-dominant students, the mimetic faculty gave them the power to portray themselves as knowledgeable of the Spanish language and culture, which is what the dual immersion model wants them to ideally portray as well. Yet, a physiological sense of closeness was also produced from the mimetic faculty between the perceiver of music, the English-dominant students, and what was being perceived, the Spanish music, as the rhythms from the music palpitated inside the perceivers' bodies and unconscious. In *Reflections* (1978), Walter Benjamin states that language provides the highest level of mimetic power, defined by him as the capacity to produce similarities and the gift of seeing resemblance. When we are imitating another language, we are in turn establishing closer ties between our own personal identities and Other foreign identities. Through the constant habit of singing mostly the same songs in Spanish every Thursday afternoon, the mimesis of Spanish words in the songs allowed the English-dominant students to further model the correct identification, representation and expression of sounds, words, grammar and vocabulary in Spanish, as well as coming to a better understanding of the cultural and geographical origins of the Spanish folk songs. Moreover, their acquisition of Spanish through music was radically different from their acquisition of Spanish during formal academic discourse because of a mediating bodily connection between mind and sound that was not necessarily logical and axial but residual within their flow of consciousness. Thus, the use of Spanish music in dual immersion schooling can greatly enlarge the capacities for second language production of Spanish, especially for the English-dominant students.

The musical performances also allowed the English-dominant students to become and behave like somebody else, somebody other than their English-dominant selves, somebody outside of themselves. Yet, what does becoming the Other through the mimesis of Spanish music imply for the English-dominant students' sense of Self? What are they really imitating? By slipping in and out of Otherness, are the English-dominant students just playing the Spanish-dominant Other in a collective space where they are being tempted to diminish their sense of Self by losing its boundedness amidst the Spanish-dominant others – but only for a short period of time? Are they just trying on the Other for the sake of appearances or are they putting their pure self-identity into becoming the Other? It is within these musical experiences, at that moment when the listening self plunges forward into the Spanish music and songs, that we take notice of the splitting of the ontic self for the English-dominant students, of being Self and of being Other, of English-dominant students yielding to the surrounding Spanish environment and becoming the Other. Yet, even though the English-dominant students were indeed yielding to the Spanish music and becoming the Other, this yielding was not passive.

Instead, it was an active yielding because most of the English-dominant students, minus a few, were playing an active role in imitating the songs verbally, as well as contorting their bodies to dance to the music: "The active yielding of the perceiver in the perceived – the perceiver is trying to enter into the picture and become one with it, so that the self is moved by the representation into the represented" (Taussig, 1993: 61). By singing with the Spanish-dominant students and dancing with them, the English-dominant students tried to situate themselves into the picture. Their faithful imitation of the Spanish songs and dance through a great degree of similitude produced an image on the rug space in which there was a heightened likeness between the Spanish-dominant and English-dominant students. For the Spanish-dominant students, however, the musical experiences allowed them to dive further into their Spanish Self by reconnecting with music and dance from their respective homelands. For them the Spanish-dominant Self was not the Other, rather it was the known. Most of the Spanish-dominant students immediately recognized the songs that Lourdes introduced to them. Thus, there was no distance/difference for the Spanish-dominant students between music that was foreign to them and music that was indigenous to their native homelands.

Furthermore, mimesis is not only a matter of one being another being but it is also about this *tense yet fluid theatrical relation of form and space* (Taussig, 1993: 34). The rug space where the musical experiences occurred, for example, allowed for the spatial production of a form of fluidity and porosity in which the English-dominant students were able to blend together with the Spanish-dominant students through their mimetic excess, by way of their sensuous likeness, and their equivalent reproduction of the Spanish language. The collective bodies of both the English-dominant and Spanish-dominant students were in closer contact with each other in the rug space during the musical lessons. Yet, the English-dominant students' contact with the Spanish music also extended beyond the rug space since many of these students continued to sing the songs and hum the music even at a physical distance from the rug space, even after the physical contact with Lourdes was severed. Furthermore, after completing a song in Spanish, there were moments throughout Lourdes' lessons in which the English-dominant students asked questions regarding the textual meanings within the Spanish songs, thus exhibiting an active role in their acquisition and imitation of Spanish music and its meaning. Sometimes Lourdes would spend time explaining the meanings of the songs, especially songs that had veiled or ambiguous meanings that only a native Spanish speaker from the Hispanic Caribbean can know as a cultural insider. In turn, by explaining the hidden meanings within the songs, Lourdes no longer made the text the unknown. By means of Lourdes' defined explanations of the songs, the English-dominant students were also able to mimetically gain control over the reality that was represented in the songs:

Lourdes: *Okay . . . yo tengo una nueva canción . . . esta canción es muy popular . . . especialmente para los portorriqueños . . .* [Lourdes begins to sing the song and plays the guitar.]
"El jolgorio esta . . .
Ay por la maceta
Vamos a gozar . . . aja!!!
Vepa, vepa, vepa!!"
Qué es "por la maceta"? Qué quiere decir "por la maceta"?

English translation:
[Okay . . . I have a new song . . . this song is very popular . . . especially for Puerto Ricans . . . [Lourdes begins to sing the song and plays the guitar.]
"The party is
So cool
Let's enjoy ourselves . . . *aja*!!!
Vepa, vepa, vepa!"
What is *"por la maceta"*? What does *"por la maceta"* mean?]

Students: *No se.*
English translation:
[I don't know.]

Lourdes: *Hay alguien que quiere decir algo? Qué quiere decir "por la maceta"?*
English translation:
[Is there someone who wants to say something? What does *"por la maceta"* mean?]

Yolanda: Cute?

Lourdes: *No . . . no . . . que esta bueno . . . bueno . . . que el chico por ejemplo esta bueno . . . cuando piensas que algo esta bueno . . . esta por la maceta . . . esta buenisimo . . . ponen atención . . . cuando yo estoy hablando de las palabras . . . especialmente los norteamericanos . . . para que entienden lo que estan cantando . . . okay . . .* [Lourdes sings the song again but the students join in this time.]
English translation:
[No . . . no . . . it is good . . . good . . . the boy for example is good . . . when you think that something is good . . . it is *"por la maceta"* . . . it is very good . . . pay attention . . . when I am talking about the words . . . especially the Americans . . . so that you understand what you are singing . . . okay . . .] [Lourdes sings the song again but the students join in this time.]

Lourdes and students:
"El jolgorio esta . . .
Ay por la maceta
Vamos a gozar . . . aja!!!
Vepa, vepa, vepa!!"

English translation:
"The party is
So cool
Let's enjoy ourselves . . . *aja*!!!
Vepa, vepa, vepa!"

Lourdes: *Qué quiere decir "vepa, vepa, vepa"?* [There is no response from the students.] *Eso es simplamente una expresión . . . no es una palabra . . . "vepa" is como "ve-pa"!* [Lourdes exclaims the word.] *Es una cosa buena . . . es como "hay hombre!" . . . es para brincar el sonido. Se usa para el sonido pero solamente es un expresión . . . vamos a cantar otra vez . . .*

English translation:
[What does *"vepa, vepa, vepa"* mean? [There is no response from the students.] This is simply an expression . . . no it is a word . . . *vepa* is like *"ve-pa"*! [Lourdes exclaims the word.] It is a good thing . . . it is like "oh man!" . . . it is for pumping the sound. You use it for sound effects but it is also an expression . . . let's sing it another time . . .]

Lourdes and students:
"El jolgorio esta . . .
Ay por la maceta
Vamos a gozar . . . aja!!!
Vepa, vepa, vepa!!"

English translation:
"The party is
So cool
Let's enjoy ourselves . . . *aja*!!!
Vepa, vepa, vepa!"

Lourdes: Okay . . . *bueno . . . esta canción tiene una otra parte . . .* [Lourdes sings the second verse.]
"Si me dan pasteles
Demelos calientes
Que pasteles frios
Empachan la gente."
Qué quiere decir esta canción? Los portorriqueños? La segunda parte . . . "Si me dan pasteles" . . .

English translation:
[Okay . . . good . . . this song has a second part . . .] [Lourdes sings the second verse.]

"If you give me pastries
Give them to me hot
Because cold pastries
Give people a stomachache."
What does this song say? The Puerto Ricans? The second part . . . "If you give me pastries" . . .

Roberta: If you give me pastries . . .

Lourdes: *Que bueno . . .*
English translation:
[Oh good . . .]

Roberta: But there's no such equivalent in English . . .

Lourdes: *Okay . . . chicos . . . escuchan . . . esta información es para los estudiantes que no son portorriqueños . . . los pasteles son . . . es algo que comen . . . es salado . . . se hace con tubérculos que son plantas de la tierra . . . como papas . . . es una cosa . . . que tiene carne adentro . . . se ponen en unos papeles especiales . . . esa es mi comida favorita . . . es buen rico . . . entonces qué quiere decir esta canción . . . Juana . . . sabes que es en íngles? Qué son pasteles . . . más o menos?*

English translation:
[Okay . . . boys . . . listen . . . this information is for the students who are not Puerto Rican . . . the pastries are . . . it is something you eat . . . it's salty . . . they make it out of tubers that are plants from the ground . . . like potatoes . . . it is something . . . that you put meat inside . . . then they put it inside special papers . . . it is my favorite food . . . it is really rich . . . so what does this song say . . . Juana . . . do you know what it is in English? What are *"pasteles"* . . . more or less?]

Juana: *Son . . .*
English translation:
[They are . . .]

Roberta: *No . . . porque la verdad es que no hay algo como pasteles en íngles. Un pastel . . .* which does not have an English equivalent . . .
English translation:
[No . . . because in truth there isn't anything like *"pasteles"* in English. A *"pastel"* . . . which does not have an English equivalent . . .]

Lourdes: Dígale maestra . . .

English translation:
[Tell them teacher ...]

Roberta: It's an indigenous food to the Caribbean ... it's made out of *"plátanos"* which are like bananas but they are huge ...
Jose: Plantains.
Roberta: Yes ... plantains ... and you can't eat them raw. You have to cook them. But to make *"pasteles"* ... which is a very complicated thing to do ... you have to grate ... you have to grate ... you have to grate the plantains ... and then you can add a little bit of ... uh ... they are tubers ... they're like ... they're like potatoes ... but when I say tubers I mean a plant that grows in the ground. So yucca is a tropical plant that grows in the ground ... they're tubers okay ... so you take some of those and you grate them. Then you make like a soft ... uh ... it looks like batter ... and then you put inside and it's wrapped in paper ... sometimes ... actually it was originally wrapped in banana leaves ... and then you boil them for an hour ... yum ....
Lourdes: They're the most delicious thing that you can eat ... that's one of my favorite foods ... ever ... ever ... ever.
Students: Heh! You're speaking in English! [Jose and Yolanda start pointing at Lourdes.]

Lourdes: *Perdóname ... perdóname ... entonces ... los pasteles necisita comer cuando son caliente porque cuando son fríos ... esta cosa tiene grasa ... empachan por el estómago ... entonces ... que quiere decir esta canción Yolanda? Ya te pregunte. Puede explicar en íngles? Que quiere decir la canción? Yolanda nos diga.*

English translation:
[Forgive me ... forgive me ... so ... the *"pasteles"* need to be eaten when they are hot because when they are cold ... this thing has a lot of grease ... it sticks to the stomach ... so ... what does this song say Yolanda? What does the song say? Yolanda will tell us.]

Yolanda: The song is about ... the fatty food from Puerto Rico ... and they say that come give it to me hot and not cold ... because if you eat it cold ... you get a stomachache.

Lourdes: *Muy bien ... que esta frío ... le da doler en el estómago ... nos fuimos otra vez!* [They sing both verses of the song once again.]
English translation:
[Very good ... when it is cold ... it gives us a stomachache ... let's go one more time! [They sing both verses of the song once again.]

Nostalgic Music: Moving Toward the Sublime

The revelation of the textual meaning of a song often produced an awakening in the English-dominant students when they discovered the themes of the songs. Yet, most of the songs revolved around themes of nostalgia for the homeland. The lyrics of the mournful songs that Lourdes sang were often penned by homesick migrants who left the Puerto Rican pastoral behind and came to New York City. Songs of the pastoral depend on the distant memory of the mostly male Hispanic migrants, regardless of whether their recollections could be misleading and falsified for the listener. The oversimplified image of simple peasants listening to rustic, homegrown, timeless music was often reproduced in Lourdes' Spanish songs. However, the reality of Puerto Rican music is much more complicated than what Lourdes presented since there are several different musical genres in Puerto Rico that represent distinct heterogeneous geographical regions on the island. In the mountain area of Puerto Rico, one can find the *seis* and *aguinaldo* musical genres and on the coastal plains one can find the *bomba* and *plena* musical genres. African derived call-and-response vocal styles, as well as African instruments, are both used in the *bomba* and *plena* musical genres ever since the African slaves who were brought over to Puerto Rico by the Spaniards reproduced them for their slave celebrations on the one day during the week when they were not enslaved to work on the sugar plantations (Glasser, 1995):

Lourdes: *Hay otra canción . . . miren . . . hay otras canciones . . . estas canciones son parte de la música de porto rico . . . de música popular . . . que se llama "bomba" y "plena" . . . esta música . . . le dije eso la semana pasada . . . pero yo voy a decir otra vez . . .*

English translation:
[There is another song . . . look . . . there are other songs . . . these songs are a part of Puerto Rican music . . . of popular music . . . that they call "*bomba*" and "*plena*" . . . this music . . . I told you this last week . . . but I will say it again . . .]

Jose: *Yo quiero decir . . . que . . . que . . . una gente venieron en la nueva york . . . y hicieron un canto de baile . . . que se llama "bomba" . . .*

English translation:
[I want to say . . . that . . . that . . . a group of people in New York City . . . and they made up a dance . . . called "*bomba*" . . .]

Lourdes: *Si . . . el es más seguro . . . el mayor hicieron en nueva york . . .*

English translation:
[Yes . . . he is correct . . . the majority was made in New York City . . .]

Students: They did?

Lourdes: *Sí.*
English translation:
[Yes.]

Ya Me Voy was one of the many traditional Puerto Rican folk songs performed every Thursday, which reinforced the idea that Lourdes' selection of songs was autobiographical in nature. Oftentimes, musicians select songs that reveal their own values and sensitivies toward life and thus the selection of songs reveals how identities of the self are formed (Lippman, 1999). The pain of nostalgia felt during the performance of this song was just as strong for the students as the pain of being estranged from one's native country was for adults such as Roberta and Lourdes. Whenever *Ya Me Voy* song was performed, there were always some Spanish-dominant students who became emotional out of nostalgia while others were crying over their recent estrangement from their native homelands. The folk music stirred their imagination and produced an effect that aroused extreme emotions from within their spirits. By finding the homeland in Lourdes' musical performances, the students were beginning to understand how music takes root in the Self. At times, the more folkloric the song then the more nostalgic the students became for their respective homelands:

Ya Me Voy

Me voy, ya me voy
pero un día volvere
a buscar mi querer,
a sonar otra vez
en mi viejo San Juan

Pero el tiempo paso
y el destino burlo
mi terrible nostalgia

Y no puede volver
al San Juan que yo ame
pedacito de patria

Mi Cabello blanqueo
ya mi vida se va
y la muerte me llama,

. . . Y no quiere morir
alejada de ti
Puerto Rico del alma

English translation:

I Am Leaving Now

I am leaving, I am leaving now
But one day, I'll return
To find my love,
To sound again in
My Old San Juan

But time went by
And fate clouded
My terrible nostalgia

And I could not return
To the San Juan I loved,
Little bit of homeland

My hair turned white
Today, life is leaving me
Death is calling me

And I do not want to die
So far from you,
My Puerto Rico

In addition to music being symbolic for the individual listener, many people feel that music allows us to transcend our present situations by permitting us to travel in the past and recollect our initial experiences with that music and its particular sounds. Music transcends life when it moves above the words and images defining it in the present moment. Music is thus played in the real time of the present as well as in the memory of the past and serves to organize temporal patterns of cognition within the listener. In turn, music allows us to both escape from our present-day lives; it also gives us the power to release our feelings, escape into another world and gives expression to unconscious emotions that cannot manifest themselves in any other medium. Some feel strongly that music should be classified within the category of the sublime because of its potential power to blind our vision and all other senses while listening to its sounds. Beautiful music has the bewitching potential to become the sublime through its spellbinding powers that leave music for students elusive and unmemorizable: "Music . . . a beauty of being that is outside the subjective, aimed at making us forget our moods, our passions and pains, ourselves . . . to make us plunge into ourselves, feel the self with a terrible intensity, and forget everything outside" (Kundera, 1995: 74).

The emotions generated from sublime music often reach a climax in which the listener identifies intensely with the present moment of sensation to the point of the sublimation and negation of Self, sometimes returning to the past and forgetting the future. Devotional music, such as the Sufi music performed by Islamic devotees, is intended to produce an ecstatic and sublime state of mind in the listener so that through the performers' words and music the listeners lose their sense of mind, leading to the sensation of actualized religious transport. Soon, Lourdes was known throughout the school for her nostalgic, romantic and patriotic ballads that often produced moments of the sublime. The song *Compadre Pedro Juan* was another nostalgic song that allowed the students and teacher to travel into the past to a mythical Puerto Rico from another time:

Compadre San Juan

Compadre Pedro Juan, baile el jaleo
Compadre Pedro Juan, que esta sabroso
Aquella niña de los ojos negros
que tiene el cuerpo flexible
bailala en la empaliza

Compadre Pedro Juan, no pierda el tiempo
Compadre Pedro Juan, saque su dama
Se acabara el merengue y si no anda con cuida'o
se quedara como un perico atasca'o
Sí señor!

Coro:

Baile – Compadre Pedro Juan
baile – de aquí pa'lla
baile – de alla pa' 'ca
baile – de medio la'o
baile – medio jinca'o

baile – y a pambicha'o
baile – aco' taito
baile – de madruga'
baile – aquí en la escuela
baile – y en la ciuda'

English translation:

My Friend Pedro Juan

My friend Pedro Juan, dances the rhythm
My friend Pedro Juan, because it's so good.
That girl with the black eyes
And the agile body,
Dance with her at the fence.

My friend Pedro Juan, don't lose any time.
My friend Pedro Juan, ask your lady for a dance!
The *merengue* dance will end and if you don't move
You'll end up like a stuck parrot,
Yes sir!

Chorus:
Dance – my friend Pedro Juan.
Dance – this way and that
Dance – that way and this
Dance – sideways
Dance – on bent knees

Dance – close together
Dance – lying down a bit
Dance – in the early morning
Dance – here at school
Dance – and in the city

The following transcript describes how the musical performance of *Compadre Pedro Juan* created a sublime moment that allowed the teacher, Roberta, to plunge into her Self, and feel the Self with terrible intensity via this Puerto Rican folk song:

Roberta: *Esta canción . . . me llevaste . . . me llevaste . . .* [Roberta starts crying and Yolanda is holding her hand to console her] *a mi juventud . . . y a mi mamí . . . y puerto rico . . .* [Roberta is gasping for air as she continues to cry. The students are listening in silence] *. . . gracias Lourdes . . .* [Roberta wipes her tears away.]

English translation:
[This song . . . brought me . . . brought me . . . [Roberta starts crying and Yolanda is holding her hand to console her.] to my youth . . . and to my mother . . . and Puerto Rico . . . [Roberta is gasping for air as she continues to cry. The students are listening in silence] . . . thanks Lourdes . . . [Roberta wipes her tears away.]

Lourdes: *Gracias . . . la música tiene el poder . . . no se . . . por la canción nosotros recuerdamos cosas lindas . . .*

English translation:
[Thanks . . . music has the power . . . we don't know . . . through the song we remember beautiful things . . .]

Roberta: *Lindísima*

English translation:
[Very beautiful things]

Lourdes: *Bueno . . . el poder de música . . . cuando vengo aquí y toco la música . . . como la música transporta uno en la historia . . . transporta a nosotros en el pasado . . . cuando cantaban Compadre Pedro Juan . . . los versos transportan a nosotros a puerto rico . . . solamente la música puede transportar a nosotros . . . que honor . . . que Compadre Pedro Juan transporta a su maestra . . . que honor tiene esta canción . . .*

English translation:
[Good . . . the power of music . . . when I come here and play music . . . the music transports one into history . . . it transports us into the past . . . when we were singing *Compadre Pedro Juan* . . . the verses transported us to Puerto Rico . . . only music can transport us . . . what honor . . . that *Compadre San Juan* was able to transport your teacher . . . what honor this song has . . .]

Yet, perhaps the folk songs Lourdes performed for the dual immersion classroom were reproducing a *sentimental folk* in which the songs were overflowing with dramatized feeling and nothing else (Kundera, 1995). By uncritically adopting folk music for its nostalgia, Lourdes imbued her performance of songs such as *Ya Me Voy* and *Compadre Pedro Juan* with a longing for a bucolic Puerto Rico or an imagined *Borinquen*, evoking the image of a unified and cohesive utopian Puerto Rican nation-state in which authentic music is made only by genuine members of the real ethnic community. The ethnic identity produced by folk music, such as in the *Ya Me Voy* and *Compadre Pedro Juan* songs, projects a false image of ethnic cohesiveness and unity by not taking into account the evolutions of ethnic identity and the cultural production of music as stuff that is constantly made and remade as the nation-state changes itself.

Most Americans have had very little exposure to Puerto Rican music, even though Puerto Rico is still seen as an American colony due to its sovereignty over the nation-state. On the other hand, Cuban music has made a greater impact on the development of American music, much more so than Puerto Rican music, and its sounds have dominated the Latin American music scene. Furthermore, the limited understanding we do have of Puerto Rican music is often tainted by a cultural deficit framework in which cultural outsiders in the past have defined the Puerto Rican culture as weak in folk arts, unsure in its cultural traditions and without a powerful faith (Glazer & Moynihan, 1963). The political and cultural hierarchies between former colonies and neo-colonies such as Puerto Rico, first colonized by Spain and then the United States, have led to the denial of a shared musical history amongst postcolonial Caribbean nations such as Cuba, the Dominican Republic, Haiti and Puerto Rico, as well as the subsequent dominance of one group of ethnic sounds over another. Furthermore, the musical identity of the indigenous ethnic groups that existed in the Caribbean prior to the arrival of Spaniards, such as the Taino and Arawak populations in Puerto Rico who were the first groups to be decimated by colonialism, has been erased from the musical narrative due to the erasure of indigenous languages and cultures from the national identity. However, the influence of the Taino language and musical culture was felt by the dual immersion students when Lourdes decided to introduce *Otinyo* into the repertoire. At first, the students assumed the lyrics were in Spanish but then were surprised to find that they did not recognize most of the words in the song. Any essentialist understanding of music from the Hispanic Caribbean was eliminated when the students were exposed to a proliferation of musical styles and genres that exemplified the differentiation of Hispanic music.

Otinyo

Otinyo-Sarawe (4X)
Sara-sara-sarawe
Otinyo-Sarawe
Sara-sara-sarawe
Otinyo-Sarawe

Se me metio Belie Belcan
Otinyo-Sarawe

Se me metio Metresile
Otinyo-Sarawe

Otinyo-Sarawe (4X)
Sara-sara-sarawe
Otinyo-Sarawe
Sara-sara-sarawe
Otinyo-Sarawe

However, most of the nostalgic songs and ballads that Lourdes played reflected the *jibiro* style of Puerto Rican folk music. *Música jibara* developed over several centuries in the mountainous regions of Puerto Rico where small farmers cultivated its native sound (Glasser, 1995). Indigenous genres such as *música jibara* and indigenous instruments were often used in Lourdes' music lessons. *Jibaro* music came about when coffee, fruit and tobacco farmers in the mountains of Puerto Rico celebrated their ethnic identity as independent of other sectors of mainland Puerto Rican society and thus *jibaro* music produced a counterculture to the Spanish colonial government in San Juan, the capital, and the government's extensions throughout the island (Glasser, 1995). When Lourdes performed *jibaro* music, she used the *maracas*, a rattle instrument made from gourds whose genealogy can be traced to the African diaspora, along with the colonial Spanish guitar to create music that reflected diverse ethnic roots as well as diverse socioeconomic and geographical backgrounds.

Yet, sometimes when she played *jibaro* music, Lourdes would request the sole black student in the classroom, Shakima, to perform a traditional dance that often accompanied *jibaro* music. Standing in the center of the rug circle, no longer connected to the circle of her peers on the periphery, Shakima would dance to the African-derived rhythms found in *jibaro* music. But nobody questioned why Shakima was the sole dancer selected to perform to the *jibaro* music, almost caricaturing the source of this music. Shakima herself was startled at first as to why she alone was selected to dance to the *jibaro* song; however, she soon took on the repeated role with bemusement. In this way, Shakima as the sole black student was stereotyped as being naturally rhythmic and dance-orientated by Lourdes, a semi-conscious decision that was not questioned by the other students and classroom teacher.

In the following *jibaro* song that Shakima often danced, *Duerme Negrito*, the semantic meanings derived from the lyrics reflect the oppression of the Afro-Puerto Rican population enslaved to the sugar plantations. It is actually a lullaby in which someone is singing to a black baby whose mother is working in the plantation fields. The narrator wants the black baby to sleep so that *the white devil* will not come and eat its feet. The white devil is a euphemism for the white slave owner who does not pay the slaves enough for their work, even though they keep working harder for him, according to the lyrics. The meanings in the text of this song are present both literally in its words and also when the meaning is transformed into its tonal shape. When *Duerme Negrito* is performed in a collective form, its performance takes on the lamenting rhythms and movements found in *jíbaro* music:

Duerme Negrito
(*de la cultura africana de Puerto Rico*)

Duerme, duerme negrito
que tú mama esta en el campo, negrito.
Duerme, duerme movila
que tú mama esta en el campo, movila.

Te va a traer codornices para ti.
Te va a traer carne de cerdo para ti.
Te va a traer ricas frutas para ti.

Y si negro no se duerme,
viene el diablo blanco y Zazz!
le come las patitas chicapun, chicapun,
a pun, pun, pun,
chicapun, chicapun

Duerme, duerme negrito
que tú mama esta en el campo, negrito.
Duerme, duerme movila
Que tú mama esta en el campo, movila.

Trabajando, si
trabajando duramente
trabajando, si
trabajando, y no le pagan
trabajando, si
trabajando negrito chiquito
trabajando, si
trabajando, si

Coro:
Te va a traer codornices para ti.
Te va a traer carne de cerdo para ti.
Te va a traer ricas frutas para ti.

Y si negro no se duerme,
Viene el diablo blanco y Zazz!
Le come las patitas chicapun, chicapun,
A pun, pun, pun,
chicapun, chicapun

English translation:

Sleep, Little Black Boy
(from Puerto Rico's African culture)

Sleep, sleep, little black boy,
Your mommy is in the fields, little black boy

She is going to bring quails for you
She is going to bring pork meat for you
And she is going to bring you delicious fruit.

And if the little black boy does not go to sleep
The white devil is going to come and Zazz!
He will eat his little feet sheek-a-boom, sheek-a- boom
boom, boom, boom
Sheek-a- boom, sheek-a- boom.

Chorus:
She is working, yes,
She is working hard
Working, yes
Working, and they don't pay her
Working, yes
Working, little black boy
Working, yes
Working, yes

The Afro-Hispanic Element in the Folk: Deconstructing *Duerme Negrito*

Den Tandt (1999) states that folk music and dance in Puerto Rico often appropriates its *afro-portorriqueño* (Afro-Puerto Rican) heritage and consequently uses this folk music to allude to the offensive cultural politics dividing a Hispanic Caribbean nation such as Puerto Rico with a

tripartite ancestry that produces a hierarchical *difference* in its racial identity: Spanish, Taino and African. The *negrista* (black) aesthetic found in
songs such as *Duerme Negrito* produces a discursive construct that reifies
black culture in folkloric celebrations of Afro-Caribbeanness of the past
while obscuring the present-day inequalities experienced by black Puerto
Ricans in the everyday. Moreover, it also brackets a dehumanizing
and degrading *negrista* identity that is commensurate with the white,
Anglophile nationalism found in Puerto Rico that wants to erase its blackness and *indígenismo* (indigeneous culture). However, at the same time,
these *negrista* songs produce a *schizophrenic consciousness* in which a black
and African presence in the musical texts consciously undermines the
white, Anglophile discourse always, in the end, under siege (Den Tandt,
1999: 77). Furthermore, the *negrista* aesthetic does not allow for a *mestizo*
(Native Indian mixed), Creole and mulatto space where race and ethnicity are made far more complex than the formulaic, premodern and essentialist race categories of Spanish, Taino and African. Unfortunately, the
afrocubanismo (Afro-Cubanism) movement that started in Cuba during the
1930s never found its equivalent in Puerto Rico where the race consciousness movement never flourished to the degree that it did in com-
munist Cuba, even though both nations share a similar history of African
slavery and Spanish colonialism (Glasser, 1995). Yet, *jibaro* music and
songs such as *Duerme Negrito* are also seen as a form of lyrical protest by
the working-class peasantry in which they express their struggles of
oppression and in which they embody a storytelling form that speaks to
immediate conditions and events in the *jibaro*'s life such as the platform
for agrarian reform, anti-poverty campaigns and the effects of modernization while never abandoning their discourse of slavery and *negritud*:

> *"Lamento Borincano"* tells the story of a Puerto Rican *jibaro*, a subsist-
> ence farmer from the mountainous interior of the island who goes into
> town to sell . . . "the bag or two of tubers" that his "scrappy patch of
> land has thrown up." Unfortunately, when he goes into town, he
> discovers that it is closed up, a casualty of the Depression and increas-
> ingly difficult subsistence for Puerto Rican farmers since the American
> invasion in 1898. The *jibaro* returns to his home crushed, his dreams of
> a better life shattered. (Glasser, 1995: 163)

In *The Black Atlantic* (1993: 100), Paul Gilroy critiques music from
the African diaspora and points to the need for critical dialogue that
challenges the *ethnic essence of blackness* often portrayed in organic phenomenon such as music. Even though a folk song such as *Duerme Negrito*

may claim to add to a pluralistic stance toward black culture in the Caribbean, nonetheless, music needs to also be examined as a sociohistorical construct. The historical character of music must not be misrepresented or underrepresented in the critical dialogue surrounding the ethnic essence of blackness as depicted in music such as *Duerme Negrito*. Slavery forced the African diasporic community to confront early on the problem of slave production as unfree labor and dehumanization, as depicted in the song *Duerme Negrito*. Yet, through its vernacular critique, this song also produces a response in which the black baby boy resembles a free subject in a slave society. The music of the African diaspora must be brought into question when a mechanized, dehumanized, sacrificial subject such as the black mother in *Duerme Negrito* is called upon as well to postpone the self-realization of her enslavement and to labor for others (Nesbitt, 2001). In turn, musical production in the classroom is often caught in a contradictory bind between the need for unhindered, musical expression and experience and the need to stop and examine the sociohistorical construct of the music produced.

Perhaps it is here where the study of music from an ethnomusicology framework can bring insight into the cultural context and heritage of music. Ethnomusicology can add to music education by introducing an evolutionist perspective of music as well as using comparative musicology to better understand the cross-cultural contexts of music in different settings and at different times. Ethnomusicologists attach a greater degree of importance to meaningful comparisons of music cultures and to the interpretation of the musical data in order to open up the real issues concerning music production. Asking students what the songs convey and the moods and emotions felt in the music can be the initial step in allowing students to have greater control over deciding the multiple meanings underlining music, thereby enriching their music education; however, the evolution of that music and its sociohistorical construct must also be discussed from a dialectical framework.

An ethnomusicologist's interpretation of a song, for example, can mediate a discussion between the structural analysis of that piece of music, such as *Duerme Negrito*, and the social situations in which it was produced – i.e. black slave life on colonial Spanish plantations. Also, through an ethnomusicology framework, the tension between the figural and literal textual meanings of *Duerme Negrito* can also lead to a wonderful exchange between students and produce critical dialogue concerning the coded language within musical texts, and the multiple characters, events and situations represented in the musical texts. If students are given the opportunity to generate their own knowledge production of the music through collective discussions of the ideological meanings hidden in the musical texts, then they have produced a collective consciousness of the text by getting at its many significations. Thus, the reality depicted within the musical text can be deconstructed through the work of the human unconscious as it tries to ascertain the relationship between language and music in order to trace its linguistic and melodic significations (Lyotard, 1998).

By raising the students' levels of critical consciousness of sociopolitical concerns within music and within their own respective social worlds, music education can become a cue device for social agency in the classroom (DeNora, 2000). The metaphor of the white devil eating the black baby's feet in *Duerme Negrito*, for example, has a hidden ideology that needs to be uncovered through a dialectical discussion of what that metaphor signifies. One must dwell on the metaphors in the text and reflect on the multiple sides of meaning without seeking quick answers. Furthermore, the unfolding of what the text signifies also allows students to relate the songs to each other and see if they can give them a wider perspective of what historical events and processes were taking place at that time in the various Hispanic Caribbean countries. The issue at stake here is whether this form of signification should be given a privileged place in music education. If students are given interpretive freedom, then the interpretive practice of analyzing the signification of texts needs to be privileged within the music curriculum. Thus, the production of an agency-sustaining music habitat needs to become the focus of continued research in education by recording how that agency-sustaining habitat within classrooms is constructed, maintained and deconstructed as it continues to affect the bodies, hearts and social consciousness of students through their moods, energy levels, desires, pleasures and actions.

Conclusion: Music as the In-Between Space

Unlike the teaching of a foreign language such as Spanish, the teaching of music communicates something that language cannot, even though music is a language in itself with its own syntax and structure. Music is a language of a different nature because it can capture intersensory emotions and moods that language cannot do so physiologically. Music simultaneously has the power to convey measured diction through songs and presents language within its tonal texts. The unique nature of a musical experience, furthermore, allows listeners to have a *synthetic response* to music because it allows the listener to produce images and thoughts of some kind during the act of listening, thus leading to the extension of ideas from the musical text and producing a metaphysical reaction not frequently found in language education (Lippman, 1999).

The ideas inherent within a piece of music also become tangible and physical when these ideas manifest themselves in the listeners' unconscious and subsequently the music becomes symbolic, cathartic and sometimes sublime for the listener. Sometimes the words in a musical text also become symbolic of emotions and thoughts extracted from their coded meanings. Melodic patterns inherent in music, as well as actual instruments and lyrics and other elemental attributes of music such as tone and pitch, arouse feelings and moods that become symbolically attached to that piece of music. Moreover, when we listen to music that we have heard before, the music now carries with it representations of the experiences it had produced in the past because of our previous associations with it. Sometimes the perception of music is also bound up with bodily orientation when our bodies respond physically to the music such as through head motions and the clapping of hands. Others also state differences in that speech allows us to convey our internal thoughts while music allows us to convey our internal emotions and feelings because the words in a song are attached to a melody and this metrical and rhythmical dualism has the power to produce radical changes in emotions – such as the sublime. The tonal experience of listening to music with our auditory and visual sensations is in turn different from listening to linguistic speech because the emotional character of music produces extramusical emotions represented structurally in the sounds.

Even though vocal music and speech both have a common origin, singing a song in Spanish does not necessarily resemble or represent uttered speech in Spanish (Lippman, 1999). Even though singing in Spanish is modeled on Spanish speech patterns, vocal songs are instead a product of heightened speech. From the standpoint of the voice, vocal music also becomes distinct from speech from the aspect of quantity because when a single person is speaking an utterance only a single voice can be heard at a time in order to comprehend the conveyed message. However, in music, a number of polyphonic voices come together in unison to produce a symbolic whole. Furthermore, some theorists feel that music conveys what language cannot by representing the unspeakable in verbal language, by representing subtleties that language cannot. Still others state that music is located in the right hemisphere of the brain where creativity is situated while language is located in the left hemisphere where a sense of control is situated (Langer, 1953).

Thus, we can state that music lies somewhere between language and thought and occupies an in-between space where it achieves its effects independent of the human will and through a stream of flowing consciousness. Music stands outside of conscious thought, and at the other end, music stands outside of language because of its abilities to produce physiological responses, via emotions and moods, that are not necessarily approximated and contingent in reality. Furthermore, in a dual immersion program, the imitation and mimesis of Spanish music can produce a liminal space or a *third space* in which both sociocultural student groups, English-dominant and Spanish-dominant, are positioned and situated alongside each other at one and the same time. In this episode, the third space is the space where difference is neither One nor the Other but something else besides – an in-between space where the One and the Other come together in a dynamic and evolving interaction: "The concept of third space represents the act of encounter which is always in a fluid state since it is always in a state of becoming and hence, cannot be fixed into any stable final formulation" (Bhabha, 1994: 208).

Even though music is not a visual medium defined by spatial constructs, it can nonetheless produce a virtual, metaphorical third space in which there is a border-crossing flow and movement of languages and cultures; music thus can be an agent for understanding the emergent third space. Bhabha (1994: 209) further notes that we must find "those words with which we can speak of Ourselves and Others. And by exploring this hybridity, this 'Third Space' we may elude to the politics of polarity and emerge as the others of our selves." Processional and performative acts, such as Lourdes' Spanish music performances, in turn become mean-ingful cultural engagements between *Ourselves and Others* that can result in a realized third space through the articulation of words that explore the hybridity between *Ourselves and Others*.

The performative production of Spanish music allowed the English-dominant students, for example, to explore the cultural hybridity between the English-Self and the Spanish-Other, while the Spanish-dominant students more so explored the ethnic hybridity between the Puerto Rican-Self and the Dominican-Self. Thus, the mimetic space of Spanish music can be posited as a third space that produces an interzone between the various student social groups, as well between the multiple ethnic Spanish-dominant groups, who otherwise at times remained socially segregated from one other during the school year. The mimesis of music in turn produces an epistemic moment when the listening subject occu-pies the space in-between multiple social worlds. The mimetic space allowed the English-dominant students to slip into becoming Other, becoming a Spanish Self, through the copying, reproduction and per-formance of Spanish music and dance – an in-between space of Self and

Other where linearity and homogeneity are rejected in favor of heterogeneity and discontinuity. The mimetic space also allowed the Spanish-
dominant students to slip into becoming the Spanish Self, becoming
perhaps another kind of ethnic Spanish Self, through the copying of music
that crossed national and geographic borders and boundaries across
the Spanish-speaking world. Thus, the realization of identity in the interstitial, third space is not fixed, since the Self is always emerging and
processual:

> Mimesis plays the trick of dancing between the very same and the very
> different. An impossible but necessary, indeed an everyday affair,
> mimesis registers both sameness and difference, of being like, and of
> being Other. Creating stability from this instability is no small task, yet
> all identity information is engaged in this habitually bracing activity
> in which the issue is not so much staying the same, but maintaining
> sameness through alterity. (Taussig, 1993: 129)

The imitation of Spanish verse also produced a space of excess for the
Spanish language, which for the most part had been marginalized within
the normative curriculum, as evident in the previous classroom episodes.
The music program attempted to resolve some of the earlier contradictions and polar binaries cited within this dual immersion classroom,
especially by the dual immersion parents who kept pointing out the
contradictions throughout the school year. Now, the students were
singing in Spanish for at least an hour a week with minimum interference in the English language; they were crossing linguistic and cultural
borders and overcoming the unequal set boundaries between Spanish
and English within the everyday life of this classroom. The restoration of
the Spanish language through these musical experiences attempted to
restore the balance between the two languages as defined by the structural integrity of true dual immersion programs. The transgressive power
of the return to Spanish, a return to what was repressed, thus occurred
through the ritualization of Lourdes' musical performances when the
students used their mimetic faculties to slip into their Spanish selves
and transform themselves within the fluid, folk-healing space of the rug
area. In doing so, they were able to cross over thresholds and enter into
a third space beyond the borderland where they were able to lose the
polarity between Spanish selves and English selves by swimming into
a pool of Spanish excess where the imitator becomes what is being
imitated through the mimetic power of language. The unequal border and
boundary between the Spanish and English language destabilized and

dissolved during these musical performances and expanded to cover more Spanish territory along the borderland.

Yet, the return to Spanish through music does not necessarily guarantee a definitive control and stability over second language acquisition; it does not guarantee mastery over the second language. Nevertheless, the musical performances led to the birth of a radically different border between the Spanish and English language, between the Spanish and English selves, the Spanish cultured being and the English cultured being, thus changing the reality of this dual immersion classroom. In turn, music can be thought of as a curriculum area in which the boundaries between the material world of the classroom and the personal world of its subjects can be subverted so that their differences can be dissolved during these social encounters with others in music. In this dual immersion classroom, music was able to subvert the borders and boundaries set up schematically between the two languages by imagining the upper limits of Spanish production, as well as loosening the social boundaries between the two student groups.

Furthermore, another type of third space was also produced during those moments of flight and transcendence when the listening subjects escaped from the present moment, from their bodily contingencies, and traveled to the cultural past. Bhabha (1994) notes that border art, such as the performance of Spanish folk music in this dual immersion classroom, demands an encounter that creates the sense of the now but also renews the past, refiguring it as a contingent *in-between space*, that innovates and interrupts the performance of the present. The *past present* then becomes the third space. Thus, the experience of traveling into the cultural past through the performance of folk songs such as *Ya Me Voy* also produces a temporal in-between space in which the listening subject is performing in the present moment but traveling metaphysically to a distant place in past memory. Many of the folk songs that the class performed were nostalgic and alluded to a utopian homeland in the folk past, thus producing different planes of temporality. Through this process of abstraction, the possibility of experiencing the sublime becomes possible when one leaves one's own bodily self and enters a moment when the listener is moving beyond what is known and familiar to new arenas of transcendence (Cumming, 2000).

Edward Said (1991: 55) defines musical transcendence as the "means to cross over . . . that chiefly involves moving from one domain to another, the testing and challenging of limits, the mixing and intermingling of heterogeneities, cutting across expectations, providing unforeseen pleasures, discoveries, experiences." The transgressive element in music has a nomadic quality, which according to Edward Said, allows music to attach itself to and become a part of the social formations within the sonic space so that the transgressive element moves from the musical to the social. Music thus has the potential of transcending social boundaries, regardless of the audience, because music can be socially empowering when the music is not entirely about music and is about *something else* outside of music (Adorno, 1985).

Chapter 6

Conclusion: False Binaries and True Dialectics

Contradictions, Rupture and Slippage: Examining the Reality of Linguistic Equity

The previous chapters examined how the dual immersion classroom subjects in this particular fifth-grade classroom initiated critical discussions that examined the tensions and fracture lines between the Spanish and English language, as well as the slippages, gaps and disjunctions between how the two languages are actually *represented* in the classroom reality versus their contingency to the true *representation* of both languages in an ideal 50/50 dual immersion model. The contradictory nature of the 50/50 language demarcation held the two languages suspended within the same discursive space; however, the two languages remained under constant tension because there was never an equal representation of both languages. Constant slippage, for example, between dedication to the equal representation of both languages and the domination of the English language occurred often throughout the academic year. If there had been a perfect balance of Spanish and English in this dual immersion classroom, then the purpose of a critical ethnographic depiction would not have been met. Furthermore, a critical ethnography would look very different in a 60/40 model because the structural tensions along the borderland of a 50/50 model seem to be much more heightened due to the need for equitable proportions of the two languages and thus more likely to rupture and open gaps – dilemmas that are implicit in the very nature of representing two languages equally through a binary, structuralist schema – an abstract mathematical oscillation between Spanish and English, of a 1:0 and 0:1 ratio.

The internal contradictions within this dual immersion classroom produced tensions throughout the academic year between and within the two languages as well as between and within the different sociocultural student groups. However, individual students and sociocultural student groups mobilized themselves best when found in such contradictions and thus this study attempted to capture the mobility of the subjects when caught up in moments, events and episodes based on conflicts and contradictions around language use (Harvey, 1996). The dual immersion subjects in this classroom came to understand themselves and their classroom reality when they had to confront salient contradictions within the informal and formal curriculum. As individual students and distinct sociocultural student groups subsequently became engaged in resolving these contradictions and tensions, as the researcher, I became aware of the slippages that can occur between moments of student agency within particular classroom episodes and moments leading to structural change along the borderland.

Furthermore, the dilemmas over linguistic equity highlighted in this study also elucidate critical issues related to the spatial mapping of the bilingual classroom, the nature of shared power and the shape of student agency in relation to teacher authority (Keane, 1997). The four distinct chapters chronicle multiple events that occurred within Roberta's fifth-grade, dual immersion classroom at PS 2000 in which discussions and dialogues related to language use and linguistic borders were enacted. The first chapter introduced the rug space as a fluid space for critical discussions and dialogues such as the debate over the importance of the Spanish spelling bee and the amount of time designated for Spanish language production during the Reading Buddies sessions. The second chapter examined how the students produced and presented a classroom cheer that was intended to represent their collective identity as a bilingual and multicultural classroom but how the final performance failed to include the diverse pastiche of song, step and acrobatics found in the three initial cheers. The third chapter followed the production of a Cuban play, based on primitive protagonist, which allowed a few dual immersion students to challenge linguistic and gender borders within its production. The final chapter recorded the musical performances of Spanish folk music and how these musical experiences moved the subjects toward the production of a hybrid and ideal third space in which students were able to move in-between languages, temporal frameworks and subjectivities of Self and Other.

Each of the four chapters explored how power and agency were exercised in particular *scenes of encounter* within particular classroom spaces and where, when and how specific, border-crossing students were able to tap into their student agency in order to confront, speak about and interactively redefine the relationship between the two languages – thus transforming themselves from social actors to social agents who enacted power, oftentimes in the performative space of the communal rug (Keane, 1997: 5). Scenes of encounter are face-to-face encounters, often constant and contested, which mark the everyday interactions of classroom life and are governed by a complex web of micropolitics in which turn-taking, silences and ruptures become fruitful in examining these scenes of encounter for their power dynamics between students and teachers. Scenes of encounter in this study often occurred in the rug area: the debate regarding the Spanish spelling bee, the aesthetic judgments made of the classroom cheers, and the use of improvised Spanish during the rehearsals for the Cuban play. Within these scenes of encounter, a few border-crossing students voiced their dissidence toward the often-shifting boundaries between the two languages and the subsequent marginalization of the Spanish language. Throughout the school year, even though the students were consciously aware of the modes of resistance and tactics they were utilizing in order to voice their dissidence, the students were very much aware of when and where to make counter-discursive contestation possible – during the communal gatherings on the rug area where they were discovering the power of mediation, for example. Thus, in order to locate the counter-discursive dialectic, the analysis of metalanguage allowed a researcher like myself to capture how the dominant discourse can be reconfigured and potentially transcended through language about language. Gaining a consciousness of language use in the bilingual classroom requires a reflective movement in which subjects stand distant and apart from themselves and examine as objective outsiders what is being said and what still remains unsaid in their discussions surrounding language as an object of discussion, which is often not the focus of bilingual education research.

The subject's acts of speaking during these scenes of encounter in turn needed to be interrogated by language, and thus the subjects found themselves in a perpetual circulatory movement in which they had to depend on language to talk about language, constantly drawing themselves back into a circular use of metalanguage (Gadamer, 1976). By tracing the occurrences of these metalinguistic discussions, the researcher is able to project a narrative map of counter resistance, and from this topographical map, with its multiple layers of counter-discursive production and reproduction, truths about the social formation of the dual immersion classroom inevitably emerge and then reveal and show its hidden vulnerabilities (Terdiman, 1985). Sometimes the metalanguage used within these scenes of encounter and their mediating dialectics led to the shifting of linguistic borders, thus opening up the possibility of transcending beyond the

Spanish/English structural binary found in dual immersion classrooms and moving toward a hybrid, third space where the subjects can situate themselves in-between the two languages and not identify themselves with solely one absolute language. For example, the students in this classroom were able to refute the contradictions between what they were doing in this classroom and what they appeared to be doing in this classroom – that contradiction in which one is either using one language or is not using that language at all and that contradiction in which Spanish is used less than English in their everyday classroom discourse. By constantly reflecting on what was and was not happening in their classroom, the students were able to illuminate self-contradictions such as the devaluing of the Spanish spelling bee and other perplexities related to producing linguistic inequity such as the lack of attention given to the Spanish cheer.

Dialectics: A Move Toward Dynamic Change

Yet, not all the metalinguistic discussions during these scenes of encounter led to transformational changes in language use and linguistic borders within the dual immersion classroom. By examining each of the four chapters according to whether change was actualized, we can better understand how the dialectics within the metalinguistic discussions at times led to transformational changes while at other times they remained stagnant or repressed. Dialectics can be defined here as an exchange of questions and answers while discussions are seen as the medium through which the dialectic is recorded – dialectics are practiced within discussions but not all discussions are dialectical in nature. Dialectics can also be seen as a method of inquiry that allows the subjects to use it as a tool and also as a form of discussion, oftentimes performing the dialectic before a large group of listeners. The questioning and learning in dialectical discussions can lead to a philosophical inquiry beyond everyday ordinary experiences; to seek knowledge actively; and to exercise courage in asking difficult questions. In ancient Greek philosophy, the dialectic was used to criticize each other's beliefs within conversations in order to discover and expose possible hidden contradictions within the belief system (Dunning, 1997). Thus, a dialectician exposes the weaknesses of names, definitions, propositions and words, such as the proposition for linguistic equity in a dual immersion model, in order to overcome these contradictory limitations in the actual process of the dialectic.

Furthermore, what has been cast aside but has not been absorbed theoretically, such as the full and equal inclusion of the Spanish language, will often yield its repressed truth content later, but until then, it festers almost like a sore unless situations are contextually changed (Adorno, 1973). When a dual immersion classroom suppresses the contradictions between the languages, it perpetuates antagonisms between the two languages until they fester. Contradictoriness is a category of reflection and can lead to the confrontation between the concept of a true dual immersion classroom and the thing itself: "Regression of consciousness is a product of its lack of self-reflection" (Adorno, 1973: 149). Truth is hidden in the dialectics and the development of the dialectic brings forth the contradictions even though the contradictions have already filtered into the object – e.g. the dual immersion classroom. Oftentimes subjects are given the power to remove the contradictions one by one through a movement of dialectics. Ideally, within dialectical movements, there is an inclination to incorporate the ideal such as the utopian ideal of linguistic equity and remain averse to what cannot be incorporated. In turn, to proceed dialectically, it means to think in and through contradictions. Adorno also states that equality mongering, as found in the dual immersion models, has the potential to reproduce the contradictions it had initially hoped to eliminate. There needs to be a critique of the inevitable manifestation of inequality within the equity aims of a dual immersion model and its identitarian binary logic. Yet, human experience often forbids the resolution of what is contradictory: "Objectively, dialectics means to break the compulsion to achieve identity, and to break it by means of the energy stored up in that compulsion and congealed in its objectifications" (Adorno, 1973: 157).

Critical dialectical discussions challenge the reification of systems and orders such as a dual immersion model that can at times produce a false consciousness because of its inherent binary structure. Reflexivity allows one to challenge the false objectivity of the dual immersion model and challenge the reigning consciousness by allowing for dialectics that resist reification. When the dual immersion classroom becomes an object of cognition and there is a retroactive questioning of its truth judgments, the dual immersion model comes to appear false because of the tensions and contradictions between the different components of the model. The ratio between the two languages produces a mathematical objectivity within the dual immersion model that then is questioned by the subjects who want to reinterpret that objective ratio. Thus, the subjects transcend the formal definition and order of their dual immersion classroom by producing a logic of non-contradictoriness through a critical consciousness. Yet, at what point, does this logic of non-contradictoriness negate the whole truth of the dual immersion model in itself? By criticizing the dual immersion model, then are we reducing the model to solely its contradictions and tensions as opposed to also focusing on its wholeness, totality and its absolute identity that also have positive strengths? By focusing on certain moments of dialectical discussions, then are we avoiding the examination of the total process?

Moreover, Adorno states that emancipatory thought must think against itself to illuminate truth through what he terms *negative dialectics* so that contradictions are never truly resolved harmoniously (Jay, 1973). In turn, to negate a negation does not necessarily bring about its reversal toward a more positive-thing-in-itself but that one should not just allow for the negation to pass. Yet, can the contradictions be removed from a dual immersion model? Or do contradictions always filter their way into the object and remain insoluble? Adorno proposes the implementation of certain actions that remove contradictions, do not comply with the power structure and instead "embody the contradictions, pure and uncompromised, in its innermost structure" (Adorno, 1973: 224). By generating critical thinking and disrupting the dominant ideology, subjects can potentially challenge the status quo and gain access to the meaning of a dual immersion classroom through the powers of reflexivity and consciousness-raising. Yet, it is only through the analysis of such critical discussions that we gain a better understanding of the power relations played out in the dialectical discussions and arrive at a deeper idea of what it means to be truly bilingual.

On the other hand, the choice of a third space simultaneously can be x and *not-x*, thus producing a non-contradiction and allowing for the affirmation of both x and *not-x*. Instead of accepting the contradictory nature of how languages are actualized in a dual immersion model, which bifurcates and separates the two languages into x and *not-x*, even though the two languages are not treated differently in any sense since they are seen as the same in value within the dual immersion model, the third space accepts both x and *not-x* and integrates them into a hybrid form. Thus the third space avoids the initial contradiction between the two languages. For example, in the chapter on the cheers production, if the students had performed a pastiche cheer that combined the Ducks in Black cheer, the Spanish cheer and the Valley Girl cheer, then they would have moved toward a hybrid third space in which the class cheer accepts at the same time and in the same space what is x and what is *not-x*. In turn, dialectics refers by definition to some sort of mediation of binary oppositions; here it was a debate between the two languages and multiple cultures and the conflicts inherent in balancing two languages and multiple cultures equally. However, even though dialectics always deals with binary oppositions, there are multiple types of dialectics and we must be cognizant of our manner of thinking about the dialectical dispositions produced in this particular dual immersion classroom.

Dialectical Readings of a Dual Immersion Classroom

According to Dunning (1997), theoretical contradictions and oppositions can only be *inverted* but never *subverted*. For example, some of the subjects in this dual immersion classroom were able to invert the binary relationship between the two languages by giving more time and space for the Spanish language at certain moments and subsequently lessening the time and space allotted for the English language, in turn reversing the original binary relationship between the two languages. However, the basic binary relationship remained situated in a dialectic of contradictions that was kept intact throughout the academic year, even after several attempts to reverse the unequal relationship between the two languages. The original linguistic framework for the dual immersion model resisted being influenced completely by the counter discourse of the students, parents and teacher.

The depiction of uneven development of Spanish in a dual immersion classroom demands for the development of structures and discursive patterns that explain the tense conjecture and unsettling contradiction of languages within it and subsequently attempt to create new regulated structures and discursive patterns that can sustain both languages equally. However, the sense of dislocation exhibited by the Spanish language in this study was felt situational so that specific moments and events that problematized the representation of Spanish could be recorded. Yet, these situational moments, events and episodes never led to drastic changes in the composition and structure of the dual immersion classroom. For example, even after much protest that Spanish was being marginalized, there was never a dialectical movement to increase the presence of Spanish in the formal curriculum. Throughout the academic year, it was as if this dual immersion classroom had forgotten off and on that the Spanish language was not being equally represented and thus the classroom subjects were overcome by what it had forgotten. Since my role as the researcher was to inquire into the theoretical relationship of the two languages, I soon determined that this dual immersion classroom did indeed follow the theoretical paradigm of binary oppositions.

The overall goal is to produce a dual immersion classroom identity that dissolves differences between the two languages but at the same time unites them in a paradoxical unity, thus affirming the opposing Spanish and English poles but without collapsing them onto each other so completely that their particularities cannot be united. Transformational dialectics embraces the concept of an *undifferentiated identity* rather than an internalized tension between two languages bonded together within a paradoxical unity (Dunning, 1997). But the plausibility of a radical transformational dialectic is only possible when there are radical changes put into place and these changes subsequently produce a new reality. Oftentimes, radical changes are put into place because the contradictions and oppositions become so unrelenting. For example, a dynamic confrontation between the oppositional nature of the two languages in a dual immersion classroom and the mutual reciprocity between the two languages must occur simultaneously in order for the dialectical unity to manifest itself in the midst of such radical change. A transcendent spirit overtakes this process of radical change as efforts are put into place to overcome both paradoxes and reciprocities. Furthermore, the transcendent spirit often results in a change of power dynamics so that the weaker language triumphs over the stronger language via this transcendental power, thus transcending all preexisting relationships between the two languages.

On the other hand, a transactional dialectic occurred in the last chapter on the Spanish music program because here the two languages and student groups were two consenting parties to a *hermetical transaction* of music and culture (Dunning, 1997: 8). The transactional dialectic opposes the sterile oppositions between the two languages and attempts to bring about some sort of reciprocal reconciliation or balanced compromise between the two languages so that they exist side by side in harmony. A higher dual immersion truth was found in the reciprocal interaction and harmony between the two languages during the Spanish music lessons and in the mutual communication between the Spanish-dominant and English-dominant students, between English Self and Spanish Other and vice versa during the music lessons with Lourdes. The social borders between the Spanish-dominant and English-dominant students dissipated during the music lessons and *a social plasticity* replaced the natural social divisions between these two student groups (Dunning, 1997: 30). In this episode, the analysis was more concerned with the discussion and exchange between the two languages and cultures, as well as the methods and pedagogy used by the Spanish music instructor to initiate such border-crossing discussion.

All of the episodes highlighted in the previous chapters were in turn based upon the dialectic of paradox in which a higher truth of what the dual immersion ideology represented in their classroom was sought through questions of meaning, through a give and take of arguments in a communal space, through conflicts regarding the contingencies of reinforcement between the two asymmetrical languages. Yet, the resolution for the paradox cannot be found within either a binary opposition of languages and cultures or the reciprocal harmony between two languages and cultures. This constant oscillation between clearly marked linguistic contradictions and the harmonious reciprocity of languages does not follow the either/or logic and instead perpetually maintains both poles of opposition in a radical tension, refusing to choose one pole over the other. The transformational dialectic does not want to flatten out the paradox inherent in dual immersion models by proposing a fixed nature to linguistic representation; rather, the transformational dialectic wants to preserve the freedom to switch back and forth between the two languages when needed and where needed. Thus, hybrid language practices and the hybrid mixing of cultures do not give into the binary opposition nor give into a reciprocal harmony between the two languages.

In turn, the typology of dialectics becomes a linear roadmap in which there is one clear route marked – even if this map is radically different from previous maps. Progress toward changing the linguistic borders in this classroom and its language practices cannot be seen as a linear progression in which the class is moving toward the transformational dialectic from the theoretical. Rather, the focus was on episodes that cumulatively highlighted some form of dialectics and should be reconceived as moments or revelations of particular dialectics.

Even though the episodes mentioned above clearly led to the polemic discussion of language usage and the subsequent subversion of linguistic borders, the episodes highlighted did not necessarily produce radical changes in the classroom life that subsequently inverted the structuring of language in the classroom. The face-to-face interactions in the scenes of encounter during these episodes did draw out polemics regarding the boundaries between the two languages due to the charismatic power and agency of specific classroom subjects. But these dialectical discussions were not able to forever resolve the internal conflicts and schisms through radical changes that changed the conceptual and concrete order of language use. When the means for resolving the internal conflicts and schisms are not adequate enough, then the conflicts are often repressed and resurface later. Thus, the ambiguities regarding linguistic representation were never resolved and subsequently these ambiguities became residual and did not permit the final resolution of problems to which episodes such as the cheers production and the Spanish spelling bee had previously drawn attention.

For example, the classroom curriculum and instruction were not radically altered so that each language was represented in equal proportions throughout the week after the dialectical discussions over language use. Tuesdays and Thursdays still remained the only two days in which the instruction was supposed to be in Spanish, and as the class became more involved in end-of-year events, such as graduation practice and standardized testing, the amount of time for the Spanish language diminished further. At times, the tensions between the two languages were never fully dissolvable, even after exposing the hidden paradoxes between the two languages and how they are represented in the classroom. Even though dialectics allow for a process of questioning and investigating, a dialectical discussion does not necessarily guarantee final answers to fundamental questions. Thus, even within the different forms of dialectics, the dialectical movement within each might lead to final resolution while at other times the dialectic might remain suspended and repressed within the life of the classroom.

Some episodes in turn did not produce a dialectical reconstruction in which the original contradictory nature between the languages was overturned; instead, the contradictoriness remained residual. Even though the four chapters single out episodes that allowed the dual immersion classroom to reflect upon its linguistic form, the episodes themselves did not play a central role in reorganizing its structural form and the unequal binary between Spanish and English. The dialectical discussions surrounding language use were at times radically self-critical of the dual immersion classroom, especially in comparison to the everyday language of the classroom. But it is impossible to predict whether these dialectical discussions will necessarily revise and restructure the next phase of classroom life in the dialectical movement.

Implications for Bilingual Education: Moving Away from the Binary

Oftentimes, classrooms change radically when there are large-scale crises, which often occur quickly and are inexplicable afterwards. Such large-scale changes produced after a crisis event can suddenly switch the gestalt of language education within the classroom. At the end of the school year, a radical change did occur that subsequently changed the dual immersion model at PS 2000 and how the two languages were to be taught in the future. A few of the dual immersion teachers decided to leave the school for various reasons and there was still a lack of Spanish-speaking activity teachers in art, music and physical education, given the amount of effort and pressure from parents. Thus, in the following academic year, the school decided to change its dual immersion model into a Spanish enrichment model and had an outside instructor come in daily for an hour to teach Spanish as a content subject in all the previous dual immersion classrooms. The teacher turnover, as well as the lack of a clear focus for the dual immersion model, was just one of the reasons for the radical changes. These events ended the long and agonizing period of doubt about what the dual immersion model at PS 2000 represented to all its school community members.

However, the decision to change the dual immersion education model was fairly well received by the remaining dual immersion teachers because, according to them, it lessened their burden in terms of balancing the curriculum and instruction in both languages. But the parents and the district officials were quite disappointed, especially since PS 2000 had gained a reputation over the years for their successful dual immersion program. The culminating decision to change the program disregarded the struggles and tensions that took place earlier throughout the school year and was paradoxically not the result of a long and gradual process of self-reflection. Rather, the decision to change the dual immersion model came suddenly and was irrevocable due to administrative pressures. There were no transformational visions at the end of the school year that addressed the present linguistic inequity between Spanish and English. The introduction of a new name – the Spanish enrichment model – created a new state of affairs at PS 2000 for the following academic school year. The text below is the last set of field notes recorded during this research study that highlight the decision to dissolve the dual immersion model:

At 9:45, I joined Roberta for the end-of-the-year dual immersion meeting in the principal's office. Janet, the school's dual immersion coordinator, was leading the staff meeting. This Thursday is the staff development day for all the dual immersion teachers. Alice, the fourth-grade dual immersion teacher, and Jill, the first-grade dual language teacher, are both staying another year. But Laurie, the second-grade dual language teacher, is leaving the school and will not continue teaching there. Janet proposes a "roller coaster" dual immersion model for next year in which half the day is in Spanish and the other half is in English and with both the monolingual and dual language teachers working together at each grade level, as opposed to remaining isolated as they are now.

At this point in the meeting, the members ask the following questions: (a) Do we want to change the dual immersion model? (b) How drastically? and (c) Do we change from a dual immersion model to a "Spanish enrichment model"? Roberta says that it is hard for her to plan if they don't have all the components in place. Roberta says she does not want to be "locked into the Spanish model" if they go with the snake method of dividing the day 50/50 into the two languages as opposed to alternating days. I can sense that the other members in the meeting are frustrated with Roberta's cynicism. Roberta states that she feels "overwhelmed" when she brings Spanish into the model. Roberta also says that she is not in the "right frame of mind" because they shouldn't be discussing these important issues on the last day of school. She says, "This discussion should have happened earlier in the school year." Then she adds on that the dual immersion teachers want someone who can speak Spanish during the enrichment periods: "We have been saying this for years. We have no control over who they hire for those positions." [In fact, the March 27 newsletter highlighted a dual immersion meeting for parents in which the topics of discussion were concerns of the model, budget allocation, status of the enrichment person, and Pan American week.] Roberta continues saying she wants to keep the model they have now with one day in English and one day in Spanish. In reference to Roberta's comment that the students are losing Spanish starting from the early grades, hinting at the ineffective third-grade dual language teacher, Janet says that it is difficult to get rid of the staff in place now. Janet now begins to ask whether they should even have a dual immersion model since they are losing some teachers next year. The level of frustration is increasing in the staff meeting as is evident from the contorted facial expressions.

Janet asks, "Do we continue with the dual immersion model? Do we assess the model next year before making any drastic changes? Do we understand why weren't doing enough of Spanish?" Jill says she wants to make changes now. Parents also state that they want more Spanish in the upper grades. Jill says there is enough Spanish in the upper grades. Roberta protests against what Jill has just said and states that she teaches in Spanish. The principal says that their Thursday meeting can identify those issues for next year and says, "Here's what we need to do for the fall." However, both Laurie and Roberta state that they cannot make it to the Thursday meeting. Laurie says, "I know people want to do a little Spanish and a little English everyday." Alice says she wants to do Spanish for one and a half hours daily. Another teacher says she wants the 50/50 model. Jill says maybe instead of the

50/50 model it should be called the "Spanish enrichment model" instead. Janet says maybe they can call it a "Two-Way Spanish Enrichment Model." The principal says that this Thursday "we can start to theoretically work out the differences between each grade without calling names . . . there needs to be an overriding thread, philosophy, and mission that works itself through each grade."

Roberta then says, "If we change the name, we have more freedom to move around and feel less guilty. Last year's personality of the class was Amia who was a gung-ho Spanish leader and this year the kids cannot even connect the nouns . . . the linguistic fiber that holds the words together is missing." [Here Roberta is referring to a female student last year who was the student council president and had led many efforts to include greater amounts of Spanish in the curriculum as well as mandating that students use Spanish within informal spaces such as when they are getting their jackets from the closet or waiting in line to go down to lunch.] Laurie says that if they do one and a half hours of Spanish each day then an enrichment model makes sense. Alice says she is the one who is speaking in Spanish all the time and that the kids are not speaking enough Spanish. Jill says that they need to speak in conversation in the lower grades as well, but if they continue focusing less on conversation and more on literacy, then they're not going to have that kind of discussion. The assistant principal says that the Tuesday and Thursday Spanish model locks them in but one and a half hours everyday in Spanish is more flexible. She says that they should not being doing what a model says they should be doing; instead, they should make it work for the children in front of us: "We need to individualize the model."

Jill says that the parents want their kids to learn more Spanish: "Parents don't want a watered version of Spanish." Jill says if they do one and a half hours of Spanish a day then the parents will know that Spanish gets done everyday. Alice says, "This is something that works for me because pressures are put on the kids." Janet then asks, "How do we change the model so that we don't lose the teachers?" Roberta then states that on some Spanish days they are interrupted constantly by "English things" such as school assemblies and that "we need a Spanish enrichment person on Thursday." Lastly, Roberta states, "We should plan for a retreat in the fall where we can meet calmly. We need to have consistent moments of conversations that are built in." Janet concludes the meeting by saying, "We have to write down what each grade will be doing next year . . . third . . . fourth . . . fifth . . . If we are doing Spanish for one and half hours a day, then we need to talk."

Concerns with Expansion and Capacity Building

This administrative meeting highlighted the overarching tension between the nature of the local dual immersion program at PS 2000 and the national policy for dual immersion models described by institutions such as the Center for Applied Linguistics and bilingual education researchers. Since it was evident throughout the school year that the Spanish language was being marginalized, the staff and administrators at PS 2000 decided to change the binary and decrease the Spanish instruction as opposed to moving the border in the other direction and changing the model to perhaps a 60/40 or 70/30 model, especially in the upper grades.

The instability and ambiguity of language use and linguistic borders in dual immersion models across the country point to the complex and sometimes contradictory relations between the national goal of dual immersion models and the immediate reality of dual immersion classrooms. Whenever a new bilingual education model is created, such as the dual immersion model, the distinctive elements of that model immediately become areas for contestation and sometimes these contestations lead to the new configurations of that bilingual education model. Conflicts, however, are a natural part of educational research, as well as national policy decision-making. Thus, there needs to be increased dialogue and debate between the national and local levels to ensure greater accountability for the Spanish language.

In short, because a national, grand definition of a dual immersion model will never be able to express the true nature of a dual immersion program at the local school level and all its particularities, it will always betray its weakness when there is friction at the local level when specific well-meaning dual immersion programs do not follow the model closely. Yet, no name and definition will succeed in expressing the true being of a dual immersion model such as the one highlighted in this study because of the great degree of difference and variance from one dual immersion classroom to another. The image of what a proposed dual immersion education model should ideally look like versus the reality experienced in a particular classroom often clashes and the *true* appearance of this classroom becomes accessible to the researcher only when what was concealed and what was intended to happen manifest themselves in dialectical discussions surrounding language use and linguistic borders.

Sometimes these counter-discursive discussions can make the definition of a dual immersion model vulnerable to counterexamples. The friction between the local dual immersion model represented in this study in comparison to the national goal of linguistic equality in dual immersion models was brought to the forefront through the four episodes chronicled here as students debated which cheer they would perform to represent their collective identity, as they persisted in their claims for more Spanish lines in the production of the play and as they contested the value placed on the Spanish spelling bee in relation to the English spelling bee. Within the polemics of these dialectical discussions, the disputed matter was language usage and linguistic borders; however, when language use is placed in the middle of the debates, then we must also interrogate where the disputations over language use ever reached either a climax, conclusion and resolution, whether a hypothesis was proposed, or whether the dialectic remained stagnated and suspended in the classroom discourse.

Bilingual educators and administrators should not fool themselves into thinking that the flaws of a dual immersion program at the local level can be overcome through the construction of an ideal naming or a formal systemization at the national level. In the everyday praxis of this fifth-grade dual immersion classroom, it became evident that the idealized definition of a dual immersion model was not able to conceal the contradictions between what it represented and what the utopian representation of linguistic equity was to be. Thus, even though names, definitions and propositions are incapable of expressing truly what a dual immersion model is in its essence at the local context, this incapability allows names, definitions and propositions such as "dual immersion education" to be always open for refutation. On many levels, one can find contradictory relationships between national policies defining dual immersion models and the actual practices found in the dual immersion programs.

References

Abbeele, G. (1992) *Travel as Metaphor*. Minneapolis, MN: University of Minnesota Press.

Addis, L. (1999) *Of Mind and Music*. Ithaca, NY: Cornell University Press.

Adorno, T. (1973) *Negative Dialectics*. New York City: Continuum Press.

Adorno, T. (1985) *Philosophy of Modern Music*. New York City: Continuum Press.

Adorno, T. (1998) *Aesthetic Theory*. Minnesota, MN: University of Minnesota Press.

Amor, T. (1969) Afro-Cuban folk tales as incorporated into the literary tradition of Cuba. PhD thesis, Columbia University.

Apple, M. (1995) *Education and Power*. New York City: Routledge.

Auge, M. (1995) *Non-places: Introduction to an Anthropology of Supermodernity*. London: Verso.

Baker, C. (1993) *Foundations of Bilingual Education and Bilingualism*. Philadelphia, PA: Multilingual Matters.

Bakhtin, M. M. (1981) Forms of time and chronotope in the novel. In M. Holquist (ed.) *The Dialogic Imagination. Four Essays by M. M. Bakhtin* (pp. 84–258). Austin, TX: University of Texas Press.

Banks, J. (1997) *Educating Citizens in a Multicultural Society*. New York City: Teachers College.

Bannet, E. T. (1989) *Structuralism and the Logic of Dissent*. London: Macmillan Press.

Barreda, P. (1979) *The Black Protagonist in the Cuban Novel*. Amherst, MA: The University of Massachusetts Press.

Barthes, R. (1992) The structuralist activity. In H. Adams (ed.) *Critical Theory Since Plato* (pp. 1127–1133). Fort Worth, TX: Harcourt Brace Jovanovich.

Bauman, Z. (1993) *Postmodern Ethics*. Oxford: Blackwell Publishers.

Benjamin, W. (1986) *Illuminations*. New York City: Schocken Books.

Benjamin, W. (1978) *Reflections*. New York City: Schocken Books.

Bernier-Grand, C. (1994) *Juan Bobo: Four Folktales from Puerto Rico*. New York City: Harper Trophy Publishing.

Berthold, M., Mangubhai, F. and Batorowicz, K. (1997) *Bilingualism & Multiculturalism: Study Book*. University of Southern Queensland, Australia: Distance Education Centre.

Bhabha, H. (1994) *The Location of Culture*. London: Routledge.

Bialystok, E. (2001) *Bilingualism in Development*. Cambridge: Cambridge University Press.

Boal-Palheiros, G. M. and Hargreaves, D. (2001) Listening to music at home and at school. *British Journal of Music Education* 18 (2), 103–118.

Bourdieu, P. (1977) *Outline of a Theory of Practice.* Cambridge: Cambridge University Press.

Bourdieu, P. (1982) *Language and Symbolic Power.* Cambridge, MA: Harvard University Press.

Bourdieu, P. (1987) *Distinction: A Social Critique of the Judgment of Taste.* Cambridge, MA: Harvard University Press.

Bourdieu, P. (1990) *In Other Words: Essays Toward a Reflexive Sociology.* Stanford, CA: Stanford University Press.

Bourdieu, P. (1992) *Rules of the Art.* Stanford, CA: Stanford University Press.

Bowman, W. (1998) *Philosophical Perspectives on Music.* New York City: Oxford University Press.

Britzman, D. (1998) *Lost Subjects, Contested Objects.* Albany, NY: State University of New York Press.

Burrows, D. (1990) *Sound, Speech, and Music.* Amherst, MA: University of Massachusetts Press.

Butler, J. (1993) *Bodies That Matter.* New York City: Routledge.

Calderon, M. (1996) *Preparing Teachers and Administrators to Meet the Needs of Latino Students.* Paper presented at the Educational Testing Service Invitational Conference on Latino Issues. Princeton, NJ: Educational Testing Service.

Camayd-Freixas, E. and Gonzalez, J. E. (2000) *Primitivism and Identity in Latin America: Essays on Art, Literature, and Culture.* Tucson, AZ: University of Arizona Press.

Carrasquillo, A. and Rodriguez, V. (1996) *Language Minority Students in the Mainstream Classroom.* Clevedon: Multilingual Matters.

Cherryholmes, C. (1988) *Power and Criticism.* New York City: Teachers College.

Chomsky, N. (1988) *Language and Problems of Knowledge: The Managua Lectures.* Cambridge, MA: MIT Press.

Christain, D. (1994) *Two-way Bilingual Education.* Washington, DC: National Center for Research on Cultural Diversity and Second Language Learning.

Christain, D. (1996) Two-way immersion education: Students learning through two languages. *The Modern Language Journal* 80 (1), 66–76.

Collier, V. P. (1989) How long? A synthesis of research on academic achievement in a second language. *TESOL Quarterly* 23 (3), 509–531.

Cumming, N. (2000) *The Sonic Self: Musical Subjectivity and Signification.* Bloomington, IN: Indiana University Press.

Cummins, J. (1981) *Bilingualism and Minority Language Children.* Ontario, Canada: Ontario Institute for Studies in Education.

Debord, G. (1994) *The Society of the Spectacle.* New York City: Zone Books.

de Certeau, M. (1984) *The Practice of Everyday Life.* Berkeley, CA: University of California Press.

Deleuze, G. and Guattari, F. (1987) *A Thousand Plateaus.* Minneapolis, MN: University of Minnesota Press.

DeNora, T. (2000) *Music in Everyday Life.* Cambridge: Cambridge University Press.

Den Tandt, C. (1999) All that is Black melts into air: *Negritud* and nation in Puerto Rico. In B. Edmonson (ed.) *Caribbean Romances: The Politics of Regional Representation* (pp. 76–92). Charlottesville, VA: University of Virginia Press.

Dewey, J. (1934) *Art as Experience*. New York City: Putnam Publishers.

Dovey, K. (1999) *Framing Places: Mediating Power in Built Form*. London: Routledge.

Duncan, N. (ed.) (1996) *Bodyspace: Destabilizing Geographies of Gender and Sexuality*. London: Routledge.

Dunning, S. (1997) *Dialectical Readings: Three Types of Interpretations*. University Park, PA: Penn State University Press.

Eilan, N., McCarthy, R. and Brewer, B. (1993) *Spatial Representation*. Cambridge, MA: Blackwell Publishing.

Erickson, F. (1980) *Timing and Context in Everyday Discourse: Implications for the Study of Referential and Social Meaning*. Austin, TX: Southwest Educational Development Laboratory.

Fass Emery, A. (1996) *The Anthropological Imagination in Latin American Literature*. Columbia, MO: University of Missouri Press.

Firth, S. (1996) *Performing Rites*. New York City: Oxford Press University.

Foucault, M. (1970) *Order of Things*. New York City: Random House.

Foucault, M. (1972) *Power/Knowledge*. New York City: Pantheon.

Foucault, M. (1978) *History of Sexuality*. New York City: Vintage Press.

Foucault, M. (1991) *Discipline and Punish*. New York City: Vintage Press.

Gadamer, H.-G. (1975) *Truth and Method*. New York City: Seabury.

Gadamer, H.-G. (1976) *Philosophical Hermeneutics*. Berkeley, CA: University of California Press.

Gal, S. and Irvine, J. (1995) The boundaries of languages and disciplines: How ideologies construct difference. *Social Research* 62, 967–1001.

Gandera, P. and Merino, B. (1993) Measuring the outcomes of LEP Programs: Test scores, exit rates, and other mythological data. *Educational Evaluation and Policy Analysis* 15 (3), 320–388.

Gardner, H. (1999) *The Disciplined Mind: What All Students Should Understand*. New York City: Simon & Schuster.

Garner, S. (1992) *Bodied Spaces: Phenomenology and Performance in Contemporary Drama*. Ithaca, NY: Cornell University Press.

Gee, J. P. (1989) Two styles of narrative construction and their linguistic and educational implications. *Journal of Education* 17 (1), 97–115.

Gee, J. P. (1992) *The Social Mind: Language, Ideology, and Social Practice*. New York City: Bergin & Garvey.

Gee, J. P. and Green, J. (1998) Discourse analysis, learning, and social practice: A methodological study. *Review of Research in Education* 23, 119–169.

Geertz, C. (1983) *Local Knowledge: Further Essays in Interpretive Anthropology*. New York City: Basic Books.

Genesee, F. (1989) Early bilingual development: One language or two? *Journal of Child Language* 16, 161–179.

Giddens, A. (1986) *Social Theory and Modern Sociology*. Stanford, CA: Stanford University Press.

Giddens, A. (1990) *The Consequences of Modernity*. Stanford, CA: Stanford University Press.

Gilroy, P. (1993) *The Black Atlantic*. Cambridge, MA: Harvard University Press.

Giroux, H. (1993) *Border-crossings*. New York City: Routledge.

Glasser, R. (1995) *My Music Is My Flag*. Berkeley, CA: University of California Press.

Glazer, N. and Moynihan, D. (1963) *Beyond the Melting Pot: The Negroes, Puerto Ricans, Jews, Italians, and Irish of New York City*. Cambridge, MA: MIT Press.

Godreau, I. (1999) Missing the mix: San Antón and the racial dynamics of "nationalism" in Puerto Rico. *Journal of Anthropological Research* 41, 389–397.

Goffman, E. (1981) *Forms of Talk*. Philadelphia, PA: University of Pennsylvania Press.

Gonzalez-Jensen, M. (1997) The status of children's fiction literature written in Spanish by U.S. authors. *Bilingual Research Journal* 21, 2–3.

Gore, J. (1992) What we can do for you! What can "we" do for "you"? Struggling over empowerment, in critical and feminist pedagogy. In C. Luke and J. Gore (eds) *Feminisms and Critical Pedagogy*. New York: Routledge.

Gramsci, A. (1971) *Selections from the Prison Notebooks*. London: Lawrence and Wishart.

Greene, M. (1978) *Landscapes of Learning*. New York City: Teachers College Press.

Grice, P. (1975) Logic and conversation. In P. Coles and J. Morgan (eds) *Syntax and Semantics, Vol. III: Speech Acts*. New York City: Academic Press.

Grindstaff, L. and West, E. (2000) Gender, sport, and spectacle: Cheerleading and the bid for cultural legitimacy. Paper presented at the Annual Meeting of the American Sociological Association Conference.

Grosjean, F. (1982) *Life with Two Languages*. Cambridge, MA: Harvard University Press.

Gutierrez, K. (1995) Cultural tensions in the scripted classroom: The value of the subjugated perspective. *Urban Education* 29 (4), 410–442.

Gutierrez, K. and Reyes, B. (1995) Script, counterscript, and underlife in the classroom: James Brown v. Board of Education. *Harvard Educational Review* 65 (3), 445–471.

Hakuta, K. (1986) *Mirror of Language: The Debate on Bilingualism*. New York City: Basic Books.

Hanks, W. F. (1996) *Language and Communicative Practices*. Boulder, CO: Westview Press.

Hanson, M. (1995) *Go!Fight!Win! Cheerleading in American Culture*. Bowling Green, OH: Bowling Green State University Press.

Hartoonian, H. (2002) *History's Disquiet*. New York City: Columbia University Press.

Harvey, D. (1996) *Justice, Nature, & the Geography of Difference*. Oxford: Blackwell Publishing.

Hatch, C. and Bernstein, D. (1993) *Music Theory and Explorations of the Past*. Chicago, IL: University of Chicago Press.

Hatton, C. and Hatton, R. (1978) The sideline show. *Journal of Association for Women Deans, Administrators, and Counselors* 42 (23).

Heidegger, M. (1971) *Poetry, Language, Thought*. New York City: Harper & Row.

Hemphill, C. (1997) *The Parent's Guide to New York City's Best Public Elementary Schools*. New York City: Soho Press.

Heras, A. I. (1993) Construction of understanding in a sixth-grade bilingual classroom. *Linguistics and Education* 5 (3), 275–301.

Holloway, L. (2001) One language one day, a second one the next. *The New York Times* (Metro Section), January 24, p. B4.

Holston, J. (1989) *The Modernist City: An Anthropological Critique of Brasilia.* Chicago, IL: University of Chicago Press.

hooks, b. (1994) *Teaching to Transgress.* New York City: Routledge.

Huerta, J. (1999) Negotiating borders in three Latino plays. In M. Kobialka (ed.) *Of Borders and Thresholds.* Minneapolis, MN: University of Minnesota Press.

Huyssen, A. (1993) Monument and memory in the postmodern age. *Yale Journal of Criticism* 6 (2), 249–261.

Ivy, M. (1995) *Discourses of the Vanishing.* Chicago, IL: University of Chicago Press.

Jakobson, R. (1990) *On Language.* Cambridge, MA: Harvard University Press.

Jameson, F. (1991) *Postmodernism or the Cultural Logic of Late Capitalism.* Durham, NC: Duke University Press.

Jameson, F. (1998) *The Cultural Turn.* London: Verso.

Jay, M. (1973) *The Dialectical Imagination: A History of the Frankfurt School and the Institute of Social Research, 1923–1950.* Boston, MA: Little, Brown Publishing.

Johnson, J. (1990) *Selecting Ethnographic Informants.* Berkeley, CA: Sage.

Jung, C. (1923) *Psychological Types.* New York City: Routledge.

Kant, I. (1951) *Critique of Judgment.* New York City: Macmillan Publishers.

Keane, W. (1997) *Signs of Recognition.* Berkeley, CA: University of California Press.

Kerber, L. (1988) Separate spheres, female world's, woman's place: The rhetoric of women's history. *Journal of American History* 75, 9–39.

Kern, S. (1983) *The Culture of Time and Space.* Cambridge, MA: Harvard University Press.

Kessler, C. (1971) *Acquisition of Syntax in Bilingual Children.* Washington, DC: Georgetown University Press.

Kirby, K. (1996) *Indifferent Boundaries: Spatial Concepts of Human Subjectivity.* New York City: Guilford Press.

Kliebard, H. M. (1986) *The Struggle for the American Curriculum: 1893–1958* (2nd edn). New York City: Routledge.

Krashen, S. D. (1983) The din in the head, input, and the language acquisition device. *Foreign Language Annals* 16, 41–44.

Kroll, J. F. (1993) Accessing conceptual representations for words in a second language. In R. Schreuder and B. Weltens (eds) *The Bilingual Lexicon.* Amsterdam: John Benjamins Publishing.

Kroll, J.F. and Tokowicz, N. (2001) The development of conceptual representation for words in a second language. In J. Nicol (ed.) *One Mind, Two Languages.* Oxford: Blackwell Publishing.

Kundera, M. (1995) *Testaments Betrayed.* New York City: Harper Perennial.

Lacan, J. (1997) *The Ethics of Psychoanalysis.* New York City: W. W. Norton & Company.

Lambert, W. E. and Tucker, G. R. (1972) *Bilingual Education of Children.* Rowley, MA: Newbury House.

Langer, S. (1953) *Feeling and Form: A Theory of Art.* New York City: Charles Scribner.

Larson, C. (1991) *Language and Comedia: Theory and Practice.* London: Associated University Press.

Le Compte, M. and Preissle, J. (1984) *Ethnography and Qualitative Design in Education Research.* New York City: Academic Press.

Lefebvre, H. (1991) *The Production of Space*. Oxford: Blackwell Publishing.
Lefebvre, H. (1999) *Everyday Life in the Modern World*. New Brunswick, NJ: Transaction Publishers.
Levi-Strauss, C. (1966) *Savage Mind*. Chicago, IL: University of Chicago Press.
Levi-Strauss, C. (1976) *Structural Anthropology*. New York City: Basic Books.
Lindholm, K. and Gavlek, K. (1994) *California Reports: 1992–1993*. San Jose, CA: Project Wide Evaluations.
Lindholm-Leary, K. (2001) *Dual Language Education*. Clevedon: Multilingual Matters.
Lippman, E. (1999) *The Philosophy and Aesthetics of Music*. Lincoln, NE: University of Nebraska Press.
Lucy, J. (1993) *Reflexive Language*. London: Cambridge University Press.
Lyotard, J. F. (1984) *The Postmodern Condition: A Report on Knowledge*. Minneapolis, MN: University of Minnesota Press.
Lyotard, J. F. (1998) A few words to sing. In A. Kris (ed.) *Music/Ideology: Resisting the Aesthetic*. London: Taylor & Francis.
MacCann, D. (1998) *White Supremacy in Children's Literature*. New York City: Garland.
McDowell, L. (1996) Spatializing feminism: Geographic perspectives. In N. Duncan (ed.) *Bodyspace: Destabilizing Geographies of Gender and Sexuality*. London: Routledge: 28–44.
McGrane, B. (1989) *Beyond Anthropology: Society and the Other*. New York City: Columbia University Press.
McLaren, P. (1997) *Life in Schools: An Introduction to Critical Pedagogy in the Foundations of Education*. New York City: Addison-Wesley Publishing Co.
Marx, K. (1947) *The German Ideology*. New York City: International Publishers.
Massey, D. (1994) *Space, Place, and Gender*. Minneapolis, MN: University of Minnesota Press.
Merleau-Ponty, M. (1992) *Phenomenology of Perception*. New York City: Routledge.
Middleton, S. (1995) Doing feminist educational theory: A post-modernist perspective. *Gender and Education* 7 (1), 87–100.
Milroy, L. (1987) *Language and Social Networks*. Oxford: Blackwell Publishing.
Muldoon, P. (2001) Between speech and silence: The postcolonial critic and the idea of emancipation. *Critical Horizons* 2 (1), 32–87.
Murphey, T. (1992) The discourse of pop songs. *TESOL Quarterly* 26, 770–774.
Nesbitt, N. (2001) African music, ideology, and utopia. *Research in African Literatures* 32 (2), 175–186.
Palij, M. and Homel, P. (1987) Bilingualism and cognitive development. In P. Homel, M. Palij, and D. Aaronson (eds) *Childhood Bilingualism: Aspects of Linguistic, Cognitive, and Social Development*. Mahwah, NJ: Lawrence Erlbaum.
Parsons, M. and Blocker, H. G. (1993) *Aesthetics and Education*. Urbana and Chicago, IL: University of Illinois Press.
Patton, M. (1990) *Qualitative Evaluation and Research Methods*. Newbury Park: Sage.
Paulston, R. (1996) *Social Cartography*. New York City: Garland Publishing.
Peirce, C. S. (1986) *Writings of Charles Saunders Peirce: A Chronological Edition*. Bloomington, IN: Indiana University Press.
Pinar, W. (1976) *Towards a Poor Curriculum*. Dubuque, IA: Kendall/Hunt Publishing Company.

Pinker, S. (1994) *The Language Instinct.* New York City: W. Morrow Publishing.

Popekewitz, T. S. and Brennan, M. (eds) (1998) *Foucault's Challenge: Discourse, Knowledge, and Power.* New York City: Teachers College Press.

Quantz, R. A. and O'Conner, T. W. (1988) Writing critical ethnography: Dialogue, multivoicedness, and carnival in cultural texts. *Educational Theory* 38 (1), 95–109.

Romaine, S. (1989) *Bilingualism.* Oxford: Basil Blackwell Publishing.

Rousseau, J. (1979) *Emile or on Education.* New York City: Basic Books.

Said, E. (1991) *Musical Elaborations.* New York City: Columbia University Press.

Sarup, M. (1993) *Guide to Post-structuralism and Postmodernism.* Athens, GA: University of Georgia Press.

Saussure, F. (1965) *Course in General Linguistics.* New York City: McGraw Hill.

Schunk, H. (1999) The effect of singing paired with signing on receptive vocabulary skills of elementary ESL students. *The Journal of Music Therapy* 36 (2), 110–124.

Serafine, M. L. (1988) *Music as Cognition: The Development of Thought in Sound.* New York City: Columbia University Press.

Silverman, K. (1983) *The Subject of Semiotics.* New York City: Oxford University Press.

Smith, R. (1994) *General Knowledge and Arts Education.* Urbana, IL: University of Illinois Press.

Soja, E. (1996) *Thirdspace.* Oxford: Blackwell Publishing.

Sommer, R. (1969) *Personal Space: The Behavioral Basis of Design.* Upper Saddle River, NJ: Prentice-Hall Publishers.

Spivak, G. C. (1990) The post-colonial critic: Interviews, strategies, and dialogues. In S. Harasym (ed.) *The Post-colonial Critic.* New York City: Routledge.

Spradley, J. P. (1980) *Participant Observation.* New York City: Holt, Rinehart, & Winston.

Stewart, K. (1996) *A Space on the Side of the Road.* Princeton, NJ: Princeton University Press.

Strinati, D. (1995) *An Introduction to the Theories of Pop Culture.* New York City: Routledge.

Taussig, M. (1993) *Mimesis and Alterity.* New York City: Routledge.

Terdiman, R. (1985) *Discourse/Counter Discourse: The Theory and Practice of Symbolic Resistance in Nineteenth-century France.* Ithaca, NY: Cornell University Press.

Tillis, S. (1998) *Rethinking Folk Drama.* Westport, CT: Greenwood Press.

Torres-Guzman, M. E., Morales, S., Han, A., and Kleyn, T. (2005) Self-designated dual language programs: Is there a gap between labeling and implementation? *Bilingual Research Journal* 29 (3), 10–23.

Tsing, A. (1993) *In the Realm of the Diamond Queen.* Princeton, NJ: Princeton University Press.

Turner, V. (1967) *The Forest of Symbols: Aspects of Ndembu Ritual.* Ithaca, NY: Cornell University Press.

Valdes, G. (1997) Dual language immersion programs: A cautionary note concerning the education of language-minority students. *Harvard Educational Review* 67 (3), 391–429.

van den Bos, P. (1993) Holistic and analytical approach compared. In M. Lieth-Phillip and A. Gutzwiller (eds) *Teaching Musics of the World*. Affalterbach, Germany: Phillip Verlag.

Volk, T. (1998) *Music, Education, and Multiculturalism: Foundations and Principles*. New York City: Oxford University Press.

Weedon, C. (1987) *Feminist Practice and Poststructural Theory*. Oxford: Basil Blackwell Publishing.

Williams, G. (1999) *French Discourse Analysis*. London: Routledge.

Winnicott, D. W. (1971) *Playing and Reality*. London: Tavistock Publications.

Young, S. and Glover, J. (1998) *Music in the Early Years*. London: The Falmer Press.

Zerubavel, E. (1979) *Patterns of Time*. Chicago, IL: University of Chicago Press.

Zizek, S. (1989) *The Sublime Object of Ideology*. London: Verso.

Zon, B. (1999) *Nineteenth-century British Music Studies*. Aldershot: Ashgate Publishing.

Index